ILLEGAL ENTERPRISE

The Work of Historian Mark Haller

Mark H. Haller

Edited by Matthew G. Yeager

University Press of America,® Inc.
Lanham · Boulder · New York · Toronto · Plymouth, UK

Copyright © 2013 by
University Press of America,® Inc.
4501 Forbes Boulevard
Suite 200
Lanham, Maryland 20706
UPA Acquisitions Department (301) 459-3366

10 Thornbury Road
Plymouth PL6 7PP
United Kingdom

All rights reserved
Printed in the United States of America
British Library Cataloging in Publication Information Available

Library of Congress Control Number: 2013938652
ISBN: 978-0-7618-6061-7 (clothbound : alk. paper)
ISBN: 978-0-7618-6505-6 (pbk:alk paper)

Cover artwork by artist Paul Ygartua,
Vancouver, British Columbia, Canada.
Courtesy of Dr. Matthew G. Yeager.

∞™ The paper used in this publication meets the minimum
requirements of American National Standard for Information
Sciences—Permanence of Paper for Printed Library Materials,
ANSI Z39.48-1992

Contents

Acknowledgments		v
Introduction	A Historian of Illegal Enterprise: An Introduction to Mark Haller *by Matthew G. Yeager*	vii

Part I: Chicago

Chapter 1	Formation of the Illinois Association for Criminal Justice	3
Chapter 2	John Landesco and the Illinois Crime Survey	23
Chapter 3	Organized Crime in Urban Society: Chicago in the Twentieth Century	35
Chapter 4	Biographical Sketches	61

Part II: Philadelphia

Chapter 5	Philadelphia Bootlegging and the Report of the Special August Grand Jury	83
Chapter 6	The Bruno Family of Philadelphia: Organized Crime as a Regulatory Agency	103
Chapter 7	Loansharking in Philadelphia: Social Control in an Illegal Enterprise	121

Part III: Illegal Enterprise Theory

Chapter 8	The Changing Structure of American Gambling in the Twentieth Century	137
Chapter 9	Loansharking in American Cities: Historical Analysis of a Marginal Enterprise	165

| Chapter 10 | Bootleggers as Businessmen: From City Slums to City Builders | 199 |
| Chapter 11 | Illegal Enterprise: A Theoretical and Historical Interpretation | 219 |

Index 255
About the Author 281
About the Editor 282

Acknowledgments

The late Mark H. Haller and his family would like to thank the following persons and institutions who contributed to the making of this book.

To Mr. Dan O'Shea, Director of Creative Services at Creative Donkeys in London, Ontario, for preparation of several charts used in Chapters 1, 10, and 11.

To Mr. John Alviti, Mark's graduate student, who helped prepare Chapter 9, and was a co-author on the article which appeared in the *American Journal of Legal History* in 1977.

To Oxford University Press, Inc., for their kind permission to reprint Chapter 3, "Organized Crime in Urban Society: Chicago in the 20th Century," which appeared in the *Journal of Social History*, volume 5, number 2 (Winter 1971-1972). Oxford University Press is also thanked for allowing republication of Chapter 4. That material came from the *Oxford Companion to United States History*, edited by Paul S. Boyer (2001), and consisted of a short vignette on "Organized Crime," pages 570-573. The Press also graciously allowed reprint from their *American National Biography* (1999), edited by John A. Garraty and Mark C. Carnes, on "Meyer Lansky," "Al Capone," "Jack Guzik," "Arnold Rothstein," and "Max Hoff."

To the Historical Society of Pennsylvania for their kind permission to reprint Chapter 5, "Philadelphia Bootlegging and the Report of the Special August Grand Jury," originally published in the *Philadelphia Magazine of History and Biography*, April 1985.

To ABC-CLIO, LLC, for their kind permission to reprint Chapter 6, titled "The Bruno Family of Philadelphia: Organized Crime as a Regulatory Agency," which appeared in the *Handbook of Organized Crime in the United States* (1994).

To John Wiley and Sons for their kind permission to reproduce Chapter 8, "The Changing Structure of American Gambling in the Twentieth Century," which appeared in the 1979 issue of the *Journal of Social Issues*.

To Temple University and the *American Journal of Legal History* for their kind permission to reprint Chapter 9, "Loansharking in American Cities: Historical Analysis of a Marginal Enterprise," which appeared in April of 1977.

To the Eleutherian Mills-Hagley Foundation Inc., of Wilmington, Delaware, for their kind permission to reprint Chapter 10, titled "Bootleggers as Businessmen: From City Slums to City Builders," which appeared in the book, *Law, Alcohol, and Order: Perspectives on National Prohibition* (1985).

To the American Society of Criminology for their kind permission to reprint Chapter 11, titled "Illegal Enterprise: A Theoretical and Historical Interpretation." This article appears in volume 28 of the journal, *Criminology* (1990).

To criminologist and professor Matthew G. Yeager of King's University College, Western University Canada, London, Ontario; for writing an introduction to Dr. Haller's work for this monograph, and for acting as curator, as the book made its way to final publication.

Introduction

A Historian of Illegal Enterprise: An Introduction to Mark Haller*

In 1931, towards the end of Prohibition, Walter Lippman complained that no serious study of the criminal underworld had been made. He was careful to delineate between "common criminals" and the vast criminal underworld of "bootleggers, panderers, fixers, and racketeers" who provided the public with "drink, sex, and gambling." It was gangsters who worked for urban political machines in "the tricks of colonizing districts, of stuffing ballot boxes, and of terrorizing voters."[1] Of course, Lippman was wrong. John Landesco had published a study titled "Organized Crime in Chicago" which was secreted within the *Illinois Crime Survey* in 1929. That early work by Landesco has since become a classic in the field of organized crime. One reason is due to Mark Haller. In 1968, he persuaded the University of Chicago Press to reprint Landesco's report, to which Haller added a new introduction based on his research at the University of Chicago.

There is every reason to ask who is Mark Haller and why is his work important to the understanding of illegal enterprise, a term professor Haller preferred over "organized crime" later in his career?

---

* I am indebted to Elizabeth L. Greiner, who as a graduate student in 1994, wrote a paper for history professor John Rule at Ohio State University titled "Mark Haller and the Mafia Hypothesis: An Historiographical Essay." Ms. Greiner has graciously allowed me to borrow extensively from her unpublished paper.

Mark Hughlin Haller was born on December 22, 1928, in Washington D.C. His father, after whom he was named, worked for the U.S. Department of Agriculture as a researcher in pomology—the study of fruit. The family would later expand to a total of three boys: Mark, Robert, and Donald. When he was six, the Haller family moved to Bethesda, Maryland. There, Mark Haller enjoyed collecting lizards, frogs, toads, possums, and his favorite pet—a squirrel he named "Jackie." In 1951 he received a BA in English literature at Wesleyan University in Connecticut. "I had decided as an undergraduate that I so much enjoyed my professors that I wanted to be a professor myself."[2] He thereupon matriculated to Johns Hopkins University where he discovered that the study of history was more interesting than literature. Haller would finish his master's thesis at the University of Maryland, specifically on Roger B. Taney and the Jackson party in the United States.[3]

After receiving his master's degree in 1954, Haller spent the next two years in the U.S. Army, serving as an intelligence officer stationed in Stuttgart, Germany. According to Haller, summarizing counterintelligence activity by the U.S. military in Europe was not especially "challenging or time-consuming." So, he spent much of his time touring museums, cathedrals, operas, and drinking beer in German beer halls. Coming from a middle-class background,

> The Army was my first experience within a thoroughly corrupt institution. I have often wondered whether, twelve years after (when he began his study of crime) I could have understood the corrupt political and police structure within which the American underworld operated if I had not personally learned how to operate and survive in the Army.[4]

This led to doctoral studies at the University of Wisconsin, Madison, where professor Haller studied the history of the eugenics movement in the United States. In 1963, his dissertation was published as *Eugenics: Hereditarian Attitudes in American Thought* by Rutgers University Press. Upon finishing his doctorate in 1959, Haller immediately landed an academic appointment at the University of Chicago, which ended up being fortuitous for a number of reasons. His teaching assignment, as a freshly-minted historian, was to teach undergraduates two, core courses in the social sciences: political theory, economic theory, sociology, and cultural anthropology. "I was fascinated by cultural anthropology, sociology, as well as by economics and so on."[5] This lead to a mindset in which professor Haller now saw himself as a social scientist, using the tools of a trained historian.

Having just published his dissertation, Mark Haller was approached by Norval Morris, then head of the University of Chicago's Center for Studies in Criminal Justice, headquartered in the law school. Morris had funding for the study of crime and criminal justice in Chicago in the 1920's, and offered a handsome stipend to the young historian. Thus began Mark Haller's immersion into the world of organized crime, the police, and urban politics in the early twentieth century. It also meant that he would be exposed to the Chicago School of sociology and the papers of Ernest W. Burgess and John Landesco, housed at the Regenstein Library. This introduction to the Chicago school has influenced Haller throughout his career.

Of course, much has been written about the Chicago School, as a founding epicenter of sociology in the United States, beginning at the turn of the twentieth century. The mid-1920's saw a burst of publications emanating from students at Chicago, including Reckless' *Vice in Chicago* (1933), Thrasher's *The Gang* (1929), Sutherland's *Criminology* (1924), Zorbaugh's *The Gold Coast and the Slum* (1929), Anderson's *The Hobo* (1923), and Wirth's *The Ghetto* (1928), among others. These young scholars argued that pathological behavior, particularly in urban Chicago, was rooted in the social disorganization of interstitial areas (characterized by high population density, poverty, poor schooling, unemployment, family breakdown). An important influence was Haller's discovery of the early work of John Landesco, whose ground-breaking research had almost been forgotten.

Landesco matriculated to the University of Chicago as a mature student and undergraduate sociology major beginning in 1923. In 1925, he finished his bachelor of philosophy degree at Chicago, and came to the attention of Ernest W. Burgess—then one of the leading lights of the Chicago School. It was a time of the beer wars in Chicago—full-blown gangsterism mixed with a cocktail of city and judicial politics. Landesco was asked by professor Burgess to begin a study of organized crime in Chicago and benefited from research funding which was available to the university through both the Rockefeller and Carnegie foundations. In 1926, outraged at widespread crime in Chicago, members of Chicago's elite businessmen, lawyers, and judges formed the Illinois Association for Criminal Justice to study the breakdown of law and order in the windy city. In 1929, they published their findings as the *Illinois Crime*

Survey. Tucked in within that large volume was Landesco's own study, titled Part III: "Organized Crime in Chicago." Like his University of Chicago contemporaries—especially Frederic Thrasher—Landesco saw crime very differently. It was not an administrative breakdown for which "good" government was the solution.

Instead, Landesco wrote that

> The gangster is a product of his surroundings in the same way in which the good citizen is a product of his environment. The good citizen has grown up in an atmosphere of obedience to law and of respect for it. The gangster has lived his life in a region of law breaking, of graft, and of "fixing." That is the reason why the good citizen and the gangster have never been able to understand each other. They have been reared in two different worlds.[6]

Although not a trained historian, Landesco's account of crime in Chicago is indeed an historical analysis of urban crime in which he traced the continuity of criminal leadership and methods from the gamblers and vice lords in the late 19th century to the bootleggers and gamblers of the 1920s. Unfortunately, by the time the *Survey* was published, the civic leaders who had commissioned it had lost interest, the staff had been disbanded, and within a year the report itself was out of print and unavailable to all but the most diligent scholars.[7]

By the time Haller started his study of urban crime in Chicago, he encountered the *Illinois Crime Survey*, and decided to research the politics of that Survey. This study was to be a full-blown monograph on crime in Chicago, which unfortunately, never came to fruition. Nevertheless, we have published excerpts from that manuscript—importantly two chapters that focus on the politics of crime surveys as well as the contribution of Landesco himself. In the study of criminal organizations, or illegal enterprise as he prefers the term, it was Mark Haller who reintroduced us to the work of John Landesco. That meant, in essence, a focus on criminal enterprises and their ties to urban political machines.

To appreciate Mark Haller's contributions to the study of organized crime, one must first look at the model designed by sociologist Donald R. Cressey when Haller began his research. In 1969, Cressey published a ground breaking study of organized crime titled *Theft of a Nation: The Structure and Operation of Organized Crime in America*. This book, which was to influence policy makers and the general public, was based

Introduction

on a report Cressey had prepared for the *President's Commission on Law Enforcement and Administration of Justice* in 1967—specifically the Task Force Report: Organized Crime. As a member of a select presidential commission, Cressey was granted access to confidential materials and was permitted to interview police and FBI officials, all of whom convinced him that a nationwide alliance of Italian crime families—collectively named La Cosa Nostra—controlled a large portion of entrepreneurial crime in the United States.[8]

Cressey's position became the "corporate" model of organized crime. It consisted of about twenty-four "crime families," consisting of approximately 5000 Italians and Sicilians or men of Italian and Sicilian decent. Each individual was allegedly a member of a specific "family," and collectively, these crime families controlled almost all of the gambling, loansharking, the traffic in narcotics, and other entrepreneurial crime in the United States. Each family was organized hierarchically with specific duties (boss, under boss, capo, consigliere, soldiers) to control crime in their specified regions. These families were linked to one another and to non-Cosa Nostra syndicates by understandings, agreements, and "treaties" and by mutual deference to a "Commission" that set national policy and was made up of representatives of the most powerful families. The boss of each family directed the activities, especially illegal activities of its members. Although not all of Cressey's conclusions were new—the basics had been described by Joe Valachi during the McClellan Hearings (1963) and publicized at length in *The Valachi Papers* (1968)—they carried with them the authority of the President's Commission, and quickly became the prevailing mafia hypothesis within which scholars of crime were expected to work.[9]

When Haller began his studies of organized crime in Chicago, he was well aware of Cressey's model and was expected to document how such hierarchical control arose in Chicago. He soon discovered that Chicago did not fit into that model. As he continued his research as a faculty member at Temple University in Philadelphia, beginning in 1968, he concluded that no city did. What Haller observed was that few, if any, social scientists were studying the actual operation of illegal enterprises— here, chiefly gambling, bootlegging, narcotics, loan sharking, and labor racketeering.

As a result of this gap, he wrote a series of articles, some of which are reprinted here, describing the structure of gambling, bootlegging, and loan sharking and the relationship of organized crime to the community—especially political connections. The more he studied these enterprises, the more he concluded they did not fit a "corporate" ethnic model of organized crime. Indeed, for a brief period, Haller doubted the existence of Italian-American crime families. However, with the availability of wiretaps in the mid-1970's and the release of other previously confidential material, Haller reconsidered his skepticism, albeit he did not accept the widely-held belief in their pervasive power. This led to a second stage of writing in which Haller hypothesized an alternative model of organized crime. This has since become the illegal enterprise model, and excerpts from that theorizing are reprinted here.

Haller's early work, clearly influenced by John Landesco's "natural product" approach, reflected a certain methodological and epistemological bias. Haller argued that historians had mistakenly looked to reformers for understanding the nature of organized crime, rather than listening to criminals and how they operated in the underworld. Reformers, he argued, lived largely outside the world of criminal justice, and had a limited, often simplistic and moralistic view of gangsters. Thus, Haller questioned the very foundation upon which the study of organized crime had been based, and began to deconstruct—or at least modify—the dominant Mafia hypothesis.

An example is the article reprinted here titled "Organized Crime in Urban Society: Chicago in the Twentieth Century." Haller argued that the activities which sustained criminal organizations, or partnerships, were based on illegal goods and services demanded by sectors of the so-called "legitimate" public. This demand from legitimate clientele created the infrastructure for capital investment, manufacture, distribution and the sale of products—especially illegal alcohol during the roaring Twenties. By the very nature of the enterprises, this led to an ever-changing framework in which agreements (and payoffs) between gangsters, the police, and local politicians acted as a regulatory system for organized crime. Ethnic and lower-class involvement in bootlegging—as Landesco had so wisely observed—functioned as a subaltern economy and source of political power in urban America.

As Haller continued his research, he challenged the traditional assumption that organized crime originated with the bootlegging gangs of the Prohibition era—a thesis also put forward by John Landesco in 1929. He traced the development of gambling to the period just after the Civil War. According to Haller, from the 1870's to around 1905—when reform movements undermined gambling—gambling syndicates had their greatest influence on urban America, especially the police, machine politics, sports, entertainment and various businesses. Prior to World War I, gambling syndicates employed numerous workers in the neighborhoods, and were organized like political wards. Indeed, it was gambling profits that often financed local political campaigns and precinct captains were often bookmakers and policy (numbers gambling) writers.

When Prohibition took hold in 1920, a younger group of ethnic Americans filled the void. Many grew up in urban slums. Of the leading bootleggers, about fifty (50%) percent were Jewish, twenty-five (25%) percent were Italian, and the rest were mainly of Polish or Irish descent. The relative youth of these entrepreneurs had long-term effects on the nature of organized crime in America. As members of the gambling fraternity died or retired, ex-bootleggers took over their enterprises, thus giving a false impression that organized crime grew out of Prohibition.[10]

In the chapter reprinted here titled "Bootleggers as Businessmen: From City Slums to City Builders," Haller documented how bootleggers "learned to use partnerships in order to pool resources and share risks in setting up a variety of legal and illegal enterprises." Early in their careers, bootleggers began to diversify their activities. Liquor importers might smuggle opium, French perfume, or illegal aliens. Because they were often sports fans and gamblers themselves, these gangsters invested in gambling houses, numbers syndicates, slot machines, race tracks, nightclubs, and speakeasies. For Haller, the leading bootleggers were "primarily hustlers, makers of deals, partners in businesses, coordinators of markets—not executives presiding over bureaucratic organizations."[11]

In two articles reprinted here ("Illegal Enterprise," and "The Bruno Family of Philadelphia") Haller challenges Cressey's idea of a rationally structured bureaucracy with a boss and individuals performing specialized functions within that bureaucracy. Haller argues that so-called "family" members and their associates are involved in independent legal and illegal activities. The crime family is largely separate from a member's economic ventures. It is, so to speak, comparable to a Rotary Club or fraternal organization. The two, most important functions of this fraternal organization are the (1) status and the opportunity to network with other members and distribute risks, and the (2) quasi-shadow government role that provides a set of norms or rules as well as occasional dispute resolution services. Hence, most underworld "deals" require low capitalization, few personnel, and an informal management style that involves personal trust. In Philadelphia, active Bruno family members carried on activities within a relatively independent cluster of business partners and associates.

After reading innumerable wire tap transcripts, Haller concluded that family members, more than most Americans, have control over their time and enjoy negotiating deals, taking risks, and plotting legal or illegal schemes to make money. A member, on a typical day, might "negotiate a loan to a small businessman in the morning, take calls from number runners in the afternoon, meet for gossip in a restaurant for dinner, and oversee a high stakes craps game until early morning." Men, in organized crime, are hustlers and dealers with no bureaucratic inclination or skill to oversee Cressey's hierarchy, a structure for which partnerships are ideally suited.

The corpus of Haller's work, in many respects, owes its source to the Chicago School of Sociology, and to the work of John Landesco. While his early articles did not openly challenge the Mafia hypothesis, Haller showed how organized crime was indigenous to ethnic neighborhoods and urban politics. With the names of Jewish and Irish gamblers and bootleggers sprinkled generously throughout his early research, he did not address the Italian Cosa Nostra per se. Instead, he focused—like Landesco—on neighborhood friendships, political connections, ethnic and class ties, and business partnerships. From these findings and his later work, Haller developed an alternative hypothesis that "bureaucracy and hierarchy become less important as explanatory tools; and various informal systems of cooperation and competition emerge as crucial factors that structure criminal enterprise."[12]

Although Haller conceded that the Bruno family was ultimately subservient to a National Commission (out of New York City), and that some sort of hierarchy did exist within the Bruno formation (but often not adhered to); the evidence supported a general separation between "family" activities and independent coalitions and partnerships. When in 1980, gangster Nicky Scarfo assassinated Angelo Bruno in front of his home and attempted to take over and redefine the role of Boss—where partnerships and members were to be subservient to him—the Bruno formation fell apart amid violent opposition to Scarfo. This ultimately lead to Scarfo's indictment and imprisonment, and the weakening of the old Bruno formation in Philadelphia.[13]

This monograph of major works by the historian Mark Haller is long overdue. In a career that spanned almost fifty years of research on illegal enterprise, he presents us with a legacy of his mentor from the Chicago

School—John Landesco.[14] This monograph further contributes to the literature on the enterprise model of organized crime. It adds a much-needed historical perspective to understanding the structure and operations of organized crime. And, in my humble view, it reiterates the importance of political economy to understanding the crime-politics nexus which is a classic characteristic of traditional organized crime anywhere in the world.[15]

Mark H. Haller passed away in September 2012, just as this book was going to press. His contributions to the field will be sorely missed by colleagues, his students, and future students of illegal enterprise.

Notes

1. Lippman, Walter J., "The Underworld as Servant," in *Organized Crime in America,* ed. Gus Tyler. (Ann Arbor: University of Michigan Press, 1962), p. 61, 65.

2. Yeager, Matthew G., "Fifty Years of research on illegal enterprise: an interview with Mark Haller," *Trends in Organized Crime* 15 (March 2012): 2, No. 1.

3. Haller, Mark, "The Rise of the Jackson Party in Maryland, 1820-29," *Journal of Southern History* 28 (August 1963): 307-326.

4. Greiner, Elizabeth L. "Mark Haller and the Mafia Hypothesis: An Historiographical Essay." Unpublished paper submitted to History 786, Ohio State University, June 1994, p. 4-5.

5. Yeager, *Ibid.* at p. 3.

6. Landesco, John. "Organized Crime in Chicago." Part III of the *Illinois Crime Survey* (Chicago: Illinois Association for Criminal Justice, 1929; republished by Patterson Smith in 1968, p. 1057).

7. Mark Haller, Introduction, *Organized Crime in Chicago.* Part III of The Illinois Crime Survey 1929 by John Landesco (Chicago: University of Chicago Press, 1968). p. ix-xvii.

8. Cressey, Donald R. *Theft of a Nation: The Structure and Operations of Organized Crime in America.* (New York: Harper & Row, 1969).

9. For a description of the fluctuating interest in the area of organized crime see Fox, Stephen, *Blood and Power: Organized Crime in Twentieth-Century America.* (New York: William Morrow and Company, 1989), p. 7. Fox, an independent scholar who has written a survey account of organized crime, with an emphasis on the Mafia, believes that public perceptions of the underworld have gone through four distinct phases: a long period of denial;

tentative recognition after the Appalachian debacle, the Valachi hearings and *The Godfather* movies; a second period of denial and romanticization; and since 1980, the present level of understanding informed by government reports and the publication of gangster memoirs.

10. Haller, Mark. "Bootleggers and American Gambling, 1920-1950," In Commission on the Review of National Policy Toward Gambling, *Gambling in America*, Appendix I (Washington, DC: GPO, October 1976), p, 102, 106, 109-113.

11. Bell, Daniel. *The End of Ideology: On the Exhaustion of Political Ideas in the Fifties*. (Glencoe: The Free Press, 1960), p. 117. Haller, Mark. "Bootleggers as Businessmen: From City Slums to City Builders," chapter 10 in this book.

12. Haller, Mark. "Bureaucracy and the Mafia: An Alternative View." *Journal of Contemporary Criminal Justice* 8 (Feb. 1992), p. 6.

13. Haller, Mark. "Life Under Bruno: The Economics of an Organized Crime Family" (Conshohocken, Pennsylvania: Pennsylvania Crime Commission, July 1991, p. 27).

14. Yeager, Matthew G., "On the Importance of Being John Landesco." Paper presented at the annual meeting of the American Society of Criminology, Washington, D.C., November 16, 2011. Publication pending in *Trends in Organized Crime*.

15. Vold, George B. "The Organization of Criminals for Profit and Power" *Theoretical Criminology* (New York: Oxford University Press, 1958, Chapter 12).

Part I
Chicago

Chapter 1

Formation of the Illinois Association for Criminal Justice

According to the official story, the formation of the Illinois Association for Criminal Justice was a relatively painless and almost spontaneous event. At the initiative of the Illinois State Bar Association, a meeting of various civic associations was called for February 6, 1926, and—so the story goes—"The result of this meeting was the formation and incorporation of the Illinois Association of Criminal Justice."[1] In reality, however, the formation of the Illinois Association occurred only after long, bitter, and complex negotiations extending over a period of more than a year and involving most of the state's prestigious civic leaders and civic organizations with problems of crime and criminal justice. An examination of the Illinois Association will explain much concerning the strengths and weaknesses of the movement that resulted in the *Illinois Crime Survey*.

The Illinois Association for Criminal Justice

The official parentage of the Illinois Association for Criminal Justice lay with the Illinois State Bar Association. At its annual meeting in July of 1925, the State Bar Association had been much concerned with the administration of criminal justice and desired to involve other civic groups in seeking solutions. After the meeting, John R. Montgomery, president of the State Bar Association and a prominent Chicago lawyer, established a prestigious Special Committee on Enforcement of Criminal Law, under the chairmanship of Amos C. Miller, also a prominent Chicago attorney. The Special Committee included the Speaker of the House and two other members of the General Assembly; two justices of the State Supreme Court; four justices of the Superior or Circuit Courts; Chief Justice Harry Olson of the Municipal Court of Chicago; Charles R. Holden, president of the Chicago Crime Commission; Andrew A. Bruce, president of the Institute of Criminal Law and Criminology; Albert J. Harno, James Parker Hall, and John H. Wigmore, Deans of the Illinois, Chicago, and Northwestern law schools; plus many other prominent members of the State Bar Association. The Special Committee, in turn, established a five-man committee on planning, which began preparation of recommendations to present to the full committee in January.[2]

At the same time, in Chicago, a similar movement was undertaken by the prestigious Presidents' Council—an organization consisting of the presidents of the city's most respected civic organizations. Among the approximately twenty-five organizations represented were the Association of Commerce, Chicago Bar Association, Chicago Church Federation, Cook County Real Estate Board, Rotary Club, Northwestern University, and University of Chicago. No labor unions or ethnic organizations were included, however. The Presidents' Council had first been called into existence during the World War in order to provide civic leadership in a time of crisis. After the War it had passed out of existence but was revived in 1925 by William R. Dawes, president of the Chicago Association of Commerce, to provide leadership in the new crisis confronting the city.[3]

At a meeting on July 9th at the University Club, the Presidents' Council discussed a proposal to survey the crime situation in Chicago and finally authorized Dawes to appoint a Special Committee on the Crime Situation to undertake such a survey. By autumn the Special Committee had been organized under the chairmanship of Joseph T. Ryerson, president of Joseph T. Ryerson and Sons iron and steel company. While membership of the so-called Ryerson Committee changed over time, its active participants included Sewell L. Avery, president of U.S. Gypsum; Rush C. Butler, a prominent corporation lawyer and soon to become head of the Illinois Association for Criminal Justice; John R. Montgomery, president of the Illinois State Bar Association; Andrew A. Bruce, president of the Institute for Criminal Law and Criminology; Henry P. Crowell, president of the Quaker Oats Company; Edward M. Skinner, general manager of Wilson Brothers; and other prominent Chicago civic leaders. Because of the presence of Montgomery and Bruce on the Ryerson

Committee, there was communication between this committee and the Special Committee established by the State Bar Association.[4]

The Ryerson Committee examined not only the best means for conducting a survey of criminal justice but also the adequacy of existing private organizations engaged in the fight against crime—especially the Chicago Crime Commission. Many members of the Ryerson Committee were quite dissatisfied with what they regarded to be a lack of vigor and aggressiveness by the Crime Commission. As a result, the Committee asked Henry B. Chamberlin, Operating Director of the Crime Commission, to attend its meeting on October 19th. Chamberlin defended the work of the Crime Commission and argued that the Commission's work could be expanded only if more money were provided. In reply, according to the minutes of the meeting, "opinion was expressed that if the Commission were more aggressive the public would contribute larger funds."[5]

Another factor influencing several businessmen on the Ryerson Committee was a desire to consolidate many of the privately supported organizations dealing with crime, thereby increasing their efficiency. Such an interest had its origin especially among businessmen associated with the Committee of Fifteen. When Samuel Thrasher, Superintendent of the Committee of Fifteen, became ill in 1925, the Committee of Fifteen faced a crisis; for it was clear that a number of businessmen were losing interest and would take this opportunity to reduce their commitment to the Committee. Mr. Skinner, a member of the Ryerson Committee, was urging by early March of 1925 that the Committee of Fifteen be merged with the Juvenile Protective Association, Illinois Vigilance Association, the Law and Order League, and others. By April, Rosenwald, who was one of the major contributors to the Committee, threatened to reduce his contributions. Reacting to such pressures, Henry P. Crowell, the businessman who was president of the Committee of Fifteen, appointed a committee in November "to take the subject of merger with other allied organizations under consideration and to arrange for joint meetings for the discussion of the problem." In pushing for such a merger, the business leaders had the example of the Chicago Council of Social Agencies, established about 1914 to coordinate the various charitable organizations within the city.[6]

The Ryerson Committee report, dated December 30, 1925, assumed an increase in crime and a breakdown in the deterrent effect of law enforcement: "But while crime has increased the punishment of crime has diminished, and this in turn adds to its burden." The report urged the formation of a Chicago Association for Criminal Justice with a board of directors representing a wide selection of elite civic organizations. The work of the Association would be carried out through nine divisions, including: finance, legislation, investigation, criminal procedure, juvenile, and pardons and probation.

"The investigation division," said the report, "should embody the Chicago Crime Commission as now constituted," while "the Juvenile Division should take over the Juvenile Protective Association and extend its work so as to completely cover the juvenile field." The Executive Committee itself would perform many of the law enforcement activities of the Committee of Fifteen. As part of an extensive war upon crime, the Chicago Association for Criminal Justice would make surveys and conduct a broad education and publicity campaign.[7] Thus, the report's recommendations reflected the coming together of efforts to undertake a thorough survey of the administration of justice and to bring coordination to the many private, crime-fighting organizations.

On the 31st of December, leading members from the Ryerson Committee and the Special Committee of the State Bar Association met to discuss and coordinate their plans. The members of the Ryerson Committee argued that the crime situation in Chicago was so acute that the city needed a separate organization to deal with the situation. Amos Miller, chairman of the Bar Association Committee, countered with the claim that "the jealousy which is sometimes manifested downstate toward Chicago might be dealt with more effectively if the crime problem were met as a state problem." Furthermore, any state organization, to be successful, would need financial assistance from Chicago sources. But despite his efforts at the meeting and in subsequent correspondence with Ryerson, he was unable to persuade the Ryerson Committee of the advantages of a single organization with state-wide responsibility.[8]

Hence, at a meeting on January 23rd, the State Bar Association Committee recommended the formation of two organizations: state-wide Illinois Association for Criminal Justice and a city-oriented Chicago Association for Criminal Justice. As the report stated: "no survey of conditions in the Chicago area will be required of the state-wide organization, because that work will be done by the Chicago Association for Criminal Justice now being formed, which will be amply financed." Nevertheless, "it is expected that the Chicago Association for Criminal Justice will join in the expense of statewide surveys in which it has an interest" and, therefore, the two organizations would work closely together. The Bar Association Committee took as its model the survey by the Missouri Association for Criminal Justice, which was just at this time being completed. Like the Missouri survey, the Illinois report would highlight the failure of police, prosecutors, and courts—failure being defined as failure to place a suspected criminal in jail with dispatch.[9]

This, then, became the official program of the Ryerson Committee and of the State Bar Association committee—a state-wide association to survey criminal justice in the state and to bring pressure upon the legislature and a Chicago organization to study the administration of justice in the city, to provide most of the financial backing for both organizations, and to carry on the programs necessary to meet the special problems of crime in the city. To bring the two organizations into existence, Amos C. Miller called a meeting of representatives from the state's most prestigious civic groups to meet in the Chicago Bar Association rooms on February 6, 1926. From this meeting, according to the official history, the Illinois Association for Criminal Justice emerged.[10]

Meanwhile, behind the scenes, a deadlock had in fact occurred because of the firm opposition by the Crime Commission to any loss of its autonomy. The first formal statement of opposition came at a January 14th meeting of the Presidents' Council, called by Dawes to approve the Ryerson Committee report of December 30th. Edward Gore, newly elected president of the Crime Commission and a Crime Commission representative to the Presidents' Council, requested that the Crime Commission not be mentioned in the report. At this point, a special committee, including Ryerson, Gore, and Rush C. Butler, retired to redraft the report. As released to the newspapers, the report did not call for the consolidation of the Crime Commission, Juvenile Protective Association, and Committee of Fifteen into the Chicago Association for Criminal Justice but rather called merely for their cooperation with the proposed Association.[11]

Despite a number of civic summit conferences concerned with the issue, the Crime Commission remained firmly opposed to the formation of new organizations. This opposition was made formal and official in resolutions passed by the Executive Committee of the Crime Commission on February 25th.[12] Henry B. Chamberlin, the Operating Director, was bitter in his attacks. He opposed a state organization, for fear that it might slight the needs of Chicago; and he feared formation of a new association for the city since, if the Crime Commission remained outside, it would lose financial support; and, if it joined, it would lose autonomy. While Chamberlin's opposition was more bitter and inflexible than that of most members of the Crime Commission, in general the members felt, quite rightly, that the effort to form a new association in the city reflected unfavorably upon the work of the Crime Commission and that; further, the Crime Commission, if given increased finances, could perform the functions that were planned for the new association.[13]

Indeed, Gore, in order to break the deadlock, specifically proposed that the Crime Commission be expanded to perform all of the functions proposed for the new Chicago Association for Criminal Justice.[14] The continued deadlock in Chicago, as Montgomery pointed out in a long and plaintive letter to Dawes, also created a deadlock in the formation of a state-wide organization. So long as it was unknown how much financial and other support could be expected from sources in the city, no definite commitments could be made concerning an Illinois Association for Criminal Justice.[15]

To break the deadlock, Ryerson, Crowell, Dawes, and other civic leaders considered the possibility of forcing the Crime Commission into cooperation by withholding the endorsement of the Association of Commerce from the fund-raising campaign of the Crime Commission. By withholding such an endorsement, which the Crime Commission intended to seek at the April 30th meeting of the Association, these leaders could reasonably expect that the Crime Commission would either pass out of existence or else agree to some form of consolidation.[16] Thus, unknown to the Crime Commission, its days of independence were apparently numbered—until it was rescued by the actions of organized crime. On April 26th occurred the McSwiggin murder. No incident in the two-year gang warfare so excited the city as the killing of the young Assistant State's Attorney in the company of gangsters. When the prestigious Presidents' Council met on April 30th in an atmosphere of crisis, it "decided to proceed with the general plan of the Ryerson Committee report and complete the organization of the proposed Illinois Association for Criminal Justice as circumstances would permit." But more important for the future, "in the present emergency, however, the Council in its desire to strengthen the hands of the Crime Commission and to increase its field of usefulness, decided to back the work of the Commission and to approve the intention of the Crime Commission to appeal to citizens of Chicago for increased revenue." On the same day the Association of Commerce also passed a resolution supporting the Crime Commission.[17]

While Ryerson regarded the situation with some optimism, events soon doomed the formation of a separate Chicago Association for Criminal Justice. First of all, the Crime Commission voted on May 6th some $250,000 to help support the grand jury investigation of the McSwiggin murder, and also voted to back the formation of a state-wide Illinois Association for Criminal Justice. In private conversations with John R. Montgomery and Amos C. Miller, Edward E. Gore promised not only cooperation but even the possibility of financial support. Thus the Crime Commission moved to refurbish its image and to cooperate in the formation of a state, but not a city, association for criminal justice.[18] When Ryerson, during the same period, approached the Juvenile Protective Association about coordinating its activities with a city wide crime fighting organization, Mrs. Louise de Koven Bowen refused on the grounds that her organization, with its emphasis upon prevention, had a philosophy quite different from the Crime Commission and the Committee of Fifteen. "I feel, therefore" that we do not properly belong in a union of this kind," she wrote, "and therefore regretfully must decline the moral support which organizations of this kind might give us." Soon afterwards, Ryerson left for his summer vacation and postponed further negotiations until the autumn.[19]

Then in August, at the initiative of Amos C. Miller and other leaders of the State Bar Association, an Illinois Association for Criminal Justice was incorporated in the state. By the time that Ryerson returned in the fall, a state-wide organization had already begun organizing and there was little motivation to set up a parallel organization for the city. [20]

By autumn, then, it was clear that there would be a single Illinois Association for Criminal Justice. On September 9th, some thirty temporary directors, representing many of the leading civic associations of the city and state, met in the City Club to adopt by-laws and to take steps toward permanent organization of the association. Rush C. Butler, vice-president of the State Bar Association, became temporary chairman, and a committee headed by Sewell Avery began to select permanent officers and to establish committees to investigate particular areas of the administration of criminal justice. Eventually Rush C. Butler was chosen as the permanent president.[21] He, in turn, began negotiations with the Industrial Club to secure financial backing for the Illinois Association.

At a Club dinner in December, the president of the Missouri Association for Criminal Justice gave a talk on the results of the Missouri survey. Then at a closed meeting on January 27, 1927, the Industrial

Club voted an initial donation of $100,000 to finance a survey of the crime situation in the state.[22]

Then, in late March, the Crime Commission and the Illinois Association negotiated a contract to define the relationship between the two organizations. The contract provided that employees of the Illinois Association could use the files of the Crime Commission; and if properly reimbursed, the Commission would assist in preparation of the survey. The contract provided further that "the reports of such surveys shall be published as the joint work of the Illinois Association for Criminal Justice and of the Chicago Crime Commission." [23] Peace returned among the crime-fighting elite.

Meanwhile, the Illinois Association took steps to recruit staff and to open an office. Most of the permanent staff were persons who had been involved in crime surveys in other states and had therefore had long experience. Arthur Lashly, a former prosecutor for St. Louis county and director of the Missouri survey, would perform similar services in Illinois. Raymond Moley, a professor of public law at Columbia University who had served as Director of the Cleveland Foundation during the Cleveland survey, had acted as research director for the New York Crime Commission, and had been consultant to the Missouri survey, was selected as consultant to the Illinois survey. By now Moley was a recognized figure in the study of criminal justice. Finally Mr. C.E. Gelhke, a professor at Western Reserve University who had been statistician for the Cleveland and Missouri surveys, became statistician for the Illinois Association. In April of 1927, the Association opened its offices on the eighth floor of a building at 300 W. Adams Street in Chicago—one floor below the Crime Commission, whose offices were in the same building.[24]

Beginning in the early spring and working through the summer, the survey committee assembled the experts to supervise or prepare the various portions of the survey committee. It was chaired by Amos C. Miller of the State Bar Association, and consisted of Deans Harno and Hinton of the University of Illinois and University of Chicago Law schools, Andrew A. Bruce of the Institute of Criminal Law and Criminology, and the usual assortment of prominent business leaders. On the whole, the committee's standards were high, and its search for capable men was not limited to the state. From out-of-state, the survey committee chose Raymond Moley to study the Municipal Court. To survey the police systems of the state, the committee chose Bruce Smith of the National

Institute of Public Administration in New York. Later, however, Smith was asked to survey only the rural police. August Vollmer, the reform chief of Berkeley, California, who had consulted with many cities and states concerning police reorganization, was then given responsibility to study the Chicago police.

Most of the survey projects, however, were given to local scholars or legal experts. John J. Healy, a former State's Attorney for Cook County, undertook the examination of the State's Attorney's office while William D. Knight, State's Attorney for Winnebago County, assumed a similar position with regard to prosecution downstate. After Henry B. Chamberlin, Operating Director of the Chicago Crime Commission, declined to undertake the study of the criminal courts of Cook County, the survey committee persuaded E.W. Hinton, Dean of the University of Chicago Law School and a former Circuit Court Judge in Missouri, to undertake the task. For the appellate courts, the survey committee selected another law school dean, Albert J. Harno of the University of Illinois. To survey the jury system, the committee chose Gustave F. Fischer, chairman of the Industrial Club's jury service committee and the Crime Commission's jury committee.

For studies of such fields as organized crime, juvenile delinquency, and parole, the Illinois Association turned to scholars closely associated with the Chicago school of urban sociology. The study of juvenile delinquency, for instance, was given to the Research Bureau of the University of Chicago. In fact, the study consisted primarily of a report by Clifford Shaw and Henry McKay on their continuing and highly influential studies of delinquency at the Institute for Juvenile Research. The study of organized crime in Chicago was delegated to Professor Ernest W. Burgess of the University of Chicago's Department of Sociology.

His graduate student, John Landesco, had already begun such a study. Financial arrangements for Landesco's work were made through Northwestern's Institute of Criminal Law and Criminology. Finally Bruce Harno and Ernest W. Burgess had been asked by Hinton T. Claybaugh, State Supervisor of Paroles, to make a report to him concerning parole and probation. Their report, with some revision, then became part of the survey.

By autumn, 1927, most of the experts had begun research or were about to do so. Rush C. Butler, president of the Illinois Association, took the opportunity to call a state-wide meeting of judges, prosecuting attorney, bar association dignitaries, and other legal leaders to meet in the

Stevens Hotel in Chicago on December 30th. While the stated purpose of the meeting was to provide guidance to the survey staff, a further purpose was to give widespread support to the Illinois Association. The day-long discussions highlighted once more the generally punitive and deterrent atmosphere within which the survey leaders and staff were operating.[25]

Much of the research went on through the winter and spring of 1928. By spring, some of the studies were far enough along so that drafts could be submitted to the revision committee for final criticism and then release to press. Under the chairmanship of Amos C. Miller, the revision committee met frequently over lunch at the Union League Club to criticize and approve the various reports as they were completed by the persons responsible for them.[26]

Beginning in late April, Chicago newspapers began to publish news stories concerning the findings of the survey. These stories appeared during the period of the 1928 election campaign, following the "Pineapple Primary." They provided general exposure of the corrupt relationship between crime and politics that dominated the news of the period. The first report released by the Illinois Association for Criminal Justice was the statistical breakdown of what happened to felony charges in Cook County—a report showing that only 3.13 per cent of those charged with a felony were eventually imprisoned for the felony with which they had been charged. About ten days later, the report on Prosecution in Cook County received the following headline in the *Tribune:* "Find Chicago Crime Laughs at Law—Survey Shows How Justice is Defeated—Blame is Placed on State's Attorney." The report provided another opportunity for the *Tribune* to attack Robert Crowe for his administration of the office of State's Attorney. On July 6th the *Tribune* carried another story from the survey under the headline: "Easy to Bomb Foe in Chicago, Survey Shows." Not all of the stories were unfavorable to Chicago, however. Under the headline, "Survey Lifts Crime Cloud from Chicago," Arthur Lashley, director of the Illinois Association, was quoted as having made the following optimistic statement: "There have been no convictions in gang murder in the past two years, but such crimes are seldom solved in any large city, and so long as the gangsters only kill each other the public is not likely to get very badly excited about it."[27]

Once the various reports of the survey had been completed, however, the Illinois Association for Criminal Justice rapidly disintegrated on the assumption, apparently, that its task was completed. Those who had prepared the various parts of the survey, returned to their normal occupations. The Illinois Association retained sufficient office staff to oversee the publication of the *Illinois Crime Survey* in the spring of 1929. For a few months longer, a secretary remained in the office to handle routine clerical tasks and to provide copies of the Survey to those willing to pay the $6.00 price. By late October or early November, even the office closed. For a few more months, it was possible to secure a copy of the Survey by sending $6.00 to Rush C. Butler at his law office, but by early 1930 even that became impossible. When asked for a copy of the Survey in 1932, Henry B. Chamberlin could only write: "the Association appears to have gone out of business. I do not know of any subsequent meetings. It closed its offices, discharged its staff, and made no further effort to carry on its ambitious program.[28]

The dissolution of the Illinois Association for Criminal Justice was important, for it meant that no organization existed with any commitment to secure the reforms advocated by the *Illinois Crime Survey*. The dissolution was also ironic, for the major recommendation of the Survey had been that the Illinois Association take on the crucial task of mobilizing an intelligent public opinion and of coordinating the many private activities in the realm of crime-fighting. By disbanding, the Illinois Association failed to carry out its own major recommendation.[29]

Implications

Such is the chronology of the formation and dissolution of the Illinois Association for Criminal Justice. In order to understand many of the strengths and weaknesses of the organization, it is necessary to highlight some of the important factors involved in the leadership and organization of the Association.

The first factor is that the Illinois Association for Criminal Justice, despite its claims to statewide interests, was in fact brought into existence and dominated by persons from the Chicago metropolitan area. Of the two groups that had cooperated in the formation of the Illinois Association, the Ryerson Committee was entirely Chicago-based and concerned with Chicago problems. While the Special Committee on Enforcement of Criminal Law of the State Bar Association had a broad membership; its chairman (Amos C. Miller) was a Chicago lawyer. It held its meetings in Chicago, and the initiative lay with Chicago lawyers. Finally the Illinois Association itself, while its formal membership was drawn from various parts of the state, had its offices and staff in the Chicago metropolitan area. Chicago was perceived to be the major problem, and the Association focused upon crime and criminal justice there. It did not become what had been planned: an organization that might educate and rally good citizens throughout the state.

While the leadership behind the survey centered in Chicago, it was far from representative of Chicago. In fact, the Illinois Association was created and dominated by the top men in business, banking, and corporation law. Of the forty-nine members who can be identified as being from the Chicago area, fully seventy-five per cent fall into these categories. If we add law school professors—who were closely associated with the corporation lawyers—then the figure tops eighty per cent. The remainder of the members were scattered in a number of occupations, including three labor leaders, two university presidents, a sociologist, a Methodist minister, the Director of the Juvenile Protective Association, the secretary of the Central Howard Association, and others. Except for Ernest W. Burgess, the famed University of Chicago sociologist, there is no evidence that any of these were influential within the Association. The leaders of the Illinois Association were, then, the elite of the Chicago industrial and banking world—men who met together at exclusive clubs, were leaders of the bar and of the Association of Commerce, and dominated the leading civic organizations of the city.[30]

Not only had these men reached an elite status but their life experiences had differed considerably from those of their fellow citizens. In a city that was heavily Catholic, only one of the twenty-three for whom religious preference is known was a Catholic. In a city heavily immigrant in origins, only four of the forty-nine had been born in a foreign country of foreign parents—and two of those were born in Canada, one in England. At least thirty-seven of the forty-nine had some college education. A further sign of their elite status is their place of residence. The prestigious Hyde Park and Woodlawn areas around the University of Chicago, the Gold Coast along the lake on the near North Side, and the elite northern suburbs such as Evanston and Winnetka account for at least thirty-six of the forty-nine. Almost all of the rest lived in other upper income areas dominated by native-born Americans. Only Jessie Binford, Director of the Juvenile Protective Association and a resident of Hull House, can be identified as living in an "ethnic" neighborhood. If one examines the backgrounds of those who took leading roles in the founding and operation of the Illinois Association, their elite status and separation from the rest of the society is even more accentuated. It was the less influential members of the Association who were Catholic, or foreign born, or lacking in a college education.

It is interesting to compare the members of the Illinois Association with other groups in the city that were involved in criminal justice or criminal activity.

The following chart suggests that both crime and the administration of criminal justice involve persons with life experiences and values quite different from those of the members of the Illinois Association for Criminal Justice. Even the attorneys active in the Illinois Association seldom appeared in criminal court or associated with lawyers who did. Those who committed crimes and those who handled criminal justice procedures lived in a world apart from the social elite who set out to survey crime and criminal justice in the city. [31]

But if the elite reformers were separated by social distance and life experience from the criminal justice process, they were also separated from the political culture of the city and county. Of course, many of the elite reformers were good citizens and joined citizens' committees in support of the reform elements in each party. But they were generally separated in values, experience, and social distance from the men who constituted the dominant political organization of each party—the Brennan faction in the Democratic Party and the Thompson faction in the Republican Party.

In short, the members of the Illinois Association possessed great social prestige and economic power, but were separated from the criminal processes they hoped to change and from the political organizations through which the changes would have to take place.

While estranged from politics and criminal processes, the members of the Illinois Association had excellent contacts in the academic world. One area of contact was the close relationship between the elite lawyers and the prestige law schools in Illinois. Another line of contact is suggested by the fact that six of the more active members of the Illinois Association were trustees of the University of Chicago.[32] More directly, professors such as Burgess, Harno, and Bruce were themselves influential within the Illinois Association. The contacts with the academic world had important results. The first was that the Illinois Association was willing to recruit the leading experts to write the various sections of the report, for there was no distrust of scholarship. The second was that, while the driving motivation behind the formation of the Illinois Associa-

Chart 1.1

Ethnic Origin of Parents of Various Occupational Groups Involved in Crime or Criminal Justice Procedures in Chicago. (Figures are percentages for each occupational group)

	1929	1929	1929	1929	1930	1930
	POLICE CAPTAINS n=55	WARD COMMITTEEMEN n=99	CRIMINAL DEFENSE LAWYERS n=128	BAIL BONDSMEN n=158	DIRECTORS OF ORGANIZED CRIME n=108	BOOTLEGGERS n=947
IRISH	76	42	33	9	29	8
GERMAN	7	20	(see other)	(see other)	5	8
JEWISH	2	3	25	51	20	7
ITALIAN	(see other)	1	(see other)	10	31	25
NEGRO	0	(see other)	(see other)	(see other)	12	17
NATIVE WHITE AMERICAN	7	19	17	15	0	13
OTHER AND UNKNOWN	8	15	25	15	3	13 Polish: 8

tion was to fight crime through the deterrent effect of punishment, some sections of the Survey suggest the limitations of punishment and the importance of other factors in limiting criminal behavior. And, finally, the Survey recognized, at least intellectually, the limitations upon the Illinois Association for Criminal Justice that derived from its narrow membership. Those trained in the Chicago school of sociology were well aware of the cultural diversities and social distances that characterize urban life; they were therefore aware that the members of the Illinois Association were out of touch with major groups in the city that the Association hoped to change.

Not only did the social origins of the members of the Illinois Association influence its activities, but also factors connected with the organization and procedure of the Association. The *Illinois Crime Survey*, the key accomplishment of the Illinois Association, was addressed to everyone in general, and thus to no one in particular. No public official had any responsibility to make a decision about the Survey recommendations. So, all public authorities could therefore ignore it without even making a decision to do so. Any results from the survey would depend, as a result, upon the kind of pressure that the Illinois Association, or some other organization, could bring to bear upon public authorities. Hence it becomes important to understand why neither the Illinois Association nor any other organization rallied to support the recommendations of the Survey.

To begin with, the staff that prepared the Illinois Crime Survey consisted of persons committed to other careers. Once they had completed their part of the Survey, their primary responsibility to the Illinois Association was at an end. Indeed, those who were from out-of-town even left the city. Thus the responsibility for carrying out the reforms rested in an important sense with the business leaders and lawyers whose initiative had first led to the formation of the Illinois Association. Yet nearly four years passed between the time that they had begun plans for the Survey in 1925, and the time that the Survey was published in 1929; three years passed before the first sections of the Survey appeared, piecemeal, in 1928. That is a long time for busy men to mark time and yet remain interested. Furthermore, a good deal happened in the interim, particularly during and after the "Pineapple Primary" in the spring of 1928. There was an exciting political campaign for reform, extensive grand jury investigations, and numerous other exciting causes to be fought. Many elite reformers found outlets for their civic virtues in activities more exciting than working for the often rather technical reform advocated in the Illinois Crime Survey. By the time the Survey was completed, it did not seem so important as it had in 1925.

With the demise of the Illinois Association for Criminal Justice, the Chicago Crime Commission could have assumed the task of working for the recommendations. The two organizations had, after all, some connections. Nine of the members of the Crime Commission were also members of the Illinois Association, and the staff of the Crime Commission had assisted the staff of the Illinois Association during the early stages of data collection. During the period that Arthur Lashly and Raymond Moley were active with the Illinois Association, the Crime Commission asked each of them to prepare a critical assessment of the activities of the Crime Commission to guide the organization in its future planning. Furthermore, at the insistence of the Crime Commission, the individual reports of the Illinois Association and the final *Illinois Crime Survey* appeared with the Crime Commission as co-sponsor. Finally, of course, the Illinois Association had its office in the same building as the Crime Commission. Even as late as 1930, the Crime Commission wondered politely about the possibility that the Illinois Association might join the Crime Commission in a campaign for anti-crime legislation.[33]

Thus, while the Crime Commission did not become committed to the work of the Illinois Association, the Crime Commission was also far from hostile. Beginning in 1928, however, the Crime Commission, revitalized by the election of Frank J. Loesch to the presidency, undertook an extensive campaign of investigations and publicity to break the relationship of crime and politics in Chicago. These activities usurped the time and energies of Loesch and the entire staff of the Crime Commission, and there is no evidence that the Crime Commission ever considered working for the recommendations of the *Illinois Crime Survey*.

Notes

1. The *Illinois Crime Survey* (Chicago: Illinois Association for Criminal Justice with the Chicago Crime Commission, 1929, republished by Patterson Smith, 1968, p. 11).

2. For founding of Presidents' Council, see memo of March 10, 1927, in Chicago Crime Commission File Number 10937.

Formation of the Illinois Association for Criminal Justice 19

3. Illinois State Bar Association, Annual Report, 1925, pp. 192-98, and Quarterly Bulletin, XIV (October, 1925), 4.

4. Minutes of the Presidents' Council, July 9, 1925; letter of William R. Dawes to Sewell Avery, July 23, 1925; both in the file of the Chicago Association of Commerce, Presidents' Council, Special Committee on the Crime Situation, Chicago Historical Society, hereinafter cited as file of Special Committee C.H.S.

5. Minutes of the Special Committee on the Crime Situation, October 12 and 19, 1925, and Introductory remarks made at the first meeting of the Special Crime Committee" by Joseph T. Ryerson, in files of Special Committee; see also correspondence in Chicago Crime Commission File Number 5050-1.

6. Quotations from letter of William C. Graves (Rosenwald's Secretary) to Rosenwald, March 7, 1925, and letter of Leslie Lewis to Graves, November 3, 1925, in Rosenwald papers, University of Chicago Library. The papers contain fairly extensive correspondence on the subject through the year 1925. In founding of the Chicago Council of Social Agencies, see its Report, 1914-16, Bulletin Number 2, pp. 1-2.

7. Copy of report in Chicago Crime Commission file Number 5050-1.

8. See "Minutes of the Joint-Meeting of the Illinois State Bar Association and Special Committee on the Crime Situation, December 31, 1925"; and copies of two letters from Miller to Ryerson, January 6, 1926, in file of Special Committee, C.H.S.

9. From mimeographed "Report of the Sub-Committee on Plan Presented at the Meeting of the Committee on the Enforcement of Criminal Law of the Illinois State Bar Association, January 23, 1926," in Chicago Crime Commission File Number 295.

10. See correspondence in Chicago Crime Commission File Number 295; also Illinois Crime Survey, p. 11; also Herald and Examiner, February 17, 1926.

11. See Minutes of President's Council, January 14, 1926, in file of Special Committee, C.H.S.

12. For attempts at negotiation, see Minutes of Private Luncheon, January 25, 1926, in file of Special Committee, C.H.S.; and correspondence covering meeting of Ryerson Committee and Crime Commission on February 16th in Chicago Crime Commission File Number 5050-1. The Executive Committee resolution is in a memo from Gore to William R. Dawes, March 17, 1926, Chicago Crime Commission File Number 5050-1.

13. For Chamberlin's criticisms, see undated typewritten memo in Chicago Crime Commission File Number 5050-1.

14. Letter of William R. Dawes to Joseph T. Ryerson, March 25, 1926, in file of Special Committee, C.H.S.

15. Copy of letter, Montgomery to Dawes, April 23, 1926, in Chicago Crime Commission File Number 295.

16. See telegram of Ryerson to Crowell, March 27, 1925, and Crowell to Ryerson, March 29, 1925; and minutes of informal conference of April 12, 1925, in file of Special Committee, C.H.S.

17. See two memos of April 30, 1926, in Chicago Crime Commission File Number 5050-1; also Herald and Examiner, May 1, 1926.

18. *Chicago Tribune*, May 7, 1926; and letter of John R. Montgomery to Joseph T. Ryerson, May 12, 1926, in file of Special Committee, C.H.S.

19. Copy of letter of Charles Yeomans to Mrs. Bowen, July 2, 1926; letter of Mrs. Bowen to Joseph T. Ryerson, July 26, 1926, and copy of letter of Ryerson to Mrs. Bowen, July 30, 1926; all in file of Special Committee, C.H.S.

20. *Post*, August 16, 1926, and *Daily News*, August 17, 1926; see also correspondence of Ryerson for Autumn, 1926, in files of Special Committee, C.H.S.

21. News stories in *Herald and Examiner* and *Daily News* for September 9, 1926, and *Chicago Tribune* for September 10, 1926. During the previous months, Frank O. Lowden, former Republican Governor, had been offered the presidency and had declined it.

22. History of the Industrial Club (no author; Chicago, privately printed, 1934), pp. 66-68.

23. See a copy of the contract and extensive correspondence between the two organizations in Chicago Crime Commission File Number 10937.

24. Correspondence in Chicago Crime Commission File Number 10937.

25. Report of Proceedings, Joint Conference on Crime, held under the auspices of the Illinois Bar Association and Illinois Association for Criminal Justice, December 30, 1927 [Chicago, 1928].

26. See minutes and correspondence of survey committee in the Ernest W. Burgess papers, University of Chicago.

27. *Herald and Examiner*, April 28, 1928; *Tribune*, May 6, 1928; ibid., July 6, 1928; and *Herald and Examiner*, August 5, 1928. For many newspaper clippings concerning the survey, see the Chicago Crime Commission File Number 10937.

28. Copy of letter of Henry B. Chamberlin to Miss G. A. Churchill, November 19, 1932, in Chicago Crime Commission File Number 10937. The correspondence in this file is the only source for the last days of the Association. In 1940, Chamberlin wrote: "So far as the practical efforts accomplished as a result of the Illinois Crime Survey are concerned, I do not think that they can be emphasized. However, the book did cause some people to think and perhaps helped a bit in guiding public and official opinion." Copy of letter from Chamberlin to Harry D. Nims. December 4, 1940, Chicago Crime Commission File Number 10937.

29. See Illinois Crime Survey, especially pp. 1096-1100.

30. I wish to thank David Johnson, a student in the History Department of the University of Chicago, for assembling the statistics upon which this paragraph and the next are based.

31. Adapted from unpublished manuscript by William F. Ogburn and Clark Tibbits, "A Memorandum on Crime, and of Certain Related Criminal and Non-Criminal Groups in Chicago," July 30, 1930, pp. 9, 20-1, 42-48, in Charles E. Merriam papers, University of Chicago.

32. The University of Chicago trustees were Sewell Avery, Julius Rosenwald, Thomas E. Donnelly, Edward L. Ryerson, Trevor Arvett, and Charles R. Holden; see Annual Register of the University of Chicago, 1926-1927 (Chicago, 1927), p. 2.

33. With regard to the contract, see letters of Frank J. Loesch to Rush C. Butler, June 8, 1928, and to Henry B. Chamberlin, June 13, 1928, in Chicago Crime Commission File Number 10937. The correspondence and papers of the committee that studied the Crime Commission are in File Number 1000F-14. In the Crime Commission's newsletter, Criminal Justice, Number 58 (May, 1930), appeared the statement: "If the Illinois Association for Criminal Justice continues as a state-wide organization it will probably concern itself with legislation; something it has not yet undertaken. In order that such a legislative program may be as effective and valuable as possible, it is desirable that the Chicago Crime Commission cooperate very closely to this end." By this time, of course, the Illinois Association had already been out of existence for six months.

Chapter 2

John Landesco and the Illinois Crime Survey

The Illinois Crime Survey, despite its meager influence, was clearly the finest study of American crime and criminal justice that had been completed at the time. As published in 1929, the Survey contained nearly 1,100 pages of text, divided into sixteen sections, plus a conclusion by sociologist Ernest W. Burgess. The largest section, nearly 300 pages in length, was John Landesco's study of organized crime in Chicago. Some of the sections, by contrast, were less than twenty-five pages in length. As might be expected, the different sections varied considerably in quality. Although each section received the criticism and approval of the Revision Committee of the Illinois Association for Criminal Justice, such editorial supervision did not iron out differences of approach or even differences of opinion. Thus, while the Survey is a generally impressive document, it is a repetitive, uneven, and loosely organized document.

One way to analyze the Survey is to see it as the coming together of two generally divergent traditions. One tradition, shared by the men who formed and directed the Illinois Association for Criminal Justice, was the emphasis upon criminal justice as a punitive system designed to prevent crime through deterrence. The tradition regarded the breakdown criminal justice in the modern city as a major cause of crime; hence, improvements in the administration of criminal justice—making punishment immediate and certain—would contribute significantly to a decrease of crime. John H. Wigmore, Dean of the Northwestern University Law School and editor of the Illinois Crime Survey, summarized the tradition when

24   *Illegal Enterprise*

he wrote: "The main feature of what is wrong may be put into one word—inefficiency."[1]

The other tradition—represented in the Survey chiefly by Landesco's study of organized crime and by Clifford Shaw's study of juvenile delinquency—traced urban crime to the social structure of urban life. This tradition derived chiefly from the Chicago school of urban sociology. By placing its emphasis upon the social structure of the city, this tradition minimized the importance of criminal justice procedures in explaining the nature and extent of urban crime.

While a person could argue for both an increased "efficiency" in criminal justice procedures and an altering of the social structure of the city, the theories of crime involved in each tradition were essentially incompatible.

Social Roots of Crime

As suggested earlier, there was another tradition represented in the Survey—a tradition dealing not with criminal justice institutions but with the social roots of crime. The tradition was represented chiefly in a report on juvenile delinquency by Clifford R. Shaw of the Institute for Juvenile Research and a report on organized crime in Chicago by John Landesco of the Department of Sociology at the University of Chicago. The recommendations that resulted from these studies were more concerned with reforming social conditions and thus specifically minimized the importance of criminal justice procedures.

Landesco, for instance, hoped that the good citizen would come to realize "how deep-rooted and widespread are the practices and philosophy of the gangster in the life and growth of the city" and that, realizing this, he would pursue a program "that will not content itself with punishing individual gangsters and their allies, but will reach out into a frontal attack upon basic causes of crime in Chicago."[2] At the conclusion of the chapter on the juvenile delinquent, the Survey recommended a program of "community treatment for the prevention of delinquency." This program included a guaranteed minimum income ("a family income sufficient to maintain at least the minimum standard of living required for the health and social efficiency of the different members of the family"), a housing program for low-income families, a recreational program, and "the integration in each community of the work of existing agencies like settlements, clubs, playgrounds, in a unified plan for the treatment of delinquency."³

What sorts of analysis led to such recommendations? By plotting the residential patterns of delinquents in Chicago, Shaw demonstrated that delinquency was concentrated in certain neighborhoods which shared a number of social characteristics. These were the neighborhoods adjacent to the Loop and those contiguous to the large industrial areas near the Chicago river, the stockyards, Calumet Lake, and South Chicago.

Such areas ware "characterized by marked physical deterioration, poverty, and social disorganization." Surrounding these areas of deterioration were neighborhoods populated chiefly by immigrant groups with "confused cultural standards, where traditions and customs of the immigrant group are undergoing radical change under the pressure of a rapidly growing city and the fusion of divergent cultures." Delinquency, then, was to be understood as a normal response to such aspects of the child's social world as "the community, the family, the gang, the play group, and the school."⁴

Since delinquency was a group behavior reflecting the culture of the neighborhood, it was not surprising that the neighborhoods with high delinquency rates exhibited a heavy concentration of juvenile gangs and adult crime. Over ninety percent of juvenile thefts were committed by younger boys in large gangs; holdups and other serious crimes were committed by older and more experienced boys in groups of two or three. The gangs established a social basis by which the youth moved from petty crimes, often at the age of eight or nine, toward recruitment into adult criminal activities. In such neighborhoods, the successful criminal was often an honored figure, and a youth often gained prestige by serving time in a correctional institution.

The social disorganization and poverty of such neighborhoods prevented the development of family and community controls that might successfully prevent such developments.⁵ Although immigrants and Negroes predominated in delinquency areas, Shaw traced criminal behavior to the social characteristics of the neighborhoods and not to the culture of the immigrants. Within the same immigrant group, there would be a high delinquency rate among those living in deteriorated and disorganized neighborhoods and a low rate among those in more stable neighborhoods.

As an immigrant group improved its standing and moved to better parts of the city, then, the delinquency rate fell markedly. The following chart, showing the place of birth of parents of delinquents, indicates such changes:

Nativity of fathers of delinquent boys expressed in percentages of total number of cases[6]

	1900	1910	1925
German	20.4	14.5	3.5
Irish	18.7	12.3	3.1
Italian	5.1	7.9	12.8
Polish	15.1	18.6	21.9

Thus, the Germans and Irish, who moved out of the poor neighborhoods during the period, showed a marked decline in delinquency, while the Italians and Poles, who replaced them, showed a marked increase.

Shaw's studies of juvenile delinquency, which he summarized for the *Illinois Crime Survey*, were major contributions to our understanding of urban delinquency and urban crime. During the same period, he published his findings at greater length in such books as *The Jack-Roller* and *Delinquency Areas*. Because of a growing recognition of the importance of his sociological explanations of delinquency, Shaw was chosen by the Wickersham Commission to write the volume on juvenile delinquency in its multi-volume report on law enforcement in the United States. By the early 1940's, Shaw drew together his thoughts in a classic book, which he co-authored with Henry D. McKay, who had been his research assistant in preparing his brief report for the Illinois Crime Survey.

Thus, the treatment of juvenile delinquency in the Survey was an early summary of theories which were stated at greater length and with greater subtlety in other works.[7]

While Shaw's study of juvenile delinquency was a summary of work that he published in more complete form elsewhere, John Landesco's study of organized crime was his major research effort. Born in Rumania in 1890 and arriving in the United States at the age of ten, he studied in the public schools of Chicago and at various schools in Wisconsin and Ohio. In 1924, he received his Ph.B. [bachelor's degree] from the University of Chicago, and soon thereafter became Ernest W. Burgess' research associate on the important parole study which Burgess, Bruce Harno, and Andrew A. Bruce undertook at the request of Hinton W. Claybaugh and which eventually became part of the Illnois Crime Survey. At about the same time, Landesco also became a graduate student in sociology at the University of Chicago, where he began a study of organized crime in Chicago, financed by the Carnegie and Rockefeller Foundations. His study of organized crime, begun independently of the Illinois Association for Criminal Justice, was published as part of the Illinois Crime Survey—certainly the longest and probably the most important part.[8]

Citing evidence from a mass of newspaper clippings extending back before 1910, as well as from his interviews with individual criminals, Landesco undertook to account for the prevalence of crime and the relative immunity of members of criminal gangs in Chicago. His study showed Chicago to be a crime-ridden city. He described the organized activities in gambling, bootlegging, and prostitution carried on openly by criminal groups. He showed the influence of racketeering and strong arm methods in labor organizations and in some phases of business activities. He cataloged the innumerable murders, bombings, and extortions carried on by gangsters with impunity. He described how criminals paid off the police and exercised influence upon the prosecution and the courts. He provided example after example of cases in which gangsters intimidated jurors or silenced prosecution witnesses by bribery, threats, or assassination. He explained how criminal gangs, through their organizing ability or through intimidation and fraud, controlled elections in wide areas of the city. And he showed how the gangster was often a hero within his neighborhood and was bound by ties of loyalty and friendship to important political leaders of the city and county. Yet, in presenting a picture that the ordinary good citizen would see as lawlessness, Landesco's purpose was to reveal the social patterns that in fact existed.

To begin with, Landesco argued that organized crime was not the creation of the Prohibition era. On the contrary, he showed that the profits of prohibition attracted men already active in various phases of organized crime in Chicago—gambling, vice, and racketeering. There was, in fact, a direct line of succession from Big Jim Colosimo, who was vice overlord in Chicago prior to his murder in 1920, through John Torrio and then Al Capone.

Organized crime, then, could not be explained by prohibition but had to be explained on the basis of social characteristics of urban life that long preceded the advent of a demand for bootleg liquor. Landesco started with the assumption, rooted in the findings of the Chicago school of sociology, that Chicago was "divided into areas widely separated from one another in economic status, customs, and standards." The social distance, for instance, between the elite Gold Coast residential area along the lake and the Back-of-the-Yards area around the stockyards was tremendous, so that the residents "live as if in two worlds."

"The gangster is a product of his surroundings," Landesco wrote,

> in the same way in which the good citizen is a product of his environment. The good citizen has grown up in an atmosphere of obedience to law and of respect for it. The gangster has lived his life in a region of law breaking, of graft, and of "fixing." That is the reason why the good citizen and the gangster have never been able to understand each other. They have been reared in two different worlds.[9]

Landesco hoped, by describing the social world of the criminal, to educate the good citizen so that he or she might more intelligently confront the problem of urban crime.

In describing the social world of the criminal, Landesco recognized but did not emphasize such factors as poverty, rapid turnover of population, the immigrants' ignorance of American ways, and other such factors that characterized the disorganization of the urban slums. Rather, he emphasized the models of behavior and the social groups that gave some structure to slum life. Within slum neighborhoods such traits as family solidarity, mutual aid, and ethnic loyalties were highly valued. Thus the racketeer and the political boss—by remaining loyal to their neighborhood and by achieving an often well-deserved reputation as a person who helps a guy in need—were admired figures. They served as models of success for the youthful gangs of the slum areas. Their positions within their neighborhoods were demonstrated at testimonial dinners that marked their moments of success and at the wakes and crowded funerals that marked their passing.

The gangster and politician were inevitably linked by ties of friendship and mutual favors. The politician provided the gangster with protection and acted as a broker between the criminal world and the criminal justice system. The gangster, at the same time, provided the politician with votes and political workers, as well as with such illegal services as fraud and strong-arm tactics on election day. These ties were often hidden from the view of newspapers and the public. But, in a brilliant chapter on the funerals of gangsters, Landesco showed how "in the hour of death, personal ties are disclosed, which in life were concealed." When Big Jim Colosimo, vice overlord of Chicago, was killed in 1920, "three judges, eight aldermen, an assistant states attorney, a congressman, a state representative, and leading artists of the Chicago Opera Company are listed as honorary pallbearers, as well as gamblers, ex-gamblers, dive-keepers, and ex-dive keepers." At the funeral of Anthony D'Andrea a year later, no fewer than twenty-one judges were honorary pallbearers, while the funeral procession extended two and one-half miles. Such ostentation and honor for the city's underworld figures could only shock and amaze the newspapers and the good citizens of the city.[10]

In his emphasis upon social factors, Landesco specifically denied the importance of psychological aberration as an explanation of criminal behavior. He found, in his four-year association with criminals in Chicago, that they did not feel remorse or feel that their activities were immoral. Indeed, for a criminal, the question of justifying his activities often did not even arise unless he was confronted at some stage with the contrary values held by good citizens. Then his justification was likely to involve pointing out the virtues of the criminal—his loyalty to his friends, his services to his ethnic group, or his kindness to his wife and children. Another line of justification involved the notion that most occupations are rackets. Policemen solicit bribes, politicians take graft, businessmen cheat or bend the law in various ways. The difference between the good citizen and the criminal was that the good citizens attempted to define their "rackets" as legitimate and the criminals' rackets as illegitimate.[11]

Landesco believed that the 1920's were a period of transition in the social relations that characterized organized crime in Chicago, a change that resulted from the large profits and centralized organization of bootlegging. The personal relations of gangsters with each other and with police and politicians were less often based upon the friendships and shared values of the neighborhood and were more likely to be based on formal and business-like relationships. "The old basis in friendly relations is being superseded by a cash nexus," Landesco argued.[12]

The Capone gang was not rooted in the neighborhood but was rather an effort to systematize and centralize the organization of bootlegging, vice, and gambling in the city. In some ways, the new organization of crime was more sinister than the old: the organization was city-wide, immunity from arrest and conviction was the result of purchase rather than friendship and organized criminals were more systematically involved in exploiting the profits from illegal activities.[13]

Shaw and Landesco, then, traced urban crime to the social structure and social dislocation of certain geographical areas of the city. Shaw's chapter was an early and brief statement of views that were important and influential in the history of academic efforts to uncover the causes of juvenile delinquency. Landesco's study, while little known at the time, is nevertheless one of the most significant attempts to understand organized urban crime in this country. But Shaw and Landesco, despite the high quality of their studies, exerted little influence upon the attitudes and activities of the economic elite of the city. Much to the contrary, these leaders' continuing campaign against crime in Chicago was rooted in the deterrent tradition.

Conclusion

So far, the analysis of the Illinois Crime Survey has emphasized those themes that appeared prominently in the Survey. But something can also be learned about the assumptions of the Survey by asking what problems and topics were *not* covered by the Survey.

One theme that was largely missing was a concern for civil liberties in the criminal justice process. The dominant view was that the defendant had undue advantage, not that defendant needed his rights safeguarded. Yet if as the Survey claimed, only seventy per cent of the 13,000 persons arrested for felonies in Cook County in a given year were later indicted, this could imply that large numbers of persons were being arrested, imprisoned, and harassed by the police without legal justification. The statistics could, in other words, suggest monumental abuse of police power. Nevertheless, the official interpretation given the statistics was generally that the failures to indict were failures to bring criminals to justice.

The Survey was silent on the question of police harassment, the third degree, and wholesale arrests without cause. It did not consider the question of whether the indigent were at a disadvantage before the courts or whether a system of public defenders might be useful or necessary. In considering Constitutional issues, the Survey mildly regretted that the Illinois Supreme Court forbad the introduction of evidence secured by illegal search or seizure. (The Survey, however, did praise the Court for preventing the use of confessions obtained by third degree methods.) Finally, the whole felony waiver issue, one of the crucial procedural issues discussed in the Survey, was treated entirely as a procedure that allowed a defendant to escape his merited punishment. The blame was thrown upon the State's Attorney and the courts for allowing defendants to plead guilty to lesser offenses and thus to escape the full penalty of the law. Yet the procedure could also be seen as a method by which the State's Attorney and the courts might pressure a defendant into pleading guilty in cases where the evidence was so weak that he or she would have been found not guilty if they had stood trial on the original charge. In general, then, the individuals conducting the Survey were not attuned to the civil liberties issues involved in criminal justice.[14]

To a considerable extent, of course, the emphasis of the Survey is understandable in view of the realities of criminal justice at the time. Political favoritism, incompetence and inefficiency, and intimidation of witnesses and jurors, were obvious and widespread. The emphasis, however, was also a result of the deterrent tradition which shaped the attitudes of the men who conducted the Survey and a result of the social distance between them and the defendants caught up in the criminal justice procedures.

A second subject—purposely not studied in the Survey—was the validity of the criminal law themselves. Most notably, the Survey did not examine the wisdom of prohibition. Beyond this, no consideration was given to the question of whether such activities as gambling and prostitution should continue to be regulated by use of the criminal law rather than by some other method.

Nor did the Survey consider the possibility that the criminal laws of the state might need codifying and clarifying. The failure to examine the criminal laws was the result of a belief that crime stemmed from a failure to punish lawbreakers rather than from defects in the criminal law itself.

The specific decision to avoid the knotty problems of prohibition was, of course, largely political in origin. In Chicago, prohibition was a major political issue that bitterly divided the city. The Illinois Association for Criminal Justice shied away precisely because any firm stand on the issue would arouse antagonisms and weaken acceptance of other recommendations. Only oblique references to prohibition appeared in the Survey.

In discussing gangland murders, for instance, Arthur V. Lashly suggested that enforcement of laws against gambling and bootlegging would deprive the gangs of profits and thereby deprive them of reason to murder each other. Ernest W. Burgess picked up the same theme: "The enormous revenues derived from bootlegging have purchased protection for all forms of criminal activities and have demoralized law enforcing agencies." And he added somewhat lamely that, since enforcement was chiefly a problem of securing public support, "once the relation between the profits of bootlegging and activities of organized crime is clearly seen, there should be no insuperable difficulties in the way of some practical form of control of the situation." Any proposal which called for a change in the public attitude toward prohibition in Chicago as a prelude to enforcement was certainly not a demand for enforcement within the foreseeable future.[15]

Furthermore, the authors of the Illinois Crime Survey were so convinced that evil men destroyed the effectiveness of the criminal justice system that they gave scant consideration to other possibilities. There was little tendency to inquire whether, given the range and quantity of tasks performed by the courts, prosecutor, and police; and given the complex relationship between these institutions—many of the administrative practices were not, in fact, inevitable. In other words, could even the best of men have done much to change the institutions given the institutional tasks and relationships that then existed? In addition, the Survey did little to explore the possibility that many of the practices that were criticized by the Survey performed positive functions. Perhaps a good criminal justice system should have more flexibility than was recognized by the men who conducted the Survey.

A final problem with the Survey was that, while it contained literally hundreds of recommendations, it did not assign priorities among the recommendations and did not provide a practical program for putting the recommendations into effect. The Survey contained no estimate of the costs which many its many recommendations would involve. It viewed politics with deep suspicion; yet would surely have to use the political process to achieve many of its goals.

In the conclusion to the Survey, Professor Ernest W. Burgess attempted, with only limited success, to meet the problem by summarizing the recommendations and providing a program.

He argued that "the control of organized crime is always in the last analysis, a problem of public opinion." No single crusade, but only a long and sustained change in public attitudes, could hope to meet the challenge revealed by the Illinois Crime Survey. On the one hand, an intelligent public, armed with facts, could elect and support the sort of officials who could reorganize the criminal justice system and remove the police, the courts, and the prisons from political favoritism and corruption. On the other hand, a campaign of education might break down the barriers that separated the immigrant communities from the native American communities. "The lack of full participation on the part of many immigrant communities in general public opinion," he wrote, "is only matched by the ignorance of the native American of the lake front neighborhoods [concerning] conditions of life and thought in the river wards." Thus, through public opinion, there was an opportunity to reform the administration of criminal justice and also to reduce the social distances that separated communities in the city.[16] Burgess recommended that the Illinois Association for Criminal Justice, or some similar organization, undertake the research and educational functions necessary to reform public opinion.

There are at least two points to be noticed about Burgess' proposals. First, he continued the general tendency of the Survey to work independently of the politicians who held office and made the crucial political decisions. Instead of approaching the mayor, judges, or state's attorney with recommendations, he would first approach the public and bring about its enlightenment. Secondly, Burgess did not really suggest a program of reform based upon the Survey; instead, he proposed that either the Illinois Association for Criminal Justice or some similar organization should undertake to frame a specific and practical program.

The *Illinois Crime Survey*, then, proposed many reforms but offered little in the way of a concrete and immediate program. When the Illinois Association for Criminal Justice passed out of existence, there was no prospect that the Survey might become a platform for change. It was published stillborn.

Notes

1. *Illinois Crime Survey* (Chicago, 1929), p. 5.
2. *Ibid.*, p. 1057.
3. *Ibid.*, pp. 728 & 729.
4. *Ibid.*, pp. 652 & 650.

5. *Ibid.*, especially 650-670.
6. Adapted from chart, *Ibid.*, p. 667.
7. For other books by Shaw, see *Delinquency Areas: A Study of Geographical Distribution of School Truants, Juvenile Delinquents, and Adult Offenders in Chicago* (Chicago, 1929); *The Jack-Roller, a Delinquent Boy's Own Story* (Chicago, 1930); and *The Natural History of a Delinquent Career* (Chicago, 1931). The Wickersham Commission report can be found in Shaw and Henry D. McKay, *Social Factors in Juvenile Delinquency*, Publication No. 13, Causes of Crime of the National Commission on Law Observance and Enforcement (Washington, D.C. 1931, Volume II). The classic summary of their views is Shaw and McKay, *Juvenile Delinquency and Urban Areas* (Chicago, 1942).
8. See *Who's Who in Chicago and Vicinity* (1941).
9. *Illinios Crime Survey*, p. 1057.
10. Quotations from *Ibid.*, pp. 1039 & 1026.
11. *Ibid.*, pp. 1043 ff.
12. *Ibid.*, p. 1039.
13. *Ibid.*, especially pp. 1010, 1012 & 1021.
14. An explanation of ways in which pressure to plead guilty in order to have the charge reduced resulted in injustice will be found in Samuel Daske, "Cracks in the Foundation of Criminal Justice," *Illinois Law Review*, XLVI (July-August, 1951), especially pp. 393-395. For contemporary recognition of the abuse involved in arrest and detention of many persons who were not held for trial, see Arthur L. Beeley, *The Bail System in Chicago* (Chicago, 1927), passim.
15. *Illinois Crime Survey*, pp. 639-640, 1099.
16. Quotations from *Ibid.*, pp. 1095 & 1097.

Chapter 3

Organized Crime in Urban Society: Chicago in the Twentieth Century

Many journalists have written exciting accounts of organized crime in American cities and a handful of scholars have contributed analytical and perceptive studies.[1] Yet neither the excitement in the journalistic accounts nor the analysis in the scholarly studies fully captures the complex and intriguing role of organized criminal activities in American cities during the first third of the twentieth century. The paper that follows, although focusing on Chicago, advances hypotheses that are probably true for other cities as well. The paper examines three major, yet interrelated, aspects of the role of organized crime in the city: first, the social worlds within which the criminals operated and the importance of those worlds in providing social mobility from immigrant ghettos; second, the diverse patterns by which different ethnic groups became involved in organized criminal activities and were influenced by those activities; and third, the broad and pervasive economic impact of organized crime in urban neighborhoods and the resulting influence that organized crime did exert.

Crime and Mobility

During the period of heavy immigrant movement into the cities of the Northeast and Midwest, organized crime provided paths of upward mobility for many young men raised in ethnic slums. The gambling kings, vice lords, bootleggers and racketeers often began their careers in the ghetto neighborhoods; and frequently these neighborhoods continued to be the centers for their entrepreneurial activities. A careful study of the leaders of organized crime in Chicago in the late 1920s found that 31 percent were of Italian background, 29 percent of Irish background, 20 percent Jewish, and 12 percent black; none were native white of native white parents.[2] A recognition of the ethnic roots of organized crime, however, is only a starting point for understanding its place in American cities.

At a risk of oversimplification, it can be said that for young persons in the ethnic ghettos three paths lay open to them. The vast majority became, to use the Chicago argot, "poor working stiffs." They toiled in the factories, filled menial service and clerical jobs, or opened mom-and-pop stores. Their mobility to better jobs and to homeownership was, at best, incremental.[3] A second, considerably smaller group followed respectable paths to relative success. Some of this group went to college and entered the professions; others rose to management positions in the business or governmental hierarchies of the city.

There existed, however, a third group of interrelated occupations which, although not generally regarded as respectable, were open to uneducated and ambitious ethnic youths. Organized crime was one such occupational world, but there were others.

One was urban machine politics. Many scholars have, of course, recognized the function of politics in providing mobility for some members of ethnic groups.[4] In urban politics, a person's ethnic background was often an advantage rather than a liability. Neighborhood roots could be the basis for a career that might lead from poverty to great local power, considerable wealth, or both.

A second area consisted of those businesses that prospered through political friendships and contacts. Obviously, construction companies that built the city streets and buildings relied upon government contracts. But so also did banks in which government funds were deposited, insurance companies that insured government facilities, as well as garbage contractors, traction companies and utilities that sought city franchises. Because political contacts were important, local ethnic politicians and their friends were often the major backers of such enterprises.[5]

A third avenue of success was through leadership in the city's labor unions. The Irish in Chicago dominated the building trade unions and most of the other craft unions during the first 25 years of this century. But persons of other ethnic origins could also rise to leadership positions, especially in those unions in which their own ethnic group predominated.⁶ Another path of mobility was sports. Boxing, a peculiarly urban sport, rooted in the neighborhood gymnasiums, was the most obvious example of a sport in which Irish champions were succeeded by Jewish, Polish and black champions. Many a fighter, even if he did not reach national prominence, could achieve considerable local fame within his neighborhood or ethnic group. He might then translate this local fame into success by becoming a fight manager, saloon keeper, politician or racketeer.⁷

A fifth area often dominated by immigrants was the entertainment and night life of the city. In Chicago, immigrants—primarily Irish and Germans—ran the city's saloons by the turn of the century. During the 1920s, Greek businessmen operated most of the taxi-dance halls. Restaurants, cabarets and other night spots were similarly operated by persons from various ethnic groups.

Night life also provided careers for entertainers, including B-girls, singers, comedians, vaudeville and jazz bands. Jewish comedians of the 1930s and black comedians of our own day are examples of a larger phenomenon in which entertainment could lead to local and even national recognition.⁸

The organized underworld of the city, then, was not the only area of urban life that provided opportunities for ambitious young men from the ghettos. Rather, it was one of several such areas. Part of the pervasive impact of organized crime resulted from the fact that the various paths were interrelated, binding together the worlds of crime, politics, labor leadership, politically-related businessmen, sports figures and the night life of the city. What was the nature of the interrelationships?

To begin with, organized crime often exerted important influences upon the other social worlds. For aspiring politicians, especially during the early years after an ethnic group's arrival in a city, organized crime was often the most important source of money and manpower. (By the turn of the century, an operator of a single policy wheel in Chicago could contribute not only thousands of dollars but also more than a hundred numbers writers to work the neighborhoods on election day.) On occasion, too, criminals supplied strong-arm men to act as poll watchers. They organized repeat voters; and they provided other illegal but necessary campaign services. Like others engaged in ethnic politics, members of the organized underworld often acted from motives of friendship and common ethnic loyalties. But because of the very nature of their activities, criminal entrepreneurs required and therefore sought political protection. It would be difficult to exaggerate the importance of organized crime in the management of politics in many of the wards of the city.9

Furthermore, it should not be thought that the politics of large cities like Chicago was peculiarly influenced by organized crime. In a large and heterogeneous city, there were always wards within which the underworld exercised little influence and which could therefore elect politicians who would work for honest government and law enforcement. But in the ethnic and blue-collar industrial cities west or southwest of Chicago, the influence of organized crime sometimes operated without serious opposition. In Cicero, west of Chicago along major commuting lines, gambling ran wide open before the 1920s; and after 1923 Capone's bootlegging organization safely had its headquarters there. In other towns, like Stickney and Burnham, prostitution and other forms of entertainment often operated with greater openness than in Chicago. This symbiotic relationship, in which surrounding blue-collar communities provided protected vice and entertainment for the larger city, was not limited to Chicago. Covington, Kentucky, had a similar relationship to Cincinnati, while East St. Louis serviced St. Louis.10

The organized underworld was also deeply involved in other areas of immigrant mobility. Organized criminals worked closely with racketeering labor leaders and thus became involved in shakedowns, strike settlements and decisions concerning union leadership. They were participants in the night life, owned many of the night spots in the entertainment districts, and hired and promoted many of the entertainers. (The comedian Joe E. Lewis started his career in Chicago's South Side vice district as an associate and employee of the underworld; his case was not atypical.)11 Members of the underworld were also sports fans and gamblers and therefore became managers of prize fighters, patrons at the race tracks and loyal fans at ball games. An observer who knew many of Chicago's pimps in the 1920s reported:

> The pimp is first, last and always a fight fan. He would be disgraced if he didn't go to every fight in town. . . . They hang around gymnasiums and talk fight. Many of them are baseball fans, and they usually get up just about in time to go to the game. They know all the players and their information about the game is colossal. Football is a little too highbrow for them, and they would be disgraced if they played tennis, but of late the high grade pimps have taken to golf, and some of them belong to swell golf clubs.12

However, criminals were not merely sports fans; some ran gambling syndicates and had professional interests in encouraging sports or predicting the outcome of sports events. Horse racing was a sport conducted primarily for the betting involved. By the turn of the century, leading gamblers and bookmakers invested in and controlled most of the race tracks near Chicago and in the rest of the nation. A number of successful gamblers had stables of horses and thus mixed business with pleasure while becoming leading figures in horse race circles. At a less important level, Capone's organization in the late 1920s owned highly profitable dog tracks in Chicago's suburbs.[13]

The fact that the world of crime exerted powerful influences upon urban politics, business, labor unions, sports and entertainment does not adequately describe the interrelations of these worlds. For many ambitious men, the worlds were tied together because in their own lifetimes they moved easily from one area to another or else held positions in two or more simultaneously. In some ways, for instance, organized crime and entertainment were barely distinguishable worlds. Those areas of the city set aside for prostitution and gambling were the major entertainment districts of the city. Many cabarets and other night spots provided gambling in backrooms or in rooms on upper floors. Many were places where prostitutes solicited customers or where customers could find information concerning local houses of prostitution. During the 1920s, places of entertainment often served liquor and thus were retail outlets for bootleggers. In the world of entertainment, the distinction between legitimate and illegitimate was often blurred beyond recognition.[14]

Take, as another example, the career of William Skidmore. At age fourteen, Billie sold racing programs at a race track near Chicago. By the time he was twenty-one, in the 1890s, he owned a saloon and cigar store, and soon had joined with others to operate the major policy wheels in Chicago and the leading handbook syndicate on the West Side. With his growing wealth and influence, he had by 1903 also become ward committeeman in the thirteenth ward and was soon a leading political broker in the city. In 1912, he was Sergeant-at-Arms for the Democratic National Convention and, afterwards, aided Josephus Daniels in running the Democratic National Committee. Despite his success as gambler and politician, his saloon, until well into the 1920s, was a hangout for pickpockets and con men; and "Skid" provided bail and political protection for his criminal friends. In the twenties Skidmore branched into the junk business and made a fortune selling junk obtained through contracts with the county government. Not until the early 1940s did he finally go to prison, the victim of a federal charge of income tax evasion. In his life, it would be impossible to unravel the diverse careers to determine whether he was saloon keeper, gambler, politician or businessman.[15]

The various social worlds were united not simply by the influence of organized crime and by interlocking careers; the worlds also shared a common social life. At local saloons, those of merely local importance met and drank together. At other restaurants or bars, figures of wider importance had meeting places. Until his death in 1920, Big Jim Colosimo's restaurant in the South Side vice district brought together the successful from many worlds; the saloon of Michael (Hinky Dink) Kenna, first ward Alderman, provided a meeting place in the central business district. Political banquets, too, provided opportunities for criminals, police, sports figures and others to gather in honor of a common political friend. Weddings and funerals were occasions when friends met to mark the important passages through life. At the funeral of Colosimo—politician, vice lord and restaurateur—his pallbearers included a gambler, two keepers of vice resorts, and a bail bondsman. Honorary pallbearers were five judges (including the chief judge of the criminal courts), two congressmen, nine resort keepers or gamblers, several aldermen and three singers from the Chicago Opera. (His good friend, Enrico Caruso, was unable to be present.) Such ceremonial events symbolized the overlapping of the many worlds of which a man like Colosimo was a part.[16]

Thus far we have stressed the social structure that linked the criminal to the wider parts of the city within which he operated. That social world was held together by a system of values and beliefs widely shared by those who participated in crime, politics, sports and the night life of the city. Of central importance was the cynical—but not necessarily unrealistic—view that society operated through a process of deals, friendships and mutual favors. Hence the man to be admired was the smart operator and dealer who handled himself well in such a world. Because there was seen to be little difference between a legal and an illegal business, there was a generally tolerant attitude that no one should interfere with the other guy's racket so long as it did not interfere with one's own.[17] This general outlook was, of course, widely shared, in whole or in part, by other groups within American society so that there was no clear boundary between the social world of the smart operators and the wider society.

In a social system held together by friendships and favors, the attitude toward law and legal institutions was complex. A basic attitude was a belief that criminal justice institutions were just another racket—a not unrealistic assessment considering the degree to which police, courts and prosecutor were in fact used by political factions and favored criminal groups. A second basic attitude was a belief that, if anyone cooperated with the law against someone with whom he was associated or to whom he owed favors, he was a stoolpigeon whose behavior was beneath contempt. This does not mean that criminal justice institutions were not used by members of organized crime. On a day-to-day basis, members of the underworld were tied to police, prosecutors and politicians through payments and mutual favors. Criminal groups often used the police and courts to harass rival gangs or to prevent the development of competition. But conflicts between rival groups were also resolved by threats or violence. Rival gambling syndicates bombed each others' places of business, rival union leaders engaged in bombing and slugging, and rival bootlegging gangs after 1923 turned to assassinations that left hundreds dead in the streets of Chicago.[18] The world of the rackets was a tough one in which a man was expected to take his knocks and stand up for himself. Friendship and loyalty were valued; but so also were toughness and ingenuity.

Gangsters, politicians, sports figures and entertainers prided themselves for being smart guys who recognized how the world operated. They felt disdain mixed with pity for the "poor working stiffs" who, ignorant of how the smart guys operated, toiled away at their menial jobs. But if they disdained the life of the working stiff, they also disdained the pretensions of those "respectable" groups who looked askance at the world within which they operated. Skeptical that anyone acted in accordance with abstract beliefs or universalistic principles, the operators believed that respectable persons were hypocrites. For instance, when Frank J. Loesch, the distinguished and elderly lawyer who headed the Chicago Crime Commission, attacked three criminal court judges for alleged political favoritism, one politician declared to his friends:

> Why pick on these three judges when every judge in the criminal court is doing the very same thing, and always have. Who is Frank Loesch that he should holler? He has done the same thing in his day. . . . He has asked for plenty of favors and has always gotten them. Now that he is getting older and is all set and doesn't have to ask any more

favors, he is out to holler about every one else. . . . There are a lot of these reformers who are regular racketeers, but it won't last a few years and it will die out.[19]

In short, the world view of the operators allowed them to see their world as being little different from the world of the respectable persons who looked down upon them. The whole world was a racket.

Ethnic Specialization

Some have suggested that each ethnic group, in its turn, took to crime as part of the early adjustment to urban life. While there is some truth to such a generalization, the generalization obscures more than it illuminates the ethnic experiences and the structure of crime. In important respects, each ethnic group was characterized by different patterns of adjustment; and the patterns of involvement in organized crime often reflected the broader patterns of each ethnic group. Some ethnic groups—Germans and Scandinavians, for instance—appear not to have made significant contributions to the development of organized crime. Among the ethnic groups that did contribute, there was specialization within crime that reflected broader aspects of ethnic life. In Chicago, by the turn of the century, for example, the Irish predominated in two areas of organized crime. One area was labor racketeering, which derived from the importance of the Irish as leaders of organized labor in general.[20]

The second area of Irish predominance was the operation of major gambling syndicates. Irish importance in gambling was related to a more general career pattern. The first step was often ownership of a saloon, from which the owner might move into both politics and gambling. Many Irish saloon keepers ran handbooks or encouraged other forms of gambling in rooms located behind or over the saloon. Those Irishmen who used their saloon as a basis for electoral politics continued the gambling activities in their saloons and had ties to larger gambling syndicates.

Other saloon keepers, while sometimes taking important but backstage political positions such as ward committeeman, developed the gambling syndicates. Handbooks required up-to-the-minute information from race tracks across the country. By establishing poolrooms from which information was distributed to individual handbooks, a single individual could control and share in the profits of dozens or even hundreds of handbooks.

The Irish also predominated in other areas of gambling. At the turn of the century, they were the major group in the syndicates that operated the policy games, each with hundreds of policy writers scattered in the slum neighborhoods to collect the nickels and dimes of the poor who dreamed of a lucky hit. They also outfitted many of the gambling houses in the Loop which offered roulette, faro, poker, blackjack, craps and other games of chance. Furthermore, many top police officers were Irish and rose through the ranks by attaching themselves to the various political factions of the city. Hence a complex system of Irish politicians, gamblers and police shared in the profits of gambling, protected gambling interests and built careers in the police department or city politics. Historians have long recognized the importance of the Irish in urban politics. In Chicago, at any rate, politics was only part of a larger Irish, politics-gambling complex.[21]

The Irish politics-gambling complex remained intact until about World War I. By the 1920s, however, the developing black ghetto allowed black politicians and policy operators to build independent gambling and political organizations linked to the Republicans in the 1920s and the Democratic city machine in the 1930s. By the 1920s, in addition, Jewish gamblers became increasingly important, both in the control of gambling in Jewish neighborhoods and in operations elsewhere. Finally, by the mid-1920s, Italian bootleggers under Capone took over gambling in suburban Cicero and invested in Chicago gambling operations. Gambling had become a complex mixture of Irish, Negro, Jewish and Italian entrepreneurship.[22]

Although the Irish by the twentieth century played little direct role in managing prostitution, Italians by World War I had moved into important positions in the vice districts, especially in the notorious Levee district on the South Side. (Political protection, of course, often had to be arranged through Irish political leaders.) Just as the Irish blocked Italians in politics, so also they blocked Italians in gambling, which was both more respectable and more profitable than prostitution. Hence the importance of prohibition in the 1920s lay not in initiating organized crime (gambling continued both before and after prohibition to be the major enterprise of organized crime); rather, prohibition provided Italians with an opportunity to break into a major field of organized crime that was not already monopolized by the Irish.[23]

This generalization, to some extent, oversimplifies what was in fact a complex process. At first, prohibition opened up business opportunities for large numbers of individuals and groups, and the situation was chaotic. By 1924, however, shifting coalitions had emerged. Some bootlegging gangs were Irish, including one set of O'Donnell brothers on the far West Side and another set on the South Side. Southwest of the stockyards, there was an important organization, both Polish and Irish, coordinated by "Pollack" Joe Saltis. And on the Near North Side a major group—founded by burglars and hold-up men—was led by Irishmen like Dion O'Banion, Poles like Earl (Hymie) Weiss and George (Bugs) Moran, and Jews like Jack Zuta and the Gusenberg brothers. There were, finally, the various Italian gangs, including the Gennas, the Aiellos, and, of course, the Capone organization.[24]

The major Italian bootlegging gang, that associated with the name of Al Capone, built upon roots already established in the South Side vice district. There John Torrio managed houses of prostitution for Big Jim Colosimo. With Colosimo's assassination in 1920, Torrio and his assistant, Capone, moved rapidly to establish a bootlegging syndicate in the Loop and in the suburbs south and west of the city. Many of their associates were persons whom they had known during humbler days in the South Side vice district and who now rose to wealth with them. Nor was their organization entirely Italian. Very early, they worked closely with Irishmen like Frankie Lake and Terry Druggan in the brewing of beer, while Jake Guzik, a Jew and former South Side pimp, became the chief business manager for the syndicate. In the bloody bootlegging wars of the 1920s, the members of the Capone organization gradually emerged as the most effective organizers and most deadly fighters. The success of the organization brought wealth and power to many ambitious Italians and provided them with the means in the late 1920s and early 1930s to move into gambling, racketeering and entertainment, as well as into a broad range of legitimate enterprises. Bootlegging allowed Italians, through entrepreneurial skills and by assassination of rivals, to gain a central position in the organized underworld of the city.[25]

Although Jewish immigrants in such cities as Cleveland and Philadelphia were major figures in bootlegging and thus showed patterns similar to Italians in Chicago, Jews in Chicago were somewhat peripheral figures. By World War I, Chicago Jews, like Italians, made important inroads into vice, especially in vice districts on the West Side. In the 1920s, with the dispersal of prostitution, several Jewish vice syndicates operated on the South and West Sides. Jews were also rapidly invading the world of gambling.[26] Although Jews took part in vice, gambling and bootlegging, they made a special contribution to the organized underworld by providing professional or expert services. Even before World War I, Jews were becoming a majority of the bail bondsmen in the city. By the 1920s, if not before, Jews constituted over half the fences who disposed of stolen goods. (This was, of course, closely related to Jewish predominance as junk dealers and their importance in retail selling.) Jews were also heavily overrepresented among defense attorneys in the criminal courts. It is unnecessary to emphasize that the entrepreneurial and professional services of Jews reflected broader patterns of adaptation to American urban life.[27]

Even within relatively minor underworld positions, specialization by ethnicity was important. A study of three hundred Chicago pimps in the early 1920s, for instance, found that 109 (more than one-third) were black, 60 were Italian, 47 Jewish and 26 Greek.[28] The large proportion of blacks suggests that the high prestige of the pimp among some elements of the lower-class black community is not a recent development, but has a relatively long tradition in the urban slum. There has, in fact, long been a close relationship of vice activities and Negro life in the cities. In all probability, the vice districts constituted the most integrated aspect of Chicago society. Black pimps and madams occasionally had white girls working for them, just as white pimps and madams sometimes had black girls working for them. In addition, blacks held many of the jobs in the vice districts, ranging from maids to entertainers. The location of major areas of vice and entertainment around the periphery and along the main business streets of the South Side black neighborhood gave such activities a pervasive influence within the neighborhood.[29]

Black achievements in ragtime and jazz had their roots, at least in part, in the vice and entertainment districts of the cities. Much of the early history of jazz lies among the talented musicians—black and white—who performed in the famous resorts in the Storyville district of New Orleans in the 1890s and early 1900s. With the dissolution of Storyville as a segregated vice district, many talented black musicians carried their styles to Chicago's South Side, to Harlem, and to the cabarets and dance halls of other major cities. In the 1920s, with black performers like King Oliver and Louis Armstrong and white performers like Bix Beiderbecke, Chicago was an important environment for development of jazz styles. Just as Harlem became a center for entertainment and jazz for New Yorkers during prohibition, so the black and tan cabarets and speakeasies of Chicago's South Side became a place where blacks and whites drank, danced and listened to jazz music—to the shock of many respectable citizens. Thus, in ways that were both destructive and productive, the black experience in the city was linked to the opportunities that lay in the vice resorts, cabarets and dance halls of the teeming slums.30

In the operation of entertainment facilities and policy rackets, black entrepreneurs found their major outlet and black politicians found their chief support. Until there has been more study of comparative ethnic patterns, only tentative hypotheses are possible to explain why various ethnic groups followed differing patterns. Because many persons involved in organized crime initiated their careers with customers from their own neighborhood or ethnic group, the degree to which a particular ethnic group sought a particular illegal service would influence opportunities for criminal activities. If members of an ethnic group did not gamble, for instance, then ambitious members of that ethnic group could not build gambling syndicates based upon local roots. The general attitude toward law and law enforcement, too, would affect opportunities for careers in illegal ventures. Those groups that became most heavily involved in organized crime migrated from regions in which they had developed deep suspicions of government authority—whether the Irish fleeing British rule in Ireland, Jews escaping from Eastern Europe, Italians migrating from southern Italy or Sicily, or blacks leaving the American South. Within a community suspicious of courts and government officials, a person in trouble with the law could retain roots and even respect in the community. Within a community more oriented toward upholding legal authority, on the other hand, those engaged in illegal activities risked ostracism and loss of community roots.

In other ways, too, ethnic life styles evolved differently. Among both Germans and Irish, for instance, friendly drinking was part of the pattern of relaxation. Although the Irish and Germans by 1900 were the major managers of Chicago's saloons, the meaning of the saloon was quite different for the two groups. German saloons and beer gardens were sometimes for family entertainment and generally excluded gambling or prostitution; Irish saloons, part of an exclusively male social life, often featured prostitution or gambling and fit more easily into the world of entertainment associated with organized crime. Finally, it appears that south Italians had the highest homicide rate in Europe. There was, in all probability, a relationship between the cultural factors that sanctioned violence and private revenge in Europe and the factors that sanctioned the violence with which Italian bootleggers worked their way into a central position in Chicago's organized crime.[31]

There were, at any rate, many ways that the immigrant background and the urban environment interacted to influence the ethnic experience with organized crime. For some ethnic groups, involvement in organized crime was not an important part of the adjustment to American urban life. For other groups, involvement in the organized underworld both reflected and influenced their relatively unique patterns of acculturation.

Economic Impact

The economic role of organized crime was an additional factor underlying the impact of organized crime upon ethnic communities and urban society. Organized crime was important because of the relatively great wealth of the most successful criminals, because of the large numbers of persons directly employed by organized crime, and because of the still larger numbers who supplemented their income through various part-time activities. And all of this does not count the multitude of customers who bought the goods and services offered by the bootleggers, gambling operators and vice lords of the city.

During the first thirty or forty years after an immigrant group's arrival, successful leaders in organized crime might constitute a disproportionate percentage of the most wealthy members of the community. (In the 1930s at least one-half of the Blacks in Chicago worth more than $100,000 were policy kings;[32] Italian bootleggers in the 1920s may have represented an even larger proportion of the very wealthy among immigrants from southern Italy. The wealth of the successful criminals was accompanied by extensive political and other contacts that gave them considerable leverage both within and outside the ethnic community. They had financial resources to engage in extensive charitable activities, and often did so lavishly. Projects for improvement of ethnic communities often needed their support and contacts in order to succeed. Criminals often invested in or managed legitimate business enterprises in their communities. Hence, despite ambiguous or even antagonistic relations that they had with "respectable" members of their ethnic communities, successful leaders in organized crime were men who had to be reckoned with in the ethnic community and who often represented the community to the outside world.[33]

In organized crime, as in other economic activities, the very successful were but a minority. To understand the economic impact of crime, it is necessary to study the many persons at the middle and lower levels of organization. In cities like Chicago the number of persons directly employed in the activities of organized crime was considerable. A modest estimate of the number of fulltime prostitutes in Chicago about 1910 would be 15,000—not counting madams, pimps, procurers and others in managerial positions. Or take the policy racket. In the early 1930s an average policy wheel in the black ghetto employed 300 writers; some employed as many as 600; and there were perhaps 6,000 policy writers in the ghetto. The policy wheels, in this period of heavy unemployment, may have been the major single source of employment in the black ghetto, a source of employment that did not need to lay off workers or reduce wages merely because the rest of the economy faced a major depression. Finally, during the 1920s, bootlegging in its various aspects was a major economic activity employing thousands in manufacture, transportation and retailing activities.[34]

Yet persons directly employed constituted only a small proportion of those whose income derived from organized crime. Many persons supplemented their income through occasional or part-time services. While some prostitutes walked the streets to advertise their wares, others relied upon intermediaries who would direct customers in return for a finder's fee. During certain periods, payments to taxi drivers were sufficiently lucrative so that some taxi drivers would pick up only those passengers seeking a house of prostitution. Bellboys, especially in the second-class hotels, found the function of negotiating between guests and prostitutes a profitable part of their service. (Many of the worst hotels, of course, functioned partly or wholly as places of assignation.) Bartenders, newsboys and waiters were among the many helpful persons who provided information concerning places and prices.[35]

Various phases of bootlegging during the 1920s were even more important as income supplements. In the production end, many slum families prepared wine or became "alky cookers" for the bootlegging gangs—so much so that after the mid-1920s, explosions of stills and the resulting fires were a major hazard in Chicago's slum neighborhoods. As one observer reported:

> During prohibition times many respectable Sicilian men were employed as "alky cookers" for Capone's, the Aiello's or for personal use. Many

of these people sold wine during prohibition and their children delivered it on foot or by streetcar without the least fear that they might be arrested... During the years of 1927 to 1930 more wine was made than during any other years and even the "poorest people" were able to make ten or fifteen barrels each year—others making sixty, seventy, or more barrels.

Other persons, including policemen, moonlighted as truck drivers who delivered booze to the many retail outlets of the city. Finally, numerous persons supplemented their income by retailing booze, including bellboys, janitors in apartment buildings and shoe shine boys.[36]

The many persons who mediated between the underworld and the law were another group that supplemented its income through underworld contacts. Large numbers of policemen, as well as bailiffs, judges and political fixers, received bribes or political contributions in return for illegal cooperation with the underworld. Defense attorneys, tax accountants and bail bondsmen, in return for salaries or fees, provided expert services that were generally legal.[37]

For many of the small businessmen of the city, retailing the goods or services of the underworld could supplement business income significantly. Saloons, as already mentioned, often provided gambling and prostitution as an additional service to customers. Large numbers of small businesses were outlets for handbooks, policy, baseball pools, slot machines and other forms of gambling. A substantial proportion of the cigar stores, for example, were primarily fronts for gambling; barber shops, pool halls, newsstands, and small hotels frequently sold policy or would take bets on the horses. Drug stores often served as outlets for cocaine and, during the 1920s, sometimes sold liquor.[38]

The organized underworld also influenced business activity through racketeering. A substantial minority of the city's labor unions were racketeer-controlled; those that were not often used the assistance of racketeer unions or of strong-arm gangs during strikes. The leaders of organized crime, as a result, exercised control or influence in the world of organized labor. Not so well known was the extensive racketeering that characterized small business organizations. The small businesses of the city were generally marginal and intensely competitive. To avoid cut-throat competition, businessmen often formed associations to make and enforce regulations illegally limiting competition. The Master Barbers Association, for example, set minimum prices, forbad a shop to be open after 7:30p.m., and ruled that no shop could be established within two blocks of another shop. Many other types of small businesses formed similar associations: dairies, auto parts dealers, garage owners, candy jobbers, butcher stores, fish wholesalers and retailers, cleaners and dyers, and junk dealers. Many of these associations were controlled, or even organized, by racketeers who levied dues upon association members and controlled the treasuries; they then used a system of fines and violence to insure that all businessmen in the trade joined the association and abided by the regulations. In return for control of the association's treasury, in short, racketeers performed illegal services for the association and thereby regulated much of the small business activity of the city.[39]

Discussion of the economic influence of organized crime would be incomplete without mentioning the largest group that was tied economically to the underworld, namely, the many customers for the illegal goods and services. Like other retailers in the city, some leaders of organized crime located their outlets near the center of the city or along major transportation lines and serviced customers from the entire region; others were essentially neighborhood businessmen with a local clientele. In either case, those providing illegal goods and services usually attempted to cultivate customer loyalty so that the same customers would return on an ongoing basis and advertise among their friends. Organized crime existed because of wide customer demand, and a large proportion of the adult population of the city was linked to organized crime on a regular basis for purchase of goods and services.

Heroism and Ambiguity

Because of the diverse ways that successful criminal entrepreneurs influenced the city and ethnic communities, many of them became heroes—especially within their own communities. There were a variety of reasons for the admiration that they received. Their numerous philanthropies, both large and small, won them reputations as regular guys who would help a person in need. Moreover, they were often seen as persons who fought for their ethnic communities. They aided politicians from their communities to win elections in the rough and often violent politics of the slums and thereby advanced their ethnic group toward political recognition. Sometimes they were seen as fighters for labor unions and thus as friends of labor. And, on occasion, they fought directly for their ethnic group. There was, for instance, the case of the three Miller brothers from Chicago's West Side Jewish ghetto. In typical ghetto pattern, one became a boxer, one a gangster and one a policeman. The boxer and gangster were heroes among Jews on the West Side, where for many years Jewish peddlers and junk dealers had been subjected to racial slurs and violent attacks by young hoodlums from other ethnic groups. "What I have done from the time I was a boy," Davy Miller told a reporter,

> was to fight for my people here in the Ghetto against Irish, Poles or any other nationality. It was sidewalk fighting at first. I could lick any five boys or men in a sidewalk free-for-all.

When the Miller brothers and their gang protected the Jews of the West Side, the attacks against them abated.[40] Particularly for youngsters growing up in the ghettos, the gangsters were often heroes whose exploits were admired and copied. Davy Miller modestly recognized this when he said:

> Maybe I am a hero to the young folks among my people, but it's not because I'm a gangster. It's because I've always been ready to help all or any of them in a pinch.

An Italian student at the University of Chicago in the early 1930s remembered his earlier life in the Italian ghetto:

> For 26 years I lived in West Side "Little Italy," the community that has produced more underworld limelights than any other area in Chicago. . . . I remember these men in large cars, with boys and girls of the neighborhood standing on the running board. I saw them come into the neighborhood in splendor as heroes. Many times they showered handfuls of silver to youngsters who waited to get a glance at them—the new heroes—because they had just made headlines in the newspapers. Since then I have seen many of my playmates shoot their way to the top of gangdom and seen others taken for a ride.[41]

Nevertheless, despite the importance of gangsters and the world within which they moved, their relations to ethnic groups and the city were always ambiguous. Because many of their activities were illegal, they often faced the threat of arrest and, contrary to common belief, frequently found themselves behind bars. Furthermore, for those members of the ethnic community who pursued respectable paths to success, gangsters gave the ethnic group a bad name and remained a continuing source of embarrassment. St. Clair Drake and Horace R. Cayton, in their book on the Chicago black ghetto, describe the highly ambiguous and often antagonistic relations of the respectable black middle class and the policy kings. In his book on Italians in Chicago, Humbert S. Nelli explains that in the 1920s the Italian language press refused to print the name of Al Capone and covered the St. Valentine's Day massacre without suggesting its connection with bootlegging wars.[42]

The respectable middle classes, however, were not the only ones unhappy about the activities or notoriety of gangsters. Organized crime sometimes contributed to the violence and fear of violence that pervaded many of the ghetto neighborhoods. Often local residents feared to turn to the police and lived with a stoical acceptance that gangs of toughs controlled elections, extorted money from local businesses and generally lived outside the reach of the law. Some immigrant parents, too, resented the numerous saloons, the open prostitution and the many gambling dens—all of which created a morally dangerous environment in which to raise children. Especially immigrant women, who watched their husbands squander the meager family income on liquor or gambling, resented the activities of organized crime. Within a number of neighborhoods, local churches and local leaders undertook sporadic campaigns for better law enforcement.[43]

Organized crime, then, was an important part of the complex social structure of ethnic communities and urban society in the early twentieth century. For certain ethnic groups, organized crime both influenced and reflected the special patterns by which the groups adjusted to life in urban America. Through organized crime, many members of those ethnic groups could achieve mobility out of the ethnic ghettos and into the social world of crime, politics, ethnic business, sports, and entertainment. Those who were successful in organized crime possessed the wealth and contacts to exercise broad influence within the ethnic communities and the city. The economic activities of the underworld provided jobs or supplemental income for tens of thousands. Despite the importance of organized crime, however, individual gangsters often found success to be ambiguous. They were not always able to achieve secure positions or to translate their positions into respectability.

Notes

1. The following are probably the most useful scholarly studies analyzing the relationship of organized crime to the social structure of the city: John Landesco, *Organized Crime in Chicago,* 2nd ed. (Chicago, 1968); St. Clair Drake and Horace R. Cayton, *Black Metropolis: A Study of Negro Life in a Northern City* (New York, 1945), II, especially ch. 17 and 19; William F. Whyte, *Street Corner Society: The Social Structure of an Italian Slum,* 2nd ed. (Chicago, 1955), ch. 4 and 5; Daniel Bell, "Crime as an American Way of Life: A Queer Ladder of Mobility," *The End of Ideology,* rev. ed. (New York, 1961), ch. 7; Humbert S. Nelli, *The Italians in Chicago, 1880-1930: A Study in Ethnic Mobility* (New York, 1970), ch. 5 and pp. 210-22; and John A. Gardiner, *The Politics of Corruption: Organized Crime in an American City* (New York, 1970).

   I use the term "organized crime " for those activities involving the sale of illegal goods and services. Prostitution, gambling and bootlegging were the major types during the early twentieth century ("juice" and heroin came later). Because labor racketeering and small business racketeering were closely tied to organized crime, I also discuss them in the paper.

2. William F. Ogburn and Clark Tibbitts, "A Memorandum on the Nativity of Certain Criminal Classes Engaged in Organized Crime, and of Certain Related Criminal and Non-Criminal Groups in Chicago." Unpublished manuscript, July 30, 1930, pp. 9-11, in Charles E. Merriam papers, Univ. of Chicago Library, Chicago, Ill.

3. For statistical discussions of immigrant mobility, see Stephan Thernstrom, *Poverty and Progress: Social Mobility in a Nineteenth Century City* (Cambridge, Mass., 1964); Stephan Thernstrom and Richard Sennett, eds., *Nineteenth-Century Cities: Essays in the New Urban History* (New Haven, 1969), pp. 49-208.

4. The literature on urban politics and ethnic mobility is voluminous. For general discussions, see Harold Zink, *City Bosses in the United States: A Study of Twenty Municipal Bosses* (Durham, N.C., 1930); Robert K. Merton, *Social Theory and Social Structure* (Glencoe, Ill., 1957), especially pp. 71-2; Eric L. McKitrick, "The Study of Corruption," *Political Science Quarterly,* LXXII (Dec. 1957), 505-06. For specific discussion of Chicago, see Joel A. Tarr, "The Urban Politician as Entrepreneur." *Mid-America,* XLIX (Jan. 1967), 55-61. For social backgrounds of machine politicians, see Harold F. Gosnell, *Machine Politics, Chicago Model,* 2nd ed. (Chicago, 1968), especially ch. 3; and John M. Allswang, *A House for All Peoples: Ethnic Politics in Chicago, 1890-1936* (Lexington, 1971), especially pp. 84-90 and ch. 8.

5. For example, see Joel A. Tarr, "J.R. Walsh of Chicago: A Case Study in Banking and Politics, 1881-1905," *The Business History Review,* XL (Winter 1966), 451-466.

6. Royal E. Montgomery, *Industrial Relations in the Chicago Building Trades* (Chicago, 1927), passim; Italian involvement in labor leadership discussed in Nelli, *Italians in Chicago,* pp. 78-85.

7. The importance of boxing in local ethnic communities gathered from various news stories appearing in Chicago newspapers. A colorful and useful history is Nat Fleischer, *The Heavyweight Championship: An Informal History of Heavyweight Boxing from 1719 to the Present Day* (New York, 1961). A study of sports as a path of mobility is much needed; for tentative discussions, see David Riesman and Reuel Denney, "Football in America: A Study in Culture Diffusion," *American Quarterly,* III (Winter 1951), 309-325; concerning pool hustlers, see Ned Polsky, *Hustlers, Beats, and Others* (New York, 1969), especially 76-77.

8. Ethnic background of selected saloon keepers from *History of Chicago and Souvenir of the Liquor Interest* (Chicago [1892]), pp. 136-254; concerning Greek ownership of taxi-dance halls, see Paul G. Cressey, "Report on Summer's Work with the Juvenile Protective Association of Chicago," typewritten paper, Oct. 1925, in Ernest W. Burgess papers, University of Chicago Library, II-A, Box 39. Jewish comedians of the 1930s included Bert Lahr, Fannie Brice (who married Nicky Arnstein, a gambler and con man), Eddie Cantor, George Jessel, Groucho Marx, Willie Howard and Jack Pearl; see book review in *New York Times Book Review* (Nov. 23, 1969), p. 1.

9. Discussions of the relationship of organized crime and politics in Chicago are numerous: Landesco, *Organized Crime,* ch. 8; Lloyd Wendt and Herman Kogan, *Lords of the Levee: The Story of Bathhouse John and Hinky Dink* (Indianapolis, 1943); Ovid Demaris, *Captive City* (New York, 1969); or the various issues of *Lightnin'*, an occasional newspaper published by the Rev. Elmer L. Williams in the 1920s and 1930s.

10. For studies of Cicero, Stickney or Burnham, see Paul M. Kinzie, "General Summary" of crime in Cicero, typewritten report, Dec. 1923, in Juvenile Protective Association papers, folder 92, in Library of University of Illinois at Chicago Circle; "Commercialized Prostitution;" typewritten report, May 2-26, 1933, Ibid., folder 97; K.B. Alwood and J.L. Munday, "Stickney," unpublished term paper, March 1930, in Burgess papers, 11-A, Box 39; investigators' reports, Committee of Fifteen files, vols. X and XI, University of Chicago Library; Daniel Russell, "The Road House: A Study of Commercialized Amusements in the Environs of Chicago," M.A. thesis in sociology, University of Chicago, 1931, pp. 13-49,61-75, and 95 ff; Jack McPhaul, *Johnny Torrio, First of the Gang Lords* (New Rochelle, N.Y., 1971), especially pp. 116-18 and ch. 12; and John Kobler, *Capone: The Life and World of Al Capone* (New York, 1971), pp. 55-56 and ch. 8.

11. Art Cohn, "The Joker is Wild," in Albert Halper, ed., *The Chicago Crime Book* (New York, 1967), pp. 45-64.

12. Ben L. Reitman, *The Second Oldest Profession: A Study of the Prostitute's "Business Manager"* (New York, 1931), pp. 169-170.

13. Good social histories of horse racing and betting, like social histories of other sports, still need to be written. Perhaps the best general picture of the interrelations of betting and racing can be gotten from Hugh Bradley, *Such was Saratoga* (New York, 1940); see also Josiah Flynt, "The Pool Room Vampire and Its Money-Mad Victims," *Cosmopolitan* Magazine, XLII (Feb. 1907), 368-370. For information about Chicago, see Wendt and Kogan, *Lords of the Levee,* especially pp. 28-30 and 50-58; *New York World,* Oct. 6, 1901; Citizens' Association of Chicago, *Bulletin* No. 14 (May 24, 1905); and various stories in Chicago newspapers.

14. There are numerous descriptions of entertainment and vice areas of Chicago, by newspaper reporters and by other investigators. See, for example, the investigators' reports in the Committee or Fifteen files and the many reports on commercialized entertainment commissioned by the Juvenile Protective Association and now deposited in the Association's files. For relations of the Capone organization to the North Side entertainment district in the early 1930s, see R.H. Sayler, "Capone Faction," undated, typewritten research paper in Burgess papers, 11-A, Box 14.

15. George Murray, *The Madhouse on Madison Street* (Chicago, 1965), pp. 366-374; Chicago *Record-Herald,* Nov. 4, 1903, April 1, 4, 21, 27 and 28, 1904; Informant E, typewritten "Special Report," July 30 and 31, 1914, and Informant N, typewritten "Special Report," Aug. 22, 1914, in Charles E. Merriam papers, University of Chicago Library, Box 87, folders 2 and 3; Chicago *Daily Tribune,* Jan. 8, 1918; *Lightnin',* III (June, 1929), 3; Demaris, *Captive City,* p. 139.

16. For discussions of Colossimo's life, see McPhaul, *Johnny Torrio,* pp. 69, 115; Kobler, *Capone,* ch. 3 and 4; and Charles Washburn, *Come Into My Parlor: A Biography of the Aristocratic Everleigh Sisters of Chicago* (New York, 1936), especially ch. 11; his funeral is described in Landesco, *Organized Crime,* ch. 9. Some of the local political and criminal hangouts are described in investigators' reports, Charles E. Merriam papers, Boxes 87 and 88. Political banquets are described in Landesco, *Organized Crime,* pp. 176-78, and in *Lightnin',* I, No. 3, p. 2, and No. 5, pp. 1 and 34.

17. The philosophy is best described in Landesco, *Organized Crime,* ch. 10, but the same philosophy is expressed whenever gangsters were asked about themselves; see, for example, [anon.], "A Good Hoodlum," typewritten term paper, 1933, Burgess papers, 11-A, Box 72. For reminiscences of a person raised on the periphery of the subculture, see Joseph Epstein, "Coming of Age in Chicago"; *Commentary,* XLVIII (Dec. 1969), 61-68.

18. The use of violence described in Landesco, *Organized Crime,* Ch. 5-7.

19. Quotation from confidential report in Chicago Crime Commission, File No. 11170, Chicago, Ill. Al Capone echoed the same view when he explained

to a lady reporter: "They talk about me not being on the legitimate. Why, lady, nobody's on the legit. You know that and so do they. Your brother or your father gets in a jam. What do you do? Do you sit back and let him go over the road, without trying to help him? You'd be a yellow dog if you did. Nobody's really on the legit, when it comes down to cases, you know that." See Kobler, *Capone,* pp. 268-69.

20. For discussions of Chicago labor racketeering, see Montgomery, *Industrial Relations,* passim; John Hutchinson, *The Imperfect Union· A History of Corruption in American Trade Unions* (New York, 1970), especially chs. 4 and 9; and the extensive correspondence and printed material in the Victor A. Olander papers, folders 115 and 266-68, in Library of University of Illinois at Chicago Circle.

21. Discussion of the Irish politics-gambling complex based primarily on Herman F. Schuettler, Scrapbook of Newspaper Clippings . . . 1904-1908, 2 vols., in Chicago Historical Society; see also Citizens' Association of Chicago, *Bulletin* No. 11 (July 31, 1903), and Landesco, *Organized Crime,* ch. 3.

22. The development of gambling can best be followed in the extensive files of the Chicago Crime Commission, especially File No. 65. Negro policy is discussed in Drake and Cayton, *Black Metropolis,* II, ch. 17; see also Harold F. Gosnell, *Negro Politicians: The Rise of Negro Politics in Chicago,* Phoenix ed. (Chicago, 1966), pp. 122-35.

23. For descriptions of Italian involvement in South Side vice, see McPhaul, *Johnny Torrio,* pp. 69-155; Kobler, *Capone,* chs. 3 and 4; and investigators' reports, Merriam papers, Boxes 87 and 88.

24. Most accounts of Chicago bootlegging concentrate upon Capone and slight the contributions of other groups. The development of the other groups can be followed, however, in the extensive files of the Chicago Crime Commission dealing with each of the leading bootlegging gangs.

25. Of the many accounts of the rise of the Capone organization, the best are Kobler, *Capone,* and McPhaul, *Johnny Torrlo;* see also Fred D. Pasley, *Al Capone: The Biography of a Self-Made Man* (New York, 1930). The movement of the Capone organization into racketeering can be followed in the Olander papers, folders 266-68; a series of stories in Chicago *Tribune,* March 19, 27, 1943; and Demaris, *Captive City,* pp. 22-29. Despite their success in crime, Italians did not displace the Irish from politics; in 1929, out of 99 ward committeemen in Chicago, 42 were Irish and only one was Italian; see Ogburn and Tibbitts, "Memorandum on Nativity," p. 45.

26. On the role of Mike de Pike Heitler and other Jews in West Side vice before World War I, see Murray, *Madhouse on Madison Street,* ch. 30; and investigators' reports in Merriam papers, especially Box 88, folders 1 and 6. On Jewish syndicates in the 1920s, see the following investigative reports in the Juvenile Protective Association papers: "Law Enforcement and Police," Nov.

29, 1922, and Dec. 3, 1922, folder 94, and "Commercialized Prostitution," Dec. 10, 1922, folder 92. For Jewish gamblers, see Chicago Crime Commission File No. 65; also Demaris, *Captive City*, pp. 104-107.

27. Bradstreet reports on 30 major bail bondsmen are attached to letters of Assistant Corporation Counsel to Harry J. Olson, April 9 and 29, 1913, in Chicago Municipal Court papers, folder 24, Chicago Historical Society. Ethnicity could be established for eighteen, of whom nine were Jewish. Half of the thirty bail bondsmen were saloon keepers. By the late 1920s, Jews constituted 51 per cent of bail bondsmen (out of 158 studied); see Ogburn and Tibbitts, "Memorandum on Nativity," p. 48. Figures on Jewish fences and defense attorneys in Ibid., pp. 15 and 47-48.

28. Reitman, *The Second Oldest Profession*, pp. 167-68.

29. The interrelationship of blacks and vice districts is discussed in Chicago Commission on Race Relations, *The Negro in Chicago* (Chicago, 1922), pp. 342-48; Reitman, *Second Oldest Profession,* ch. 11; Walter C. Reckless, *Vice in Chicago* (Chicago, 1933), passim; and the many investigators' reports in the Committee of Fifteen papers.

30. For the migration of jazz to Chicago and its development there, see Nat Shapiro and Nat Hentoff, eds., *Hear Me Talkin' to Ya: The Story of Jazz as Told by the Men Who Made It* (New York, 1966), pp. 80.164; Eddie Condon, *We Called It Music: A Generation of Jazz* (New York, 1947); and Milton Mezzrow and Bernard Wolfe, *Really the Blues* (New York, 1946). An excellent general social history of jazz is Neil Leonard, *Jazz and the White Americans: The Acceptance of a New Art Form* (Chicago, 1962).

31. Italian homicide rate mentioned in Rudolph J. Vecoli, "*Contadini* in Chicago: A Critique of The Uprooted," *Journal of American History,* LI (Dec. 1964), 406. For an interesting discussion of ways that Italian criminals in the United States reflected south Italian values, see Francis A. J. Ianni, "The Mafia and the Web of Kinship," *The Public Interest,* XXII (Winter 1971), 78-100. A thorough criticism of the literature which interprets American organized crime as a transfer of the Sicilian mafia is in Joseph L. Albini, *The American Mafia: Genesis of a Legend* (New York, 1971), especially chs. 5 and 6.

32. On blacks, this is my surmise from information in Drake and Cayton, *Black Metropolis,* II, pp. 514 and 546.

33. See Drake and Cayton, *Black Metropolis,* II, pp. 492-94 and passim; Nelli, *Italians in Chicago,* especially pp. 222-34, describes gangster influence on Italian political representation.

34. Estimate of number of prostitutes from City of Chicago Civil Service Commission, *Final Report, Police Investigation, 1911-1912* (Chicago, 1912), p. 12; for a lower estimate, see Vice Commission of Chicago, *The Social Evil in Chicago* (Chicago, 1911), p. 71. Figures on Negro policy from Gosnell, *Negro Politicians,* pp. 124-25, and Drake and Cayton, *Black Metropolis, II,*

pp. 478-81. For discussions of the organization of bootlegging, see references listed in footnote 23; a description of his organization by an ex-bootlegger is Roger Touhy, *The Stolen Years* (Cleveland, 1959).

35. Fred Cotnam, "Conversations with Bell-boys," student term paper, Winter 1929; Stanley Jenkins, "Prostitution and the Prostitute in a Study Centered around Hotel Life," typewritten, undated term paper; and Morris Carl Bergen, "The City, as Seen by the Cab Driver," typewritten term paper, July 1932; all in Burgess papers, II-A.; Also Investigators' reports, Nov. 1922, in Juvenile Protective Association papers, folder 94; and Report F-2 in "Commercialized Prostitution," July 1933, Ibid., folder 98.

36. Quotation from Raymond Sayler, "A Study of Behavior Problems of Boys in the Lower North Community," typewritten research paper (1934), p. 50, in Burgess papers, II-A, Box 53. Explosions of stills in Chicago *Tribune*, Sept. 28, 1927. See also, Cotnam, "Conversations with Bell-boys," and Cressey, "Report on Summer's Work," pp. 28ff.

37. On relations of criminals to politics, see references in footnote 9. For relations to police, see especially the investigators' reports in Merriam papers, Boxes 87 and 88. Of many discussions of judges and criminals, see Judge M. L. McKinley, *Crime and the Civic Cancer-Graft,* Chicago Daily News Reprints, No. 6 (1923), in Juvenile Protective Association papers, Supplement 1, folder 58. An excellent general analysis of the bail bondsman is Arthur L. Beeley, *The Bail System in Chicago* (Chicago, 1927), especially pp. 39-46. A long description of defense attorneys for organized crime is in Sunday Chicago *Tribune,* April 8, 1934.

38. On newsstands and gambling, see typewritten memo by C.O. Rison, private detective, to Chicago Federation of Labor, July 4, 1910, in John Fitzpatrick papers, folder 4, Chicago Historical Society. For other businesses acting as fronts for gambling, see Rison's many investigative reports for June and July, 1910, in Ibid. Also Nels Anderson, "Report of Visit to Ten Gambling Houses in Hobohemia," Jan. 1, 1923, Doc. 79, in Burgess papers; Paul Oien, typewritten research notes describing a large proportion of the gambling places in Chicago, Summer 1935, in Burgess papers. On sale of cocaine at drug stores, see especially Informant No. 100, typewritten but undated lists of places for securing cocaine (1914), in Merriam papers, Box 88, folder 1.

39. Landesco, *Organized Crime,* ch. 7; Samuel Rubin, "Business Men's Associations," typewritten term paper, Winter 1926, Burgess papers, 11-D, Box 115; Philip Hauser and Saul Alinsky, "Some Aspects of the Cleaning and Dyeing Industry in Chicago—A Racket," unpublished research paper (1929), Burgess papers; also the various issues of Employers' Association of Chicago, *Employers' News,* during the 1920s, which reported business racketeering in detail; also journalistic accounts, such as Fred D. Pasley, *Muscling In* (Ives Washburn Publisher, 1931), and Gordon Hostetter, *It's a Racket* (Chicago, 1929).

40. Quotation from William G. Shepherd, "How to Make a Gangster," *Colliers* (Sept. 2, 1933), p. 12.

41. First quotation from Ibid., p. 13; second quotation from anonymous, typewritten research paper entitled "Introduction," (approx. 1934), p. 10, Burgess papers, 11-A, Box 71.

42. Drake and Cayton, *Black Metropolis II* , pp. 490-94 and 546-50; Nelli, *Italians in Chicago,* p. 221.

43. On the attitude of immigrant mothers, see the many letters to Mayor Dever (1923-27) from immigrant women reporting speakeasies and begging the Mayor to have them closed; in William E. Dever papers, Chicago Historical Society, especially folders 25-26. For a long article on the Chinese Christian Union and its campaign to close Chinese gambling dens, see Chicago *News,* May 11, 1904. On activities of black and of Polish church organizations, see Herbert L. Wiltsee, "Religious Developments in Chicago, 1893-1915," M.A. thesis in history, University of Chicago, 1953, pp. 14 and 23.

Chapter 4

Biographical Sketches

Al Capone
17 January 1899 – 25 January 1947

"Scarface," the press called him.

There's a wonderful story about the scar. In a Brooklyn saloon, he said something uncomplimentary about a woman at the bar. Her brother, a hoodlum named Frank Gallucio, took exception to Capone's remark and whipped out a stiletto, leaving an ugly triple scar on the left side of Capone's face.

Capone hated the scar, and spent the rest of his life trying to hide it with makeup. He was known to claim it resulted from shrapnel while he fought with the famed Lost Battalion in France. Interestingly, he never avenged himself on Gallucio, but actually hired the man later as a bodyguard.

It's hard to say what has made Capone endure as the epitome of the Prohibition-era gangster. Until the government managed to jail him, he did bestride Chicago like a colossus, after achieving that preeminence in wars that cost perhaps a thousand lives. And he did things that caught the imagination. Once, at a large private dinner party, he beat three men to death with a baseball bat. Later, of course, his men dressed as police to murder most of the leadership of Bugs Moran's mob. ("Only Capone kills like that," was Moran's reaction and, fortuitously enough, the incident occurred on February 14; a day earlier or later and we wouldn't know it as the St. Valentine's Day Massacre.)

There were a few lines of Capone's that resonate nicely. In an apologia for his enterprise: "If people did not want beer and wouldn't drink it, a fellow would be crazy for going around trying to sell it. I've seen gambling houses, too, in my travels, and I never saw anyone point a gun at a man and make him go inside."

"I want peace," he said on another occasion, "and I will live and let live" Yeah, right. But my favorite is this: "You can go further in this world with a kind word and a gun than you can with a kind word alone."

Al Capone, Chicago bootlegger and symbolic crime figure, was born Alphonse Capone in Brooklyn, New York, the son of Gabriel Capone, a barber, and Teresa Raiola, both immigrants from the Naples region of Italy. At age fourteen, Capone dropped out of school, joined the gang life of the streets, and soon worked as a bartender and bouncer at Coney Island. In 1917, in a brawl with a customer, he received the knife wound that earned him the media nickname "Scarface" (although his friends called him "Snorky"). In December 1918, he married Mary "Mae" Coughlin, the daughter of a laborer.

There is disagreement concerning when Capone arrived in Chicago to work in the rackets run by John Torrio, another transplanted New Yorker. Torrio was a partner of James "Big Jim" Colosimo, a famous Chicago restaurateur and entrepreneur in Chicago's notorious South Side red-light district. In May 1920, shortly after the beginning of Prohibition, Colosimo was assassinated, and Torrio thereafter oversaw the red-light activities while expanding rapidly into bootlegging. By most accounts, Capone was in Chicago in time to assist Torrio in planning Colosimo's assassination, and he certainly worked with Torrio afterward in managing red-light activities in Chicago and the suburbs, and in developing the illegal liquor business. As the bootlegging expanded, Capone brought his brothers, Ralph and Salvatore (Frank), to Chicago to assist in the operations. Emphasizing wholesaling, the Torrio operation supplied liquor to speakeasies in the downtown Loop and in several suburbs west and south of the city while also selling liquor to bootleggers in other parts of the city. By 1923 Torrio had patched together a loose territorial agreement with other bootleggers.

In April 1924, Capone began to capture the headlines that would make him America's most famous criminal. He organized gunmen to control an election in Cicero, a town west of Chicago. Although his brother Frank was killed in a shootout with the police, his candidates won, and Capone and his associates expanded their participation in Cicero gambling houses. Soon afterward the truce among Chicago bootleggers collapsed. In January 1925, Torrio pleaded guilty to an earlier bootlegging charge and a week later was shot and seriously wounded in front of his home. On release from the hospital in February, he began a nine-month sentence and made plans to return to New York. In late 1925, Capone became the most famous member of the coalition that took over Torrio's Chicago operations.

To coordinate their varied enterprises, Capone and his associates worked out a set of partnerships within an essentially decentralized system. There were four senior partners—Al Capone, his older brother Ralph, their cousin Frank Nitti, and Jack Guzik—who split their profits more or less evenly. These four supported an entourage that hung out at their headquarters in Chicago's Metropole Hotel beginning in 1925 and the Lexington Hotel in 1928. To operate their enterprises, the senior partners gave a share of the profits to those who provided day-to-day oversight of a gambling house, bootlegging operation, parlor house, or other activity. Among the senior partners, Capone often exercised leadership because of his dominating personality, his occasionally volcanic temper, and his willingness to take decisive action. Because he was frequently absent from the city, however, the other partners assumed much of the oversight.

Capone achieved notoriety in part because Chicago's bootlegging wars were more violent and persistent than those in other cities. Among the high points of the beer wars were the 10 November 1924 shooting of North Side bootlegger Dion O'Banion in his flower shop; the April 1926 assassination of Assistant State Attorney William H. McSwiggin; the widely reported October 1926 peace treaty of two months' duration, negotiated by leading Chicago bootleggers in a hotel room; the April 1928 "Pineapple Primary" bombings to aid the candidates backed by Capone ally Mayor William Hale "Big Bill" Thompson; and finally the notorious St. Valentine's Day massacre of 1929, which eliminated the North Side gang as a serious rival. Through it all, Capone was available to the press, acknowledged the cheers of the crowds at sporting events, drove down Michigan Avenue in his armored car, threw large tips to waiters and newsboys, and gloried in the attention he received.

Through it all, too, Capone and his growing network of associates expanded their business activities and political influence. As their wholesale activities grew, they developed contacts to obtain imported liquor from Detroit, New York, and Miami; diverted industrial alcohol from

Philadelphia; and purchased beer from towns in Wisconsin and downstate Illinois. After the St. Valentine's Day massacre, Capone's associates expanded the wholesaling of liquor to the growing nightclub district on the Near North Side, and some became owners of nightclubs. In 1927, in addition, the senior partners joined Edward J. O'Hare to establish the Hawthorne Kennel Club in Cicero for dog racing. Extending their influence, members of Capone's group provided protection for labor racketeers or became labor racketeers themselves.

Capone's notoriety, however, placed him under pressure and removed him from daily oversight of operations. In autumn 1927 Mayor Thompson, pursuing unrealistic presidential ambitions, ordered his police chief to harass Capone out of Chicago. That winter Capone moved to Florida and, in March 1928, purchased a mansion on Palm Island in Miami Beach. Although he periodically returned to Chicago, he mostly lived in informal exile, and his influence waned. In May 1929, after attending a conference of leading bootleggers in Atlantic City, Capone was arrested while changing trains in Philadelphia and received a year's sentence for carrying a concealed weapon.

When Capone left Eastern State Penitentiary in Philadelphia on 17 March 1930, his partners were in trouble for tax evasion, and federal authorities were under instructions from President Herbert Hoover to put Capone in prison. The Internal Revenue Service probed his Chicago and Florida finances while the Prohibition bureau investigated his bootlegging. In March and June 1931, Capone was indicted for income tax fraud. At first he agreed to plead guilty in return for a short sentence, but when the judge refused to be bound by the agreement, Capone withdrew his plea. In October a federal jury found him guilty on five of twenty-three counts. The judge sentenced him to eleven years in prison plus fines and court costs.

When the U.S. Supreme Court refused to hear his appeal on 2 May 1932, Capone was transferred from the Cook County jail to the federal penitentiary in Atlanta, Georgia. In August 1934, when a maximum-security prison was opened at Alcatraz in San Francisco Bay, Capone was among its first occupants. In early February 1938, doctors confirmed a diagnosis of syphilis of the brain. Released on 16 November 1939 (with reduced time for good behavior), he sought treatment in a Baltimore hospital and then retired to his Palm Island estate with his wife and only son. Before dying from a stroke in Miami, he alternated between periods of recovery and periods of increasing mental and physical deterioration.

Capone was a major underworld leader from late 1925 until late 1927, when his absence from Chicago reduced his involvement. At age thirty-two, Capone's influence ended completely with his last tax-fraud conviction, but his myth, exaggerating his brief career, had barely begun. Through media coverage, numerous exciting biographies, several movies, and a popular television series (The Untouchables), he came to represent the violence of Chicago in the 1920s and the place of crime in American society during and after Prohibition.

Meyer Lansky
28 August or 4 July 1902 – 15 January 1983

The image that endures is almost benign. Meyer Lansky was either a criminal genius or simply a man who applied modern business methods to areas of enterprise—whiskey, gambling—which society chose to render illegal. By the end of his long life, Prohibition was a distant memory, while gambling in one form or another was legal (and often state-sponsored) in forty-eight states. And Lansky, who had survived most of his contemporaries, somehow morphed into a wise and gentle grandfather. So why did the Feds insist on hounding this poor old man?

Well, he did kill a lot of people along the way. Lansky and Ben Siegel started out supplying hot cars to gangsters and moved into murder for hire; it was the Bugs and Meyer mob that, under Albert Anastasia, became known as Murder Incorporated.

Was Siegel one of his victims? Hard to say, but if he didn't order the hit, it's certain he at least signed off on it. "I had no choice," he's supposed to have said.

Meyer Lansky, bootlegger and gambling entrepreneur, was born Meyer Suchowljansky in Grodno, Belorussia (then Russia), the son of Max Suchowljansky, a garment presser, and Yetta (maiden name unknown). Lansky's father immigrated to New York City in 1909 and brought the family over two years later. Meyer, who left school in 1917 at age fourteen, was fascinated by the street life and crap games of the Lower East Side and while still a teenager associated with other hustlers, such as Bugsy Siegel and Lucky Luciano.

With the coming of Prohibition in 1920, Lansky and Siegel entered bootlegging, backed initially by Arnold Rothstein and using a car and truck rental company as a front. By the mid-1920s, in partnership with Luciano, Lansky was bringing liquor across the Atlantic directly into New York and New Jersey harbors. Soon his younger brother, Jake Lansky, was an active partner and assistant in his enterprises. The contacts that Lansky made with other bootleggers on the East Coast and in the Midwest provided a network of associations that were central to his later career as a casino owner.

After Prohibition, Lansky became an entrepreneur of illegal and legal gambling casinos, especially in growing tourist centers. As early as the 1920s, he was probably involved in casino operations in Saratoga Springs, New York, during the August racing season, and by the late 1930s he, along with Frank Costello and Joe Adonis, owned the Piping Rock nightclub and casino there. His main focus, though, became the growing tourist trade in the Miami area. In the mid-1950s, along with Vincent "Jimmy" Alo, his closest Italian friend after the jailing of Luciano in the 1930s, Lansky invested in the Plantation casino in Hallandale (near Miami) and in other Florida gambling ventures. He also briefly operated gambling in Cuba through an association with Fulgencio Batista, the country's dictator.

Lansky reached the apex of his casino career in the decade and a half following World War II. In 1945, with Alo, Costello, and other investors, he remodeled and reopened the Colonial Inn in Hallandale; it was one of the most important illegal casinos in the country. Lansky also had interests in the Beverly Club outside of New Orleans, renewed his partnership with Costello in Saratoga Springs, and invested with Siegel and others in the construction of the Flamingo in Las Vegas. In June 1947 Siegel was killed, no doubt because some partners disapproved of his financial management of the Flamingo. Whether or not Lansky approved of the murder of his friend, he continued as an investor in the Flamingo. As the largest and most famous of the fledgling casino/hotels on the Las Vegas strip, the Flamingo helped to launch the city's development as a national center of legal gambling and entertainment. Although Lansky invested in other Las Vegas casinos, he remained in Florida and had little direct involvement in the city.

In October 1950 and March 1951, Lansky was called to testify before the U.S. Senate committee, chaired by Estes Kefauver of Tennessee, that was investigating interstate organized crime. Because the hearings identified Lansky and other criminal entrepreneurs as central to a national coordination of "organized crime," he faced local investigations in Florida and New York (Saratoga Springs) that resulted in indictments and convictions for gambling and conspiracy in 1953 and the closing of his casinos. For the rest of his life, he was the subject of ongoing investigations by the Federal Bureau of Investigation, the Immigration Service, and the Internal Revenue Service.

Lansky's troubles in the United States coincided with the return to power in March 1952 of Cuba's Batista, who had retired in 1944. Lansky became Batista's adviser on the development of Cuban tourism through gambling. In 1955, he and Jake began running the casino at Havana's Hotel Nacional. Soon thereafter, investing his own money, Lansky built the Riviera, perhaps the largest hotel/casino in the world outside of Las Vegas. His days of glory ended abruptly after Fidel Castro took power in 1959. With the nationalization of the casinos in 1960, Lansky lost much of the money he had invested in Cuba.

Back in Florida, Lansky increasingly operated behind the scenes. By this time, he required frequent medical treatment for ulcers and a heart condition and was under the constant surveillance of law enforcement. For a while in the early 1960s he helped organize the skimming of profits from Las Vegas casinos for himself and others. He also arranged for the sale of his Las Vegas casino interests.

In May 1929, Lansky had married Anne Citron; they had three children (one son was physically handicapped). Anne Lansky increasingly soured on the marriage and divorced him in February 1947. In December 1948 Lansky entered into a happier marriage with Thelma "Teddy" Schwartz. Teddy had one child from a previous marriage, but she and Lansky had no children together. During World War II, he assisted the U.S. government in contacting the imprisoned Luciano in order to secure his aid in having the New York waterfront unions guard against German sabotage. Although he was not an observant Jew, Lansky recognized a responsibility to Jewish causes and, after the war, gave money to aid the Israeli fight for independence. Frustrated by what he saw as U.S. government persecution, he moved to Israel in 1970 and applied for citizenship. By the time his application was finally denied in 1972, he faced several indictments in the United States. Leaving Israel on a long and highly publicized international plane trip, he sought asylum in Paraguay but wound up back in the United States. Over the next few years, he underwent a number of federal trials as well as heart bypass surgery.

By 1976, he had beaten all charges and then went into retirement in Miami Beach. His medical and legal expenses, combined with the costs of caring for his increasingly handicapped son, drained much of the money he had acquired from selling his interests in Las Vegas casinos. After his death in a hospital in West Miami, the trust fund he had left for his wife and son proved to be almost worthless.

Lansky's importance derives from the central role he played among a group of criminal entrepreneurs, often ex-bootleggers from the 1920s, who developed illegal casino gambling in a number of American resort areas and who played a critical role in launching Las Vegas as the fastest-growing American city after World War II. It required considerable skill to assemble the capital required to start casinos, to negotiate deals with police and politicians, to hire and supervise a staff so that the casino would not go bankrupt through embezzlement, and to make wealthy customers feel at home while gambling. Although Lansky was often in the news because of a false perception that he was a money manager for the Italian-American mafia, he is properly understood as an independent entrepreneur whose reputation for business acumen and reliability encouraged others to invest in his projects. By the time he died, his world had vanished; the illegal casinos were gone, replaced in Las Vegas, Atlantic City, and other locations with legal casinos to feed America's fascination with gambling.

Jack Guzik
Between 1886 and 1888 – 21 February 1956

Bootlegger and gambling entrepreneur, was born probably in Russia, the son of Max Guzik and his wife (name unknown). Guzik was brought to Chicago in 1891-1892 and became a U.S. citizen through the naturalization of his father in November 1898.

By 1910, Guzik, like his brother Harry, was hustling a living in Chicago's Southside red light district. In 1914, for instance, he arranged protection for his woman, Elsie Cusick (an early spelling of his last name), at 2222 Wabash Avenue, where she oversaw two prostitutes. After a 1914 campaign to close the red light district, both Guzik and his brother moved their vice activities to blue-collar suburbs. As a vice entrepreneur, Guzik made contacts with underworld figures like John Torrio and Al Capone and with politicians, including Michael Kenna and John Coughlin, who, between them, represented the downtown First Ward in the city council until the 1940s. Such contacts were central to his meteoric rise in the 1920s.

With the onset of Prohibition in 1920, Guzik and Capone joined Torrio as he organized a coalition of bootleggers to distribute illegal alcohol in Chicago and its suburbs. On election day in April 1924, Capone-led gunmen seized the polls in Cicero, Illinois, and assured the victory of friendly politicians. Afterward, Guzik and Capone spent much time there overseeing gambling houses and bootlegging activities. Concurrently, an uneasy truce among Chicago bootleggers collapsed, and bootleg wars broke out that earned Chicago and Capone worldwide fame. In 1925, Torrio was convicted of bootlegging and was shot by rivals. As a result, he returned to New York and left the Chicago operations to his associates.

Thereafter, the varied illegal operations associated with Capone's name were in fact coordinated by four equal partners: Al Capone, his older brother Ralph, their cousin Frank Nitti, and Jack Guzik. These four, in turn, entered into partnerships with various persons to operate individual enterprises. For instance, they entered into partnership with Sam Guzik, Jack's younger brother, to operate slot machines in the western suburbs and with Louis Lipschultz, Jack's brother-in-law, to deliver beer in Cicero and nearby suburbs. This structure allowed oversight by the four partners within a basically decentralized system in which various individuals assumed responsibility for daily management of separate enterprises. After the notorious St. Valentine's Day Massacre on 14 February 1929 completed the decimation of the Northside gang, the partners not only expanded bootlegging into the northern part of the city but also became involved in the lively nightclub area on the near Northside. In 1927, too, they joined with Edward J. O'Hare to establish in Cicero the Hawthorne Kennel Club for dog racing, a popular activity that made money from illegal betting.

The murderous bootleg wars and Capone's notoriety focused government investigative efforts on the four partners, and all went to prison for income tax evasion. Jack Guzik was convicted in November 1930 and went to prison in April 1932 after the U.S. Supreme Court refused to hear his appeal. In December 1935 he emerged from prison into a new world. Prohibition was over, and Al Capone, still in prison, would never resume an underworld role. Guzik immediately returned to a central place within the Chicago underworld, first as a partner with Frank Nitti and, after Nitti's suicide in 1943, as a partner with Tony Accardo.

Guzik's chief focus was gambling. Working closely with Hymie Levin, he became and remained until his death the central figure whose permission was needed to operate bookmaking and other gambling enterprises in downtown Chicago. His relations with Alderman Kenna in the late 1930s were so close that Guzik received his mail at Kenna's city hall office. After World War II, Guzik and Accardo also used strong-arm tactics to become partners in policy gambling syndicates operated by blacks and whites out of the South-side black ghetto.

About 1940 Guzik and Levin began distributing sports information to betting parlors in and around Chicago. Later they joined with others in demanding a share in the national race wire operated by James Ragen. When Ragen refused, they established a rival company called Trans-America Publishing and News Service and recruited underworld associates in other cities to establish local outlets for their company. In 1946 Ragen was assassinated, apparently by gunmen associated with Guzik; thereafter Guzik and his partners merged their news service with the rival company.

In other ways, too, Guzik and his associates extended their business interests and influence beyond Chicago. In 1926 Guzik purchased land in Florida and began to spend time there. By the 1930s, with his Chicago associates, he had invested in Florida dog and horse tracks. In 1949, Guzik and Accardo muscled in on the S&G Syndicate, which dominated bookmaking in the Miami area. Guzik and Accardo also invested money in the Riviera, one of the casino hotels that transformed Las Vegas into America's fastest-growing city after World War II. During the famous Senate investigations into organized crime under the leadership of Estes Kefauver, Guzik was subpoenaed as a witness and at his appearance in March 1951 refused to testify on Fifth Amendment grounds.

Guzik and his wife, Rose (maiden name unconfirmed but probably Lipschultz), whom he reportedly married in the early 1920s, raised three children (one of them adopted) in their modest Chicago home. Barely five feet tall, Guzik looked like a squat penguin, and he generally avoided the notoriety of his more flamboyant partners. He may nevertheless have been the most significant criminal leader in Chicago during the twentieth century. The lack of careful attention to him is reflected by the fact that, although his friends called him Jack and he used either Jack or John as his legal name, newspaper stories and most crime histories refer to him as Jake. From the time that he and Capone became partners in 1926 until his death in Chicago—a full thirty years—Guzik remained at the center of those criminal entrepreneurs who exercised extensive influence on Chicago politics, steadily expanded their hold on the underworld of the city, and extended their interests into Florida, Las Vegas, and other locations.

Guzik has not been the subject of a biography but appears in the major secondary works on Capone or the twentieth-century Chicago underworld. Generally Guzik is not treated as an active partner but instead is inaccurately referred to as Capone's accountant or as a money handler for the mob. Discussion of Guzik can be found in John Kobler, *Capone: The Life and World of Al Capone* (1971); Jack J. McPhaul, *Johnny Torrio: First of the Gang Lords* (1970); Ovid Demaris, *Captive City* (1968); Estes Kefauver, *Crime in America* (1951), chaps. 3, 4, and 7; and Virgil W. Peterson, *Barbarians in Our Midst* (1952).

Arnold Rothstein
1882 – 6 November 1928

As Meyer Wolfsheim, Arnold Rothstein has a cameo role in F. Scott Fitzgerald's masterpiece, *The Great Gatsby*, identified as the man who fixed the 1919 World Series. It's hard to say just what prompted the author to include the scene, and my own best guess is that Fitzgerald, hardly a stranger to Manhattan nightlife, had been in the same speakeasy as the gambler. Someone must have pointed out and identified Rothstein, and the instant must have made an impression.

By all accounts, the man was extremely slick and sophisticated, a genius with numbers, and a master at profiting hugely from crime while staying clear of the law. All of this makes his sudden decline and fall in 1928 difficult to understand.

Apparently he had some sort of breakdown. Always well-dressed and perfectly groomed, he turned overnight into an unkempt man with shaking hands and a pallid face. Gambling had always been profitable for him, and now he suddenly turned into a man who couldn't win for losing. Finally, at an epic poker game at the Park Central Hotel, Rothstein lost $320,000 in a matter of hours.

He left, saying he'd pay later, then repudiated the debt on the grounds that he'd been cheated. Eventually a phone call drew him back to the hotel, where he was shot to death, ostensibly because of his refusal to pay what he owed.

Arnold Rothstein, prominent gambling entrepreneur and the suspected fixer of the 1919 World Series, was born in New York City, the son of Abraham Rothstein and Esther Kahn. The father was a successful businessman in various phases of the garment industry, and both parents were observant Jews, greatly respected within the Jewish community of the city. Unlike his siblings, Rothstein was a rebellious youth who disdained school, and he was fascinated by the excitement and gambling that he found in the street life of the city. By his mid-teens he was a pool shark and was running his own dice games. He left home at age seventeen and worked briefly as a traveling salesman, but by the time he was twenty he was building the career that would lead him to a central role as the major intermediary between the underworld and upper world of New York.

By 1902, Rothstein had become a bookmaker, taking bets on horse racing, prizefighting, and elections. By 1907 he was taking lay-off bets from other bookmakers and was increasingly respected so that big time bettors placed their bets with him. In 1904 he went to Saratoga Springs to make book during the August racing season, and in 1907, he opened a gambling house there. At the same time he operated high stakes crap games in New York City and opened a string of gambling houses. Rothstein was himself a high roller, making bets on various sporting events and becoming the owner of a stable of racing horses. As a result of his growing prominence in gambling, he made friends among the big bettors from the legitimate world and the underworld. He was or would become an associate of men like Charles Stoneham, owner of the New York Giants baseball team, newspapermen such as Bayard Swope and Damon Runyon, major figures in the underworld, and many people in theater and entertainment. Equally important, his close ties with Tim Sullivan, Charles Murphy, Jimmy Hines, and other leaders of Tammany Hall meant that by the end of World War I he was the chief coordinator between the worlds of sports, gambling, and politics.

With the famous "Black Sox" scandal in which the favored Chicago White Sox threw the World Series to the Cincinnati Reds, Rothstein achieved an unwanted notoriety. Yet whether he directly participated in the fix remains unclear. Abe Attell, a former featherweight champion and a member of Rothstein's entourage, was in Cincinnati at the beginning of the series along with Rachel Brown, Rothstein's chief accountant. Attell bet heavily on each game and was in regular contact with the players to whom he eventually gave money. Joseph "Sport" Sullivan, a

Boston sports gambler who knew Rothstein, contacted the players in Chicago. Rothstein certainly knew about the fix, as did many knowledgeable people in the gambling world, and he probably won bets on the series. For nearly a year following the World Series, Major League leaders and sportswriters carefully protected the good name of baseball rather than seek out the facts about a scandal that many knew about and many more suspected. When a grand jury in Cook County, Illinois, finally undertook an investigation, Rothstein declared: "There is not a word of truth in the report that I had anything to do with the World Series of last fall" and testified voluntarily. The grand jury indicted Attell, Brown, Sullivan, and eight White Sox players. (Because the confessions of the eight players were later "lost," no one was convicted, although the players were later banned from baseball for life.) Thereafter Rothstein, although not indicted, was branded as the man who fixed the World Series, and he came to symbolize the shadowy connections between crime and power in the nation's largest city. He was the person upon whom F. Scott Fitzgerald based the character of Meyer Wolfsheim in his 1925 novel *The Great Gatsby*.

As the baseball scandal unraveled in 1920, Rothstein announced his retirement from gambling. Although he gradually dropped his gambling houses, he remained the bookmaker for big bettors, took part in high stakes poker games, bet on the races, and sought out other opportunities for profitable bets. He also used his contacts and power to expand his business interests. With the coming of Prohibition, Rothstein provided the money and political protection that helped a number of bootleggers to launch their careers. These included Jack "Legs" Diamond, Waxey Gordon, Bill Dwyer, and Frank Costello. For a while Rothstein took an active part in bootlegging but soon largely withdrew. Nevertheless, his involvement in bootlegging led to the smuggling of opiates into the United States, and at the time of his death he had money invested in the purchase of drugs in Europe. By the early 1920s Rothstein had also entered into various shady stock market activities, including the fencing of stolen securities and the sale of worthless stocks. He also established real estate companies for investments in Manhattan real estate, and he played an important role in the labor and business racketeering that had become an important part of the garment industry in New York City.

During the 1920s Rothstein generally worked in his office in midtown Manhattan in the afternoon. In the evenings he had a regular public place where he hung out, such as the Knickerbocker Hotel or Lindy's restaurant. There he engaged in quiet conversations with people of all walks of life who knew where to find him and who wished to talk business. Rothstein did not drink, avoided profanity, and had little of the flamboyance often associated with underworld figures. Although he often had a mistress, his chief emotional support came from his wife, Carolyn Greene Rothstein, whom he had married in August 1909; they had no children. By 1928, despite his many business investments, Rothstein seemed to face a cash shortage and became uncharacteristically lax in paying off his gambling debts. On 4 November 1928, he was shot in a room in the Park Central Hotel and was found after he stumbled down to the employees' entrance. The shooting was assumed to stem from his failure to make payment on a debt. He died in a New York City hospital.

Max Hoff
29 May 1893 – 27 April 1941

Bootlegger, boxing manager and promoter, Max Hoff was born in South Philadelphia, Pennsylvania, the son of Harry Hoff and Sara (maiden name unknown). He attended the local Horace Binney elementary school and was a newsboy in the city's downtown. As a teenager, Hoff (known as "Boo-Boo") became part of a group of largely Jewish young men involved in the boxing and gambling world that centered in gyms on the southern edge of the downtown. There he developed ties central to his successes during the 1920s, including one to Charlie Schwartz, with whom Hoff probably ran small gambling establishments in South Philadelphia before Prohibition. In 1917, he married Helen Flynn. They had one son.

In the 1920s Hoff managed one of the nation's largest stables of boxers. As his stable grew, Hoff established the Arcadia Gym in a large building on North Thirteenth at Cherry Street (near the downtown) and outfitted it as perhaps the finest gym in the city. There Jack Blackburn—the former black boxer and later Joe Louis's trainer—trained Hoff's aspiring fighters. By 1924 Hoff scheduled his boxers each summer for bouts at Philadelphia stadiums. In 1928, for instance, he rented Baker Bowl, the Philadelphia Phillies baseball field, for several evenings of outdoor fights. Each winter his fighters performed in the Arena at Forty-sixth and Market Streets in West Philadelphia—the center for boxing in a city then noted for its boxing fans. Periodically, he took members of his stable on well-publicized trips as far as California to compete in important matches.

A footnote to Hoff's boxing career emerged from the famous Philadelphia bout of September 1926 in which Gene Tunney won the heavyweight championship from Jack Dempsey. In January 1927 Hoff's attorney revealed that, on the day before the fight, Tunney and his manager had signed a contract that Hoff would receive 20 percent of Tunney's earnings for that fight and subsequent fights if he defeated Dempsey. Amid charges that Hoff had obtained the signatures by improper promises, his attempts to collect dragged through the courts until he withdrew his suit in January 1931.

By the mid-1920s, Philadelphia was the major center for the diversion of industrial alcohol for bootleg liquor. Hoff and his partners, including Schwartz and Samuel Lazar, were early investors in alcohol and chemical companies and soon dominated the market. Eventually they incorporated the Franklin Mortgage and Investment Co., with headquarters in the business district, from which to operate their various alcohol companies. Their attorney was U.S. Congressman Benjamin M. Golder. The alcohol was not only diverted for use in Philadelphia but was shipped as oil, lumber, or bricks to midwestern cities such as Chicago and Minneapolis. Hoff invested in several prominent gambling houses in the 1920s. Both he and Schwartz had social and business ties to the Jewish gamblers, boxers, and bootleggers of New York. In the 1920s Hoff invested in real estate in Atlantic City and Ocean City on the New Jersey shore, and he moved into a large home in a fine, West Philadelphia neighborhood.

A series of shootings during a bootleg war led in August 1928 to the convening of an investigative grand jury. Until the grand jury, Hoff was a prominent fight manager whose bootlegging was largely unknown to the public. After several months of well-publicized hearings, in which his name appeared regularly in the headlines, the grand jury issued a report that, with some exaggeration, labeled Boo-Boo Hoff "the King of the Bootleggers." The report exposed Hoff's numerous presents of money and Christmas baskets to the police. It revealed his ownership of various alcohol companies, including the Quaker Industrial Alcohol Company and the Glenwood Industrial Alcohol Company. Indirectly, it linked him to some of the shootings through his purchases of guns, including machine guns, from the Military Sales Company on Market Street. The grand jury also mentioned his ownership of gambling houses and of the

Piccadilly nightclub. While many policemen, including the director of public safety and the captain of detectives, were fired or forced to resign, Hoff himself escaped indictment.

After 1928, however, Hoff's fortunes declined. His winnings from his fight management were attached by the court to cover debts incurred from his investments on the Jersey shore. His fine home in West Philadelphia was sold at sheriff's auction in 1929. His bootleg interests were harmed by the publicity of the grand jury and by more effective law enforcement. His fight business waned, perhaps because his rivals in the Philadelphia fight business were linked to the racketeers like Frankie Carbo who came to dominate prizefighting by the 1930s. In 1929 his first wife died. Hoff married Margaret Kaher (or Kaier) in 1929 or 1930. They had one son.

In the 1930s Hoff continued to operate a gym in downtown Philadelphia and to manage a declining stable of fighters. He owned several clubs, including The 1214 (on Spruce Street), where Jimmy Durante and Sophie Tucker performed. He continued to operate gambling clubs. One of his most prominent businesses was the Village Barn, a chaperoned dance hall that was a popular teenage hangout. He was also among the partners who owned the Philadelphia Warriors professional basketball team. A diminutive man and less flamboyant than his associates, Hoff was for two decades a central figure in the sports, gambling, and nightclub scene in Philadelphia. He died, probably of a heart attack, while sleeping at home.

Organized Crime

Organized Crime is a term that has been used selectively in the twentieth century to identify particular criminal coalitions that were often ethnically based and which others wished to define as especially dangerous, illegal conspiracies. Generally speaking, the criminal groups identified as "organized crime" have possessed neither the hierarchical structure nor the power ascribed to them. But the label has, nevertheless, strongly influenced both popular attitudes toward the groups involved and the policies of law enforcement. The history of "organized crime," therefore, must include both a history of criminal structure itself and of the use of the term.

From the 1860s until well into the twentieth century, certain types of gambling became increasingly coordinated in some urban neighborhoods.

During and after the Civil War, policy gambling—a kind of illegal lottery—enjoyed wide popularity. Fans could bet on the numbers in bars, barber shops, newspaper kiosks, and other neighborhood outlets. At the same time, policy entrepreneurs backed the local retailers, so that the retailer retained a fixed percent of each bet while the backer(s) assumed the risk when bettors won. By the 1880s, as horse racing became a national, professional sport, fans wished for an opportunity to bet off-track as well as at the track. Off-track bookmaking was coordinated much like policy, with bets taken in local retail outlets while bookmakers backed the local sellers. As a result, especially by the 1890s, policy and off-track bookmaking syndicates had the support of bettors as well as local businesses and politicians. The activities of these important criminal entrepreneurs were not yet labeled "organized crime," however.

During the Progressive Era anti-prostitution crusade, many reformers argued that the red light districts in American cities could not exist without the systematic recruitment of thousands of young girls each year. They claimed that shadowy, organized networks of "white slavers"—often with an Eastern European Jewish background—lured innocent girls from American small towns, port cities, and foreign countries to become slaves in the cities' bordellos. Again, the specific term "organized crime" was not used, though the concept, with its exaggerations, was clearly present.

The term itself was first used in the 1920s, perhaps in John Landesco's *Organized Crime in Chicago* (1929). In the period of Prohibition, the press and movies, in their treatment of the bootleggers, often ascribed to the largely decentralized and independent bootleggers a mythical centralized control and power. Chicago, where the violence of bootlegging wars was capped by the famous 1929 St. Valentine's Day massacre and where Al Capone reveled in media attention, was the focus of worldwide attention.

Capone was one of four partners who entered into partnerships with others to establish numerous relatively small bootlegging, gambling, and vice enterprises. Because he lived chiefly at his Miami home after 1927 and spent much of 1929 in a Philadelphia prison (Eastern State Penitentiary), Capone was perhaps the least important of the four partners. The media, nevertheless, defined him as the lord of Chicago bootlegging and a controlling figure in local politics. Such films as *Little Caesar* with Edward G. Robinson (1932) and Paul Muni's *Scarface* (1932) provided vivid images of the gangsters' power and ruthlessness and made Capone a symbol of "organized crime."

The most important twentieth century development involving the split between the reality of criminal structure and the mythical uses of the term "organized crime" was the creation of the idea that "the mafia" coordinated crime in the United States. An important early step came in 1950 to 1951 when the U.S. Senate's Special Committee to Investigate Organized Crime (popularly known as the Kefauver Committee after its chair, Senator Estes Kefauver of Tennessee) held widely-watched televised hearings in a number of cities and concluded officially that a secret society called "the mafia," operated across the United States to oversee crime. In 1963–1964, Joseph Valachi, a long-time member of a New York City Italian-American crime family, testified before Congress and for the first time provided a public description of the structure of such groups. He was motivated to do so because, while in prison for drug dealing, he had killed a fellow prisoner and then sought leniency by agreeing to talk. More important, perhaps, the President's Commission on Law Enforcement and the Administration of Justice published a report on Organized Crime (1967), based chiefly upon information gained from telephone wiretaps. The report claimed that 24 "Cosa Nostra" cartels in some 20 cities, with membership restricted to Italian Americans, controlled criminal activities in their own cities and cooperated across city boundaries in gambling, loansharking, and drugs. Building on such developments, Hollywood contributed vivid and exaggerated images of "the mafia" in movies like *The Godfather* (1972) and *Prizzi's Honor* (1985).

In the process of identifying a "mafia" menace, newspaper reporters and criminologists created a history of the American "mafia" that mixed myth with fact. During Prohibition, successful bootleggers, although often young men from poor neighborhoods, learned to think in terms of national and even international markets as the importers and manufacturers made deals with processors and wholesalers so that booze could be moved from its multiple sources to its millions of consumers. During and after Prohibition many bootleggers and their business associates invested in gambling casinos and other gambling enterprises; with a broadened understanding of markets, they sometimes jointly invested in tourist centers like Miami, New Orleans, or Hot Springs.

Concurrently, some Italian-American entrepreneurs, beginning probably in the late 1920s and continuing into the 1930s and 1940s, formed local membership organizations. Like the Masons, Elks, and other fraternal orders, the organizations had formal initiation rituals for members and often acted like secret societies. Like Chambers of Commerce or Rotary Clubs, they were a framework within which members, while generally remaining independent in their economic pursuits, could develop contacts, learn about business opportunities, and sometimes settle disputes under circumstances in which the legal system was not available to them.

After World War II, then, investigators discovered both the joint partnerships of independent entrepreneurs and the Italian-American "families" (which they labeled "the mafia"). They then constructed a history based upon the assumption that the generally independent businessmen in the families were instead controlled by and worked for the profit of the "mafia" and that non-Italian entrepreneurs were subservient to the Italians. In this history, the "mafia" rose to a central place in coordinating crime nationally through the power of Italian-American bootleggers. On the one hand, this ignores the fact that entrepreneurs of Eastern-European[,] Jewish background dominated bootlegging. Some 50 percent of leading bootleggers were Jewish, 25 percent were Italian-American. On the other hand, this ignores that many leading bootleggers (like Capone) were not members of "families" and that many of those who formed the families were not bootleggers. In the history, Lucky Luciano, after a series of assassinations in New York City, consolidated "mafia" control nationally. While Luciano certainly emerged, briefly, as a highly respected "don" in New York, it is an exaggeration to ascribe national power to him. After World War II, according to the dominant history, the "mafia" moved into and controlled the casinos in Nevada. No doubt many entrepreneurs who had operated illegal casinos in the 1930s and 1940s were leaders in the expansion of legal gambling in Las Vegas. But this history overlooks the predominance of Jewish entrepreneurs in the rise of Las Vegas as a national entertainment center. Equally important, it overlooks that they were largely independent, acting in their own interests and not seeking profit for a "mafia."

As the fight against the "mafia" menace became a central focus of law enforcement, the Federal government established Organized Crime Task Forces in many cities where Italian Americans were active in criminal activities. States and cities followed suit. Naturally, the focus of federal, state, and local prosecutions almost solely on Italian Americans, combined with the media attention, necessarily publicized the exaggerated notions of the power of "the mafia" while obscuring the complexity and diverse roots of criminal activities and generally ignoring similar activities by persons not of Italian American background.

In the 1970s, with the launching of the "war on drugs," drug trafficking gradually supplanted "the mafia" as the focus of law enforcement and media attention. It became clear that Italian-Americans could not bear the blame for the multiple, drug trafficking activities that provided LSD, marijuana, cocaine, and heroin to a diversity of users. As a result, the term "organized crime" was now transferred to drug "cartels," often centered in other countries like Mexico, Jamaica, or Colombia. This had the effect of again oversimplifying a complex problem while also externalizing America's drug problem by blaming it on powerful foreign organizations. At the end of the twentieth century, with the expansion of international banking and trade and the management of the international economy by computers, the term "organized crime" was expanded to encompass a variety of criminal activities embedded in the new economy, such as money laundering and investment fraud.

The term "organized crime," introduced in the 1920s, has been applied to a diversity of criminal markets and ethnic groups. While criminal entrepreneurs often enter into joint ventures or use violence as part of market competition, the effect of the term has been to oversimplify the structure of complex and loosely coordinated activities, to suggest that a danger originates abroad, and generally to exaggerate the centralized power and control of those engaged in illegal pursuits.

Part II

Philadelphia

Chapter 5

Philadelphia Bootlegging and the Report of the Special August Grand Jury

During the prohibition era of the 1920s, America's largest cities produced famous bootleggers who have become part of our historical folklore. In Chicago, Al Capone, Frank Nitti, and Jack Guzik were notorious in their own day and further immortalized by the television series "The Untouchables." New York City, during the same period, spawned "Dutch" Schultz (Arthur Flegenheimer), Jack "Legs" Diamond (originally a Philadelphia boy), Meyer Lansky, "Lucky" Luciano, and Frank Costello. Yet, who can name a Philadelphia bootlegger? The lack of famous names from what was then the third largest, American city does not reflect a lack of bootlegging in Philadelphia. Rather, it reflects the degree to which widespread corruption and lax law enforcement deprived Philadelphia's bootleggers of the publicity that might have made them underworld legends.

Two periods during the 1920s, however, found bootlegging in Philadelphia the focus of media attention. The first period occurred after Mayor W. Freeland Kendrick unexpectedly named Smedley D. Butler, a Brigadier General in the U.S. Marines, to be Director of Public Safety beginning in January 1924. "Old Gimlet Eye" had won two Congressional Medals of Honor for his service in the Spanish-American War, the Philippine pacification, and Latin American expeditions. After just two years as Director of Public Safety, though, he told reporters: "Sherman was right about war, but he was never head of police in Philadelphia."[1]

Butler completely reorganized the police department. When he had taken over, police precinct boundaries generally corresponded to political ward boundaries, so that local politicians could name the local police captain and thereby control the police in the ward. Butler reduced the forty-two police precincts to twenty-two and transferred large numbers of officers in an attempt to break the control of politicians over the police. He also instituted a series of highly publicized raids of speakeasies and distilleries. After critics charged that police raids deprived workingmen of their drinking places but left the wealthy undisturbed, Butler attempted to padlock the prestigious Bellevue-Stratford Hotel. His policies faced bitter opposition from many politicians, while magistrates sometimes refused to grant search warrants and looked with little sympathy on the prosecutions that resulted from the raids. When the Marine Corps refused to extend his leave beyond two years, Butler resigned from the Corps to continue as Director of Public Safety. The Mayor promptly fired him; Butler returned to the Marines. His two years in the city captured headlines for Butler but did not bring fame to bootleggers.

For a few months in 1928-1929, however, an investigative grand jury did briefly focus attention on Philadelphia bootleggers and their close ties with city police and local politicians. The grand jury, in turn, was convened because of the publicity resulting from a series of shootings that accompanied a war among bootleggers in the city. The killings began on May 30, 1927, when Joseph Zanghi and Vincent Coccozza were shot from a moving car near 8th and Christian Streets in South Philadelphia. The most notable assassination, however, occurred in early August 1928, when Hughie McLoon, the diminutive former mascot of the Philadelphia A's baseball team and a popular figure in the city's night life, was shot on Chestnut Street. The shooting provoked sufficient outrage that an investigative grand jury spent seven months subpoenaing witnesses and bank records, interviewing bootleggers, bankers, and cops, and preparing a final report of its findings. Excerpts from that report are published here.

But first some background. When the Volstead Act imposed national prohibition in January 1920, much of the previous structure of importation, manufacture, wholesaling, and retailing of alcoholic beverages became illegal and largely collapsed. Several results occurred. One result was that Americans drank less. Indeed, the best estimate indicates that during prohibition per capita consumption of alcoholic beverages fell to less than forty percent of the level before World War I.[2] A second result, of course, was that gradually a new set of businessmen established firms for the importation, manufacture, processing, wholesaling, and retailing of alcoholic beverages. At first, the new entrepreneurs operated on a relatively small scale and a generally *ad hoc* basis.

But as the 1920s progressed, some entrepreneurs gained increased importance as coordinators of on-going bootlegging operations. The entrepreneurs, who by the late 1920s had emerged as the leaders in various phases of bootlegging, reflected the fact that the new (and illegal) businesses offered economic opportunities for those willing to assume the risks of a criminal career. In American cities generally, the new entrepreneurs were surprisingly young—often in their early twenties or even their late teens—when prohibition began. They tended to be uneducated and unskilled, raised in the slums of the city. They were typically the children of new immigrants. A national sample of successful bootleggers from the late 1920s found that approximately 50 percent were of Eastern European Jewish background, 25 percent were Italian, and 25 percent were from other backgrounds—mostly Irish and Polish. Philadelphia's successful bootleggers, while perhaps more heavily Jewish than the national average, otherwise tended to mirror the national characteristics.[3]

Bootleg entrepreneurs, in their own day and in legend, are best known for the gang wars during which they shot each other down on the streets of American cities. Just such widely publicized shootings led to the convening of the Philadelphia grand jury in August 1928. But the gang wars have obscured recognition of what was the most remarkable characteristic of bootlegging: business cooperation. Those who established import operations, for instance, not only needed on-going relations with foreign exporters and shippers but with domestic processors and wholesalers. By the same token, wholesalers within each city provided a nexus between importers and manufacturers, on the one hand, and the thousands of retail outlets on the other. Only by a complex network of business cooperation could importers, manufacturers, and wholesalers provide the range of alcoholic beverages sold by retailers to thirsty Philadelphians. There is a paradox, then, in understanding successful bootleggers. They tended to be young men with slum backgrounds and minimal business experience; nevertheless, they rapidly established regional and even international cooperation as an inevitable feature of the bootlegging business.[4]

The 1928 grand jury uncovered important aspects of the economic and political networks that characterized bootlegging in Philadelphia. Most important, the grand jury identified Philadelphia's central role in the diversion of industrial alcohol. While the Volstead Act restricted the manufacture of alcohol for beverage purposes, alcohol was used in a variety of industrial processes and was a normal component of such diverse products as hair oil, lotions, and rubbing alcohol. Federal law required that alcohol manufactured for non-beverage purposes be "denatured"—that is, that poisons be added to the alcohol to prevent its use in products for human consumption. Because the Delaware Valley was a major center for the American chemical industry, including the manufacture of industrial alcohol, the area was also a center for diversion by bootleggers.

The grand jury discovered that "Boo-Boo" Max Hoff, Charley Schwartz, and their partners were the major figures in the diversion of industrial alcohol. Before prohibition, Hoff and Schwartz were known in South Philadelphia as operators of small gambling houses. By the 1920's, Hoff was an established figure in the city, not as a bootlegger but as a leading promoter of prize fights and the manager of prize fighters. The bar that he ran in the Sylvania Hotel in Center City was a hangout for the city's sporting crowd. Hoff was small and conservative in dress; Schwartz, by contrast, was a gaudy dresser, a conspicuous first-nighter at New York theaters, a notable fight fan with a ringside seat at major fights, and a big plunger at the race tracks and gambling houses along the East Coast. He carried a bankroll consisting mostly of $500 bills ("five yard notes"), making it difficult for him to take a taxi or buy a pack of gum.[5]

So successful were the operations of Hoff, Schwartz, and their partners by the mid-1920's that they sold illegal alcohol as far away as Chicago and Minneapolis—often shipping their products by bribing employees of the Reading Railroad. One of their manufacturing plants, Quaker Industrial Alcohol Company, produced (and presumably diverted) nearly one and one-half million gallons in 1926 alone. The partners coordinated their bootlegging enterprises through the Franklin Mortgage and Investment Company, with offices in the Bankers Trust Building at Walnut and Juniper Streets in Center City Philadelphia. Their attorney, who represented their companies and defended the partners, was Congressman Benjamin M. Golder. Hoff and Schwartz had interests in Philadelphia nightclubs and gambling houses as well as investments in real estate in Atlantic City and Ocean City, New Jersey. Documents seized in their headquarters indicated that their payments annually to the city's police and politicians may have exceeded a quarter million dollars. Their bootlegging activities, in short, were the center from which they extended their influence and business interests.[6]

While the grand jury uncovered a great deal of information about the diversion of industrial alcohol, its investigation of other sources of Philadelphia booze was less successful. In the brewing of beer for the Philadelphia region, two men were of chief importance. One was Max Hassel, known as the "Millionaire Newsboy." The son of Jewish immigrants and a newsboy on the streets of Reading, Pennsylvania, during World War I, Hassel somehow invested in a local brewery in the early years of Prohibition, and by the mid-1920s, he owned a number of breweries in the Reading area. The other major figure was Mickey Duffy, whose name concealed the fact that his parents immigrated from Poland. Duffy owned several breweries in southern New Jersey. From a headquarters in Camden, he coordinated shipment of his beer into Philadelphia and also operated a Philadelphia numbers gambling syndicate. By the late 1920s, Hassel and Duffy were partners in several breweries until Duffy's assassination in Atlantic City in 1931.[7]

Another important group of Philadelphia bootleggers was the six Lanzetti brothers, led by the eldest brother with the improbable name, Pius. The brothers organized "alky" cooking in the small row houses in the Italian neighborhoods of South Philadelphia. Within such immigrant neighborhoods bootleggers provided families with stills and corn sugar; the families manufactured alcohol in their homes; and the bootleggers then purchased the alcohol and processed it for sale. Despite their involvement in bootlegging, the Lanzettis' were better known for the operation of numbers gambling in South Philly from the late 1920s until the mid-1930s.[8]

One aspect of bootlegging importation was completely ignored by the Grand Jury. Yet Philadelphia, itself an international port and located close to ocean ports on the Jersey coast, produced a number of entrepreneurs important in financing and managing the system by which whiskey and rum from Europe, Canada, and the West Indies found markets in American cities. In the early 1920s, Atlantic City was a smugglers' paradise because of the close ties forged between smugglers, local politicians, and Coast Guard officials. Much of the booze seems to have been destined for the Philadelphia market, but it is not clear what direct involvement Philadelphians had in the smuggling. Nevertheless, some of those ties are suggested by the fact that Johnny Campbell, owner of several ocean-going vessels and known by 1924 as "King of the Bootleggers" in Atlantic City, soon moved his headquarters to downtown Philadelphia. Thereafter, he not only continued to smuggle booze into ports along the Jersey coast but imported directly into Philadelphia on coal ships.[9]

When the Coast Guard severely restricted smuggling in the Northeast during the summer of 1925, some smugglers moved their operations to Florida ports and imported liquor from the West Indies and Central America. Apparently Eddie Satinover and his wife Ella, residents of the Wynnefield section of Philadelphia, were among those who sought warmer climates for smuggling activities. Among their partners was George Long, who owned the Three Star Hennessy Chemical Company in Philadelphia and was involved in diversion of industrial alcohol. As early as December 1926, the partnership purchased liquor in Puerto, Mexico, and arranged for its shipment to Florida. In 1927, Ella travelled to Nassau and arranged for shipments from there to Florida ports. Although Eddie Satinover was indicted in 1928, he was never brought to trial.[10]

Another interesting pair of bootleggers were the brothers Charles and Irving Haim (or Haimovitz). Charles had been a city policeman before prohibition. When prohibition came, the brothers were partners with Hoff and Schwartz in the purchase of chemical companies and the diversion of industrial alcohol. Around 1927, the Haims had a falling out with Hoff and Schwartz and began to operate independently.

By 1929, the Haims appeared as partners, along with a Minneapolis bootlegger and Canadian exporters, in the establishment of the Mill Creek Distillery in Havana. This company not only manufactured bourbon and rye for smuggling to New York, Florida, and New Orleans but also coordinated shipments from Europe for the American market. The importance of the Haims in providing liquor for Philadelphia is difficult to determine, but they might well have rivaled Hoff in importance.[11]

Between the manufacturers and importers on the one hand and the retailers on the other, there was a complicated system of warehousing and wholesaling. The Grand Jury did little to analyze wholesaling in Philadelphia; only scattered newspaper stories offer a few vague details. Since beer was mostly brewed in blue-collar towns in the Philadelphia region, beer distribution necessarily involved trucking kegs into the city and storing them in warehouses before selling them to local speakeasies. In 1928 the police identified Al Hendrie as the largest beer runner in the city. The thirty-year-old Hendrie owned four trucks and made regular runs from the coal mining regions of eastern Pennsylvania to a garage located on North 11th Street. He claimed that he paid city detectives $900 weekly to operate and that he also made payments to officers in the counties through which his trucks moved. Scattered evidence suggests that whiskey wholesalers similarly kept their goods in local garages, old warehouses, and other city buildings. Trucks from the warehouses then made regular runs to retail outlets.[12]

Throughout the city, thousands of retailers purchased booze from manufacturers and wholesalers and then sold it to individual customers. Some—the local speakeasies—sold by the drink to customers who imbibed on the premises; other retailers sold by the bottle or case to customers who preferred to drink at home or to carry hip flasks. The Grand Jury, in its final report, provided a detailed description of the close relations between the numerous neighborhood speakeasies and the police and politicians. In several wards, local retailers were organized into protection associations and made regular payments to a collector. The collector, in turn, funneled the funds to the police and to the political ward leader.

In addition to the speakeasy operators, many Philadelphians—like hotel bellhops, doormen in apartment and office buildings, operators of newspaper kiosks—made money through the sale of bottles or cases. Among the more interesting of these retailers were a handful of men known as "society bootleggers," who specialized in servicing the wealthy and claimed to sell only the best imported brands. Because imported brands were assumed to be safe as well as of high quality, they commanded the highest prices. The most famous of Philadelphia's society bootleggers was Joel Kerper. A cigar importer before Prohibition, he found it more profitable in the 1920s to provide his socially prominent customers with alcohol. From his office at 341 Walnut Street, he sold what he claimed were choice liquors to brokers, attorneys, and others who often had Main Line addresses. In the summer, he made shipments to their vacation homes on the Maine coast in packages labeled "varnish" or "floor paint." When he was finally arrested in 1928, his records showed that he netted about $30,000 yearly and that his "choice liquors" were, in fact, a mixture of Canadian imports, water, and Philadelphia-made grain alcohol.[13]

Even this brief sketch demonstrates that the structure of bootlegging in an urban metropolis like Philadelphia was highly complex. Alcoholic beverages flowed from a bewildering variety of sources: from importation, diversion of industrial alcohol, from home stills and large stills hidden in old factories and country barns, from beer breweries, and from other sources not discussed here. The beverages then needed to be trucked to the city, processed, warehoused, and distributed to local outlets. Finally, in a city like Philadelphia, there were literally thousands of small-scale retailers of alcoholic beverages. Many importers, manufacturers, wholesalers, and retailers not only had ongoing relationships with each other but also with local police and politicians to ensure protection. No bootlegger or group of bootleggers could dominate such a complex economic and political network. "Boo-Boo" Hoff and his partners, although clearly the most important figures in the diversion of industrial alcohol, faced numerous competitors in the Philadelphia region alone. Max Hassel and Mickey Duffy, once they joined forces, owned between them a string of breweries stretching from Reading to Atlantic City; but numerous other brewers continued to manufacture beer for the Philadelphia market. Compared with the legal liquor business, either before or after prohibition, bootlegging remained relatively small-scale and competitive.

Historians have, thus far, done little to unravel the complex economic and political networks that characterized bootlegging in the 1920's, despite the importance of bootlegging for an understanding of American life of that decade and the history of crime in subsequent decades. This is why the report of the Special August Grand Jury is an important historical document. It is among the best contemporary attempts to understand the political and economic structure of bootlegging in an American metropolis.

Report of the Special August Grand Jury[14]

The outstanding facts uncovered by the Grand Jury were:

1. That from illegal sources a certain number of Philadelphia police were getting approximately $2,000,000 in graft a year. High ranking police officials were discovered to have bank accounts out of proportion to their salaries. With incomes ranging from $1,500 to $2,500 per year they had assets which ran from $5,000 to nearly $200,000 with no other apparent source of revenue. Two police officials were jailed and virtually all were questioned by the Grand Jury.

2. That there was a definite link between the police graft and organized politics. It was shown during the probe that prominent politicians not only closed their eyes to the liquor traffic and other forms of vice but were themselves participants in these illegal businesses. Through the activities of the Grand Jury, one Republican city committeeman was sent to jail on a charge of taking bribes from saloon-keepers for "protection" and another still waits trial on a charge of running a "number game."
3. That the trafficking of liquor was so important a business that Philadelphia, not to be shamed by Chicago, had for its very own a "King of the Bootleggers." Despite the fact that the Grand Jury subpoenaed this "boss bootlegger," whom it at various times identified as Max "Boo Boo" Hoff, to testify before it eight times, it was unable to indict him. . . .
4. That gambling was as well organized as the liquor traffic and that there were "overloads" in gambling circles as well as a "King of the Bootleggers." Locations of some of the largest of these places which were being conducted "without knowledge" of the police was given by the Grand Jury in one of its presentments. . . .

On Police Wealth

One hundred and thirty-eight policemen were found by the Grand Jury to be "unfit for service." Of that number there are still some fifty cases to be judged by the Civil Service Commission. Some of the officers declared unfit were dismissed by the Commission; others preferred to resign. . . .

Typical "Police Payroll"

During the course of the police graft investigation it developed that many police in every part of the city were on the "weekly payroll" of bootleggers and operators of stills. A typical payroll list kept by a man admittedly in the liquor traffic was released publically by the Grand Jury. The list was kept in a little black book seized by Federal prohibition agents when they raided the home of Morris Clearfield. The book contained the names of various police and mentioned a captain, who according to District Attorney Monaghan, was Charles Cohen. This man with twenty-three others was arrested and charged with bribery, extortion, and conspiracy but was freed. The police in question were, according to the probing body, attached to the Fourth Street and Snyder Avenue station and the Detective Bureau. The partial list is attached hereunto:

Week of November 2, 1927

Thompson	$ 5.00
Mitchell, cop	$10.00
Two detectives, City Hall	$10.00
Walley, Casper, Rags, 3 cops	$10.00
Lawrence, cop	$ 5.00
Jacob-helper, Sergeant Harting	$12.50
Captain	$75.00
Joe Simmons, Sergeant Haynes, Sergeant Archy, Sergeant Barras, Sergeant Kolsky	$27.50
Sam, Tom and Steve, 3 cops	$15.00
Mack-helper, Sergeant Gallagher, Sergeant Whaley	$14.00
Cells, cop	$5.00
	$204.00

Dealing with "Extra" Money

Numerous possible, but highly improbable, reasons were given by the members of the police force when asked as to the source of their wealth. This is how many of the police force made "extra money" according to their statements before the Grand Jury.

1. Being lucky in crap games and poker games.
2. Betting on the right horse.
3. Building bird cages for the retail trade.
4. Raising thoroughbred dogs for sale.
5. Lending money to dead saloonkeepers who left provisions in their will for the loan plus a large bonus.
6. Having an interest in butcher stores, restaurants, and haberdasheries.

After more than two months of intensive probing, on October 29th, the Grand Jury named twenty-four high ranking police whose bank accounts approximated three quarters of a million dollars. They gave a short analysis of each man's account arrived at from various testimony. In reference to each, the probing body said:

Case of Captain of Detectives Beckman

Investigation by the Grand Jury brought forth a statement that Captain Beckman, head of the Detectives Bureau, was the possessor of a personal fortune approximating $75,000, the source of which he was unable according to the Grand Jury to "coherently explain."

In dealing with this case, the Jury attempted to show that Captain Beckman and Mr. Boo Boo Hoff were intimate. A former employee of Mr. Hoff, Louis Elfman, told of the latter meeting Captain Beckman on several occasions. . . .

Harry A. Davis

When Director Davis' resignation was accepted publicly he had been with the force for a period nearly thirty-five years. He was appointed in January of 1893. In 1896 he was promoted to a sergeancy, in 1905 to a lieutenancy and in 1914 was given the rank of captain and detailed as Assistant Director of the Department of Public Safety.

Mayor Mackey appointed him to fill the directorship of the bureau and he held that position at the time of the Grand Jury's inception. Shortly after he severed his connection with the police department, Mr. Davis was appointed executive secretary of the Republican City Committee, which position he still holds, and which he held before going into the Mayor's cabinet. . . .

Traced Whiskey Supply

We also endeavored to trace the manner and the means whereby large quantities of whiskey were available for consumption. We recognized the maintenance of stills accounted for some small part of the available supply. This did not seem to us to explain the enormous quantity of whiskey and alcohol on the market. By dint of persistent effort we discovered the manner in which large quantities were produced and diverted into liquor channels. The method substantially involved four separate items:

1. The organization and operation of industrial alcohol plants.
2. The diversion of alcohol from such plants.
3. The sale of denatured alcohol by the industrial alcohol plants as permitted by law to perfumery and other establishments commonly known as "cover-up" houses.
4. The distribution of alcohol by cover-up houses and others.

King of the Bootleggers

A typical example of a company organized and operated ostensibly to produce industrial alcohol, but in reality to furnish alcohol for beverage purposes is the Quaker Industrial Alcohol Company. The officers of the company were dummies who had been employed in large part by the president who died prior to the inception of our investigation. The president himself was a dummy, but he held the key to the identity of the real persons back of the enterprise.

Hoff and Lieutenants Named

Certain evidence before us leads to the conclusion this plant was maintained and operated by Max Hoff, Charles Schwartz, Sam Lazar and a number of other men prominently identified with the liquor traffic. . . .

We uncovered evidence which conclusively established the fact that, during a period of a few months, 350[,000] gallons of alcohol were illegally diverted into liquor channels. We are advised this quantity of alcohol provided in excess of a million gallons of consumable liquor.

Diversion of Alcohol

One of the methods of diversion was to ship large quantities of alcohol over railroads in drums labeled as containing some other product, such as tar, asphaltum, etc. This form of diversion was possible through the bribery of railroad employees, and we believe a Federal gauger was also implicated.

An employee of the Reading Railway Co. entered into an arrangement with Fries, president of the Quaker Industrial Alcohol Company, to sign bills of lading covering the shipments from the Quaker Company without knowing or without inquiring into the actual contents of the shipments. On orders from Fries, the employee would order the necessary cars on the Bell road siding. These cars would then be loaded with drums labeled to contain tar, asphaltum, etc., whereas, in reality, they contained alcohol. The names of the consignees were fictitious. By these methods of bribery and corruption, over 350,000 gallons of alcohol were diverted into the liquor channels.

Another method of diversion practiced by this company . . . was to sell denatured alcohol to a person or company commonly known as the "cover-up" house entitled by law to receive it for perfumery or other purposes. These houses confirm the sales [by] the industrial alcohol plant and cover-up, by reason of the cloak of legality, the unlawful diversion of alcohol. Enormous quantities of so-called denatured alcohol delivered to cover-up houses require merely a process of redistillation to make it salable for beverage purposes. . . .

Cover-Up Houses

We found "cover-up" houses which claimed to have delivered thousands and thousands of gallons of hair oil, toilet waters, and perfumery to individuals far in excess of normal requirements. In one instance, five hundred gallons of "hair oil," according to the books of the "cover-up" house, were delivered in one shipment to a village of about 50 people. There can be no doubt these deliveries concealed unlawful diversion of alcohol. . . .

Gang Warfare Laid to Bootleg Protection

As diversion and distribution of alcohol was beyond the pale of the law, no legitimate method of protecting the product could be used, and it was essential that an adequate form of protection be devised which would result in the safe delivery of the product either to dealers or to the places where it was to be sold or consumed. It is to be borne in mind the Quaker Industrial Alcohol Company was only one of a number of such plants. . . . Other large industrial alcohol plants, such as Glenwood Industrial Alcohol Company, maintained similar establishments and among these constant competition and rivalry for business existed. . . .

Criminals Employed "In Racket"

The men employed by the operators of alcohol manufacturing plants and by their distributors, prior to the advent of prohibition legislation had been engaged as burglars, bandits, dope peddlers, and gunmen. They made a precarious existence, and the money which was procured was out of all proportion to the risk assumed. As the system developed these men realized the enormous financial benefit to be derived by them through connections with the liquor traffic. With such men disloyalty was followed by death and a business rival was eliminated by murder. They were ready and willing at all times to perform any act of violence on behalf of their employers which would tend to a continuance of the profits they were receiving. In many instances proprietors of saloons or cafes were visited by gunmen or toughs and vicious assaults committed upon them, either to induce them to purchase their liquor from other sources or in retaliation for real or fancied affronts. These gangs and gangsters, with money derived from these occupations, insolent in their power, and secure in the confidence of their chiefs, flaunted the law and openly defied constituted authority.

City McManus Case

Of the many instances before us of the connection and results of the liquor traffic and gang warfare, the case of a man named McManus is outstanding. McManus for sometime was employed in the prohibition department as custodian of liquor in the warehouse and later as an investigator in the prohibition department, and, as such, operated as a free lance investigator inquiring into the conditions of distilleries and other plants engaged in the diversion of alcohol. At about 1a.m., on January 26, 1926, while returning to his home, 5028 Saul Street, in the city of Philadelphia, in company with his wife and baby, he was assailed from behind by two men with caps pulled well over their faces or with masks. One of these men struck his wife over the head, rendering her unconscious. McManus was carrying their baby and, realizing the nature of the attack upon him and the probable reasons therefore, and being fearful for the life of his child, deposited the child in the snow in the bushes. He then retreated some little distance to remove the scene of the fighting from the vicinity of the child and his wife. The attackers drew revolvers and shot him. He received six bullet wounds in his legs and was taken to the hospital, where he remained for 27 weeks.

Investigated Alcohol Company

The story which led up to this attempt to murder McManus has to do with the diversion of alcohol and warfare between rival gangs. McManus had investigated the Consolidated Ethyl Solvents Corporation in which Hoff, Lazar, Schwartz, Fuerstein, the Haims, and [a] man named Robinson and one Benjamin Fogel . . . were reputed to be interested. McManus had trailed a truck supposed to contain unlawfully diverted alcohol and, entering upon the premises, tested the alcohol. After leaving the plant to enter his automobile, he saw Schwartz and Fuerstein sitting in his car and they said they wished to talk to him and asked him whether he wanted money. Upon receiving his reply that he did not want money, Fuerstein told him, "You got to cut this out" and said, "You will either cut it out or you will be removed."

Bootleggers' Power to Remove Investigator

Not long thereafter he was removed as investigator. He told us of a consultation which had taken place among the competitive elements in the alcohol traffic, which brought together Hoff, Lazar, Schwartz, Fuerstein, the Haims and many other men prominently identified with the liquor traffic. Later, some difference of opinion arose among these men and a gang was formed, composed of Hoff, Schwartz, Lazar and other associates, and another gang was organized in competition with them, including the Haims, Fuerstein and a great many other men. Irving Haim saw McManus and informed him of the formation of these cliques. Irving Haim, Charles Haim, Saller and a number of other men offered McManus the sum of $150 per week to do substantially the same work which he had done before being dismissed from the prohibition department, the information to be apparently used against Hoff and his associates and furnished to the prohibition department. He accepted the employment and thereafter Haim paid him his salary and gave him other sums of money at different times exceeding $10, 000.

The nature of his employment and the general purpose for which his information was used came to the attention of the opposing clique. Strangely coincident, the attempt to murder followed. . . .

Machine Guns Sold in Market Street Shop

The Grand Jury traced the direct connection between the sale of fire arms and their employment in the trafficking of liquor. It found that the Chicago bootleggers were not the only "racketeers" who could purchase machine guns and bullet proof vests as they would the ordinary commodities of life. . . .

We had before us a man named Goldberg, who conducted a store on Market Street, in Philadelphia. This man maintained an arsenal in his cellar. He purchased machine guns which he sold and delivered on orders of some of the prominent figures in bootlegging activities, among them Max Hoff. He dealt in bulletproof vests. The evidence before us discloses that, on orders of Max Hoff, he supplied bullet-proof vests and machine guns for which Hoff paid.

The machine guns could readily be carried concealed in automobiles or in other places. Many of the murders committed in this city were committed with the use of machine guns and such other paraphernalia as was sold by Goldberg. Ford and Bailey were notorious in their association with Hoff. They were frequent visitors to a place maintained by him in the Sylvania Hotel and to a place known as "the Ship," and the evidence indicates that each of these men received the sum of $100 per week.

Their duties consisted in terrorizing, attacking, and probably murdering competitors. They were body guards to Hoff and his satellites, and their record in this city is one of crime and violence. We are advised Hoff cannot be prosecuted for his purchase of these weapons as no law makes their sale or possession unlawful. . . .

Large Number of Saloons Running at Inception of Probe

At the time our investigation commenced there were summoned the Director of Public Safety and other high officials in the Police Department, and the reports made by them or by their subordinates covering various phases of criminal activity are before us. One report shows at that time 1170 saloons and cafes were operating in this city and thousands of speakeasies. Most of these establishments sold liquor, and the evidence is conclusive [that] they could not be profitably operated without the sale of liquor. They were maintained openly and notoriously to the certain knowledge of the citizens. Obviously each required large quantities of liquors or other beverages to supply its patrons. In many cases the merchandise was delivered openly to the saloons, cafes, and speakeasies, where it was to be sold or consumed. . . .

Organized Politics Linked with Vice and Graft

The connection between the collection of graft from the law breakers and the political system which had made that species of blackmail possible was definitely established.

Matthew Patterson was considered a political figure of some importance. He was a genial fellow well met and a familiar figure to thousands of Philadelphians. Aside from being in the State legislature for several terms, serving as a member of several extremely important committees, he was the Republican leader from the Nineteenth Ward and had a seat in the Republican City Committee.

When the Grand Jury probe opened a young lawyer, Joseph L. Ehrenreich, came into the District Attorney's office and gave Judge Monaghan a check for $4503.56. Questioned, he said that he had collected it at the instance of "Mat," as Mr. Patterson was generally called, for what he believed were campaign purposes.

Appearing before the Grand Jury, Mr. Ehrenreich proceeded to unfold a tale which caused them to gasp in amazement.

Political Boss and Police Captain Indicted

Following this recital, Mr. Patterson and Captain Charles Schoenleber, commander of the district which comprised the former's ward, were indicted and brought to trial on charges of extortion, bribery, and conspiracy.

At the trial Mr. Ehrenreich testified that he had been instructed by Mr. Patterson to call on William G. Peters, a saloonkeeper and "get some collections."

For a period of six months, the young lawyer said, he went to Mr. Peters' saloon [at] Germantown avenue and Berks street, where the latter turned over to him $1870 in March; $2090 in April; $2020 in May; $2029 in June; $2090 in July; and $2035 in August; a total of $12,195. . . .

After the collections started Mr. Patterson instructed the lawyer to give Captain Schoenleber $1240 every month, telling him to take $300 a month for himself and keep the rest in bank until such time as he was called on to produce it. . . .

Previously Mr. Peters told the court that Mr. Patterson had appointed him to collect $55 every two weeks from the saloonkeepers in the Nineteenth ward. He "kept a little book of the saloonkeepers who paid him."

On the stand Mr. Peters was asked by Major Schofied, prosecuting the case, "What was the money for?"

"Protective Association."

"What was its purpose?"

"Protection."

"What kind of protection?"

"So we wouldn't be bothered by police."

Twelve saloonkeepers who testified at the trial all admitted giving $55 every two weeks to Mr. Peters.

In the face of the evidence presented the jury found both Captain Schoenleber and Mr. Patterson guilty. . . .

Gambling Overlords

On the phase of the inquiry with respect to gambling and the part played by it in the corruption of certain elements of the Police Department, the Jury found:

1. One gambling house was maintained at the corner of Thirteenth and Market streets, in which Charles Schwartz, Max Hoff and others were reputed to be interested. Another was

the Turf Club where men and women of influence gambled nightly and was said to be owned partially by Max Hoff.

2. Another large establishment of this kind was at 1332 Walnut Street, controlled and operated by Richard Kaelker, his brother Charles, and Moses Weinbeck. This place was fitted up with elaborate gambling devices, including roulette wheels, bird cages, and dice. Liquor was served free of charge and food provided for the patrons. Every luxury was offered the frequenters of the establishment, which was hung with tapestries and oil paintings and which was peopled by quiet footed attendants.

Richard Kaelker, his brother Charles, and Moses Weinbeck for many years had been the overlords of organized gambling in this city, and without their permission or approval, no large gambling establishment could be maintained. Both the Kaelkers and Weinbeck were active for many years in the political activities of the Twentieth Ward.

All of these places . . . operated over a period of many years without molestation by police authorities. A condition such as this cannot exist except with the knowledge and connivance of those in authority. In the police districts in which these establishments were maintained police officials were affluent and other police officials known to be friendly with the overlords of the gambling syndicate were found to be in possession of enormous sums of money.

Notes

1. Fred D. Baldwin, "Smedley D. Butler and Prohibition Enforcement in Philadelphia, 1924-1925," *Pennsylvania Magazine of History and Biography,* LXXXIV July 1960), 352-368.

2. David E. Kyvig, *Repealing National Prohibition* (Chicago, 1979), 23-26; also John C. Burnham, "New Perspectives on the Prohibition 'Experiment' of the 1920's," *Journal of Social History* II (Fall, 1968), 51-68.

3. Mark H. Haller, "Bootleggers and American Gambling, 1920-1950," in Commission on the Review of National Policy toward Gambling, *Gambling in America,* Appendix I (Government Printing Office, 1976), pages 108-115.

4. Haller, "Bootlegging in Chicago: The Structure of an Illegal Enterprise," Paper read before convention of American Historical Association (Dec. 1974); also Haller, Bootleggers as Businessmen: From City Slums to City Builders," Paper read to conference on Prohibition: 50 Years Later (Eleutherian Mills, April 1983).

5. Philadelphia *Bulletin,* Sept. 14, 1928, and other newspaper clippings and data in File on Boo-Boo Hoff, Box 63, Coast Guard Intelligence files (National Archives, Washington, D.C.); Report of Special August Grand Jury [1929] in Committee of Seventy Papers, series 3, folder I, Urban Archives, Temple University Library.

6. *Ibid.*

7. File No. 5-62-52, Central Files of the Department of Justice (National Archives, Washington); Letter to Jesse L. Thompson, Feb. 16, 1926, in folder 4354-5239, Box 47, Coast Guard Intelligence Files; Letter of William J. Kelly to Harry J. Anslinger, Feb. 3, 1930, Box 49, Coast Guard Intelligence Files; Philadelphia *Inquirer,* Aug. 22, 1928, 8.

8. Jim Riggio, "Tales of Little Italy," *Philadelphia Magazine* [March 1971], 78-79; Philadelphia *Inquirer,* May 4, 7, 12, 15, and 18, 1934; Philadelphia *Bulletin,* Feb. 6, 1935.

9. Folder 400-600 in Box 46, newspaper clippings in Box 19, and Folder 4354-5239 in Box 47, Coast Guard Intelligence Files.

10. Memo "Re: Eddie Satinova," May 24, 1927, and Confidential Statement of Mrs. Ella Satinover, June 8, 1927, in Box 56, Coast Guard Intelligence Files; also File No. 23-18-218, Central Files of the Department of Justice.

11. Letter to M.W. Willebrandt, April 4, 1924, in File No. 23-30-26, Central Files of the Department of Justice (National Archives, Suitland, Md.); *Evening Bulletin,* Sep. 12, 1928; Folder 12877 on Mill Creek Distillery, Box 79, Coast Guard Intelligence Files; Letter to F.W. Cowan, July 29, 1930, in Folder 4180, Box 90, Coast Guard Intelligence Files; and Confidential Memo from American Consulate General, Aug. 15, 1932, File No. 5-39-52, Central Files of the Department of Justice.

12. Newspaper clippings in file on Boo-Boo Hoff, Box 63, Coast Guard Intelligence Files.

13. Various newspaper clippings in folder 10030, Box 63, Coast Guard Intelligence Files.

14. From typewritten Report of the Special August Grand Jury [1929], pages 1, 2-3, 41, 42-43, 44, 45-46, 47-49, 52-53, 65-66. The excerpts from the Report have been edited to correct punctuation, spelling, and typographical errors. Also, the order of some excerpts has been changed to create greater continuity.

Chapter 6

The Bruno Family of Philadelphia: Organized Crime as a Regulatory Agency

In 1959 Angelo Bruno Annalore—known during most of his life as Angelo Bruno, or "Ange" to his friends—became the boss of the South Philadelphia Italian American crime family. Born in the town of Villalba, Sicily, in 1910, he was raised in South Philadelphia, where his father owned a small grocery store. By the late 1930s, he had become a successful operator of numbers gambling and took pride in his skill and reliability as a criminal entrepreneur. His success as an entrepreneur and his political skills enabled him to assume the position of boss during a leadership crisis of the late 1950s. During his twenty-one-year leadership of what became known as the Bruno family, he was a careful, secretive boss, who even looked like a stodgy and conservative accountant.[1] As boss, he continued drawing profits from numbers gambling and loansharking, while expanding his investments in numerous legitimate businesses in the Philadelphia region, Florida, and elsewhere. His leadership abruptly ended on 21 March 1980, when· he was shot and killed in front of his home in South Philadelphia. The existence of the Bruno family and of allied families in other American cities raises the obvious question, why do men involved in a range of illegal and legal money-making activities find it useful to join and support such groups? What functions do the groups perform for members? One answer is that the families function as a sort of shadow government or regulating agency that brings some predictability and structure to their part of the urban underworld.

Because the Bruno family enjoyed a remarkable stability and held a recognized place in the underworld of Philadelphia and of several surrounding cities, it provides a good case study. An examination of the role of the family in the late 1970s, in the years before Bruno's death, can clarify the family's regulatory functions.

Introduction

In order to understand the regulatory functions of the Bruno family, it is necessary to examine two different types of structures. One is the structure of the illegal (and legal) businesses operated by the members. These businesses were owned and directed by the members and their partners and were not operated on behalf of the family. As owners, the members and their associates pocketed the profits, when there were profits; they suffered the losses, when there were losses.

The other structure was the family. The family was not a business or money-making operation, nor did it control any businesses. As one long-time member declared with reference to money-making activities: "The family don't run anything."[2] The family, instead, was like a fraternal organization. In the world in which the members operated, there was prestige in belonging to the family, with its powerful reputation and its secret ways. In the restaurants and nightspots where they hung out, they enjoyed the special attention that they received. Many members took seriously the social bonds that were forged among members and were displayed at marriages, funerals, and other occasions where they exchanged gifts and acknowledged their loyalties to each other.

Under Bruno, the family had a normal structure, which may have existed since the 1930s. There was a boss and underboss. There was also a consigliere, who was supposed to be a wise and neutral figure to advise the boss and mediate disputes among members. The family also had capos (often referred to in Philadelphia as "capis"). In theory, at least, each member reported to a capo.

The family, while not involved in money-making schemes, aided the economic interests of its members and their associates. One function was to provide a group within which members could make useful contacts, learn about business opportunities, and exchange mutual favors. But there was also a second function. The family was a sort of shadow government, providing a set of rules and expectations that facilitated the members' legal and illegal activities. A willingness of underworld wheelers and dealers to risk money in chancy enterprises and to trust others as partners or agents required that they feel confidence that commitments would be honored. For legal businessmen, regulatory structure is provided by the law and by ethical standards enforced formally and informally through bar associations or better business bureaus. The Bruno family, then, was like a bar association or better business bureau in providing a structure of rules for those who accepted its legitimacy.

It is necessary first to understand the problems and the risks faced by the members in their business activities. Then it will be possible to understand the ways in which the Bruno family provided rules that gave structure to the world in which members operated.

Illegal Businesses

In the late 1960s, the Bruno family had approximately fifty-eight active members. Of these, a few pursued only legal sources of income; some had only illegal sources of income; and others, generally those best known to the public and to law enforcement, combined legal and illegal sources of income.[3] By the late 1970s, the number of active members—as estimated by the Pennsylvania Crime Commission in 1980—had declined by about ten. The distribution of their involvement in legal and illegal activities, however, generally followed the same pattern.

The members structured their illegal businesses in order to share profits and spread the risks. There were two patterns by which this was done. Although sometimes a loan-sharking operation or numbers bank was owned by a single individual, typically the ownership was by two or more partners. The partners could include both family members and nonmembers. Usually, all of the partners invested money in the enterprise, but one member was responsible for day-to-day oversight of the business. By forming partnerships, the owners spread the risks and combined their resources and expertise.[4] While an illegal business was generally established and controlled by partners, the next level of participants was often commission agents—a system in which persons received a share of the profits from that part of the business in which they participated. In numbers gambling, for instance, a numbers writer in a barbershop or saloon received a percentage of the money that was bet at his or her retail outlet. Similarly, loan sharks made arrangements by which agents shared in the profits that they generated from loans. In effect, agents were uninvested partners in that phase of the loan shark business for which they had responsibility.[5]

There were a number of implications from the system of partnerships and commission agents. First of all, such a system meant that each person's income was tied directly to how well the activities turned a profit. This minimized the necessity for oversight since each person had a stake in doing well. Second and connected to this, the system provided for considerable decentralization of operation and therefore minimized central oversight. Each person in a numbers bank, loan shark operation, or sports book had wide discretion in carrying out his end of the enterprise. Finally, the system meant that most illegal enterprises had minimal overhead expenses or ongoing financial commitments. As an example, numbers writers sold numbers from their own bars, barbershops, or newspaper kiosks, so that the numbers bank had many outlets without the necessity of paying rent. Furthermore, since income was tied to profits, if the enterprise lost money or went out of business, there was no obligation to continue paying salaries or other expenses. This minimized risks of those overseeing the enterprise and simplified entry and exit.

The system also fit the life-style of the people in the rackets. While they often faced periods of intense activity, in general they were free of bureaucratic supervision and controlled their own time while carrying on business by cryptic telephone conversations, meetings on street corners, and exchanges of information in bars or restaurants. Written records, while important, were few and kept informally—often written by hand. These were people who spoke of their world as "being . . . on the street."

They enjoyed the life of deals, negotiations, whispered conversations; and they escaped the bureaucratic' responsibilities of overseeing formal organizations.

The major illegal business engaged in by members of the Bruno family was loan-sharking.[6] However, the members were only a minority of loan sharks in the Philadelphia region. Nevertheless, loan-sharking was significant not only because of the money earned by those who operated as loan sharks but also because, as lenders who financed various illegal activities, the loan sharks sometimes exercised a broad economic influence on the underworld of the Delaware Valley. The loans to legal businessmen, at the same time, made them important players in the small businesses of South Philadelphia.

Because some borrowers were chronically delinquent in their payments, the attempt to collect from those in default was a loan shark's most difficult and time-consuming activity. The ultimate collection tool was violence—or, more accurately, the threat of violence. For those who were members of the Bruno family, the fact of their membership increased the credibility of their threats. Regular borrowers, though, were often aware that threats were seldom followed by actual violence. In Philadelphia, loan-sharking was largely nonviolent. Unreliable borrowers, of course, lost their access to future loans—a genuine threat for those who regularly relied on loan sharks. In general, however, defaulters were threatened as a means to induce them to recognize their obligation and agree to a new payment schedule.

Important loan sharks operated within a structure in which most of the loans were, in fact, made and collected by others. One pattern was for a leading loan shark to make arrangements for others to handle the contact with customers. In this case, the loan shark and the agent would split equally the profits from those loans managed by the agent. The agent had some independence in making loans and in managing repayment. But he was typically expected to operate within guidelines laid down by the loan shark and to seek prior approval for large or risky loans. A second pattern was for the chief loan shark to lend money to other loan sharks, who, in turn, would lend to customers. In theory, the subsidiary loan shark was an independent businessman whose income, if he managed the loans skillfully, was the difference between what was collected and what was paid for the money. In reality, though, the loan could not be repaid if those to whom the money was lent reneged on their payments. As a result, the chief loan shark was consulted concerning large or risky loans and also consulted with regard to strategies for collection when borrowers were in arrears. This created complex relations of debt among loan sharks as well as with the ultimate customers.

The second most important illegal activity was numbers gambling. Most of the numbers banks in South Philadelphia were owned by members of the Bruno family and their associates. Some of the numbers banks in Northeast Philadelphia, while independently operated, were owned by persons who had friends and associates within the Bruno family. Bruno family members also had numbers banks in Trenton and Bristol. Numbers banks in the African American neighborhoods of Philadelphia were largely independent, as were many white-operated numbers banks outside South Philadelphia.

Numbers banks have existed in Philadelphia since numbers gambling was first introduced into the city in the early 1920s.[7] It is a gambling game popular in many neighborhoods. In the most common method of playing the game, bettors place their money on any three-digit number from 000 to 999. While the payoff odds have varied from time to time and from bank to bank, the standard payoff in the late 1970s was 650 to 1. Since the odds of winning were 1,000 to 1, the persons involved in the numbers game would, in the long run, earn $350 out of every $1,000 that was bet. Numbers have traditionally been sold in barbershops, bars, newspaper kiosks, and other neighborhood outlets. There are also walking writers who go door-to-door in the neighborhood. The problem for those running the business, though, is that bettors believe in lucky numbers; and, on any given day, many bettors may select the same number. If that number wins, then the seller will be unable to make payments from the money bet on losing numbers.[8] What is profitable in the long run may lead to bankruptcy in the short run.

This is the reason for numbers banks. The bank assumes the risk by agreeing to pay off winning bettors. As a result, the numbers writers take bets in the neighborhoods. They keep a fixed percent of the money bet with them (often 20 percent) and pass on the rest of the money and the betting records. They are assured a steady income based on the amount bet with them. The bank, then, assumes the risk of paying winners and is responsible for providing the writers with enough money to cover the winning bets. The bank takes on the risks in the expectation of making a profit from the bets placed with a large number of writers. Often a pickup person collects from the writers, handles payments to writers on his route, and settles with the bank every week or two.

Those who ran numbers banks, as a result, were at the center of an elaborate system for managing risk. They had to prescribe policies to the pickup men concerning "cut" numbers and betting limits and maintained daily contact with the operations that might involve dozens of numbers writers. In turn, the banker often had regular contact with an "edge-off" house as well as with a loan shark. The system operated on credit. Periodically, the pickup person settled with writers and with the banker; the banker had to settle with the edge-off house and, perhaps, with a loan shark. It was a system run on the assumption that people would meet their obligations and pay their debts.

A few members of the Bruno family operated zignetti games in South Philadelphia and floating crap games at various locations in the Delaware Valley. While these games were few in number, they constituted a significant proportion of the zignetti and crap games in the region. Almost always they were run as partnerships. It was necessary to have a bankroll present at the game in case the players had a run of good luck. (The bankroll for a high stakes craps game might run as high as $100,000.) Few entrepreneurs had that sort of money— and even fewer were willing to risk losing that much on a bad night. As a result, they pooled their investments to spread the risks. But it was standard that one partner was present at the game to hire and oversee the lookouts and operators, to make significant decisions concerning such matters as extending credit to players, and to guard against embezzlement in what was largely a cash enterprise.

There were other illegal markets in the Delaware Valley. In most, members of the Bruno family were of minor importance. A few members ran sports bookmaking—and others became involved because, as loan sharks, they made loans to bookmakers. Members of the family, though, operated a small proportion of the sports betting in the region. With regard to drugs, a handful of members had been wholesalers of heroin in an earlier period. By the late 1970s, however, they were largely absent from the dealing in heroin, cocaine, and marijuana. At the end of the decade a few trafficked in P2P, used in the manufacture of methamphetamine. Nevertheless, in drug dealing, the most lucrative (and risky) underworld market, members of the Bruno family were notable chiefly for their relative nonparticipation.[9] There were, in short, important areas of illegal enterprise in which members of the Bruno family played, at best, a marginal role.

Legal Businesses

The members of the Bruno family, their relatives, and their associates also controlled a range of small businesses in the Delaware Valley. Probably the most numerous were bars, nightclubs, and restaurants. Given a life-style that involved socializing and conducting business at restaurants and nightspots and given the traditional use of such places as centers for loan-sharking and gambling, they felt comfortable in ownership of such businesses. Probably a majority of successful members had an ownership interest in at least one restaurant or nightspot. Other businesses owned by members and associates provided services to nightspots, such as food services, vending machine companies, and financial services such as insurance and real estate. One associate ran a talent agency that placed entertainers in nightspots in the Delaware Valley. Even in the control of labor unions, the chief influence of Bruno family members was within locals of the Hotel, Restaurant and Bartenders Union.

Because so many of their businesses were connected to restaurants and nightspots, there was a great deal of mutual dealing among members and associates in legitimate businesses. They bought from each other and recommended each other's businesses to others. On the whole, their businesses were small. Often, close relatives were officers in the businesses and oversaw day-to-day operations.

Functions of the Bruno Family

Members of the Bruno family and their business associates, then, were involved in numerous independent legal and illegal business enterprises. They invested money together in risky ventures, bought and sold on credit, borrowed from each other, and owed each other favors for services rendered. For this world of small business to operate with a minimum of conflict and with reasonable cooperation, it was necessary to have a set of norms or rules and a rudimentary system of dispute settlement. The Bruno family provided such regulatory functions for those who recognized its legitimacy.

Much of the underworld in the Delaware Valley did not recognize the legitimacy of the family and operated outside its framework. Although there were some ties between a few Bruno family members and some African American criminals, on the whole, the African American underworld was independent. The same was true of the small underworld of Asian Americans. Finally, substantial portions of the white underworld—especially drug dealers and many sports bookmakers—maintained a complex but generally independent position. Nevertheless, in Philadelphia, Chester, Atlantic City, Trenton, and even Newark there were significant networks of persons in illegal and legal businesses who recognized the legitimacy of the family's norms and often operated within its framework.

An example will show how the family could provide the structure of predictability that facilitated business activities. In the mid-1970s, a Bruno nephew and an insurance dealer in northeast Pennsylvania were involved in a surety bond fraud. At one point, they decided that their scheme might be helped by a bribe of $100,000 to state regulators. Of this amount, the insurance dealer was to contribute $25,000. He was worried, though, that, if he put up the money and the bribe fell through, he might not get his money back. Consequently, he explained his problem to Albert Scalleat, whose brother Joseph was a longtime and respected member of the Bruno family operating from the Hazelton, Pennsylvania, area. Scalleat contacted Bruno and obtained his assurance that there was nothing to fear. Later the bribe scheme failed, and the insurance dealer's money was returned to him.

In this instance, Scalleat and Bruno provided the framework that made the scheme possible for two associates who accepted the family's legitimacy. The many daily transactions of members and associates would not be possible, however, if every transaction required the personal intercession of a family leader. Instead, then, the members recognized and operated within a set of formal and informal rules that had evolved over time to guide them in their business behavior.

At the initiation ceremony, new members swore their loyalty to the family and its leadership. For those who took the oath seriously, this represented a commitment to a group of men and a pattern of behavior. For most new members, having already proven themselves through business partnerships with members, admittance to the family represented formal recognition that they had proven their adherence to a code of "honorable" criminal behavior.

At the initiation ceremony, in addition, new members were solemnly informed that some criminal activities were forbidden. These included kidnapping, prostitution, counterfeiting of money, and drug dealing. There was a mixture of reasons for the bans: to maintain order within the underworld, to avoid crimes that would result in heavy penalties, and to sustain their concept of themselves as "honorable" men who disdained dishonorable activities. The mandate to shun prostitution represented a view that living off the money of a prostitute was dishonorable. Probably the mandate against kidnapping reflected the fact that in the late 1920s and early 1930s, in a number of cities such as Chicago and New York, the underworld was disrupted by gangs that kidnapped other criminals and held them for ransom. The creation of a stable underworld required stamping out such behavior.[10] The origin of the ban on drugs, probably dating from the 1950s, reflected the perception that, because drug trafficking was a federal offense, such activity presented a danger of vigorous enforcement and stiff sentences. But the ban also gave members an image of themselves as good citizens in their neighborhood and also meant that many people in South Philadelphia tolerated the family because it was seen as a group that protected the area from drug dealers.

There were other explicit elements of the code designed to maintain stability and order. As in crime families elsewhere, no member was to kill anyone without the permission of the boss. It was further understood that members were to inform their capo of their illegal ventures, so that the capo could determine whether the venture would be upsetting to another member.[11] In practice, however, this rule was not taken seriously. Another rule, according to one mob defector, was that members were not supposed to place bets with bookmakers who were members, thereby avoiding the types of quarrels that could arise if either the bettor or the bookmaker failed to make payment afterward."[12] All of these rules were intended to keep peace and stability among the members and associates.

To avoid attracting the attention of the public or authorities, Bruno pressured members to shun ostentation. Even Frank Sindone, Bruno's longtime associate and his partner in a major loan-sharking operation, found Bruno's rules stultifying. As he once exclaimed to Salvatore Merlino: "He [Bruno] don't want nobody that drinks around him, and nobody that gambles! He wants all priests around him!" When Merlino remarked, "What's the good having it [money] if you can't spend it." Sindone complained: "I've got plenty of f—king money! What am I going to do? Die and leave it to my family? I don't want to leave it to my family! I want to live, too!" He made clear: "I love this guy [Bruno]! This guy, this guy has been good to me!" Yet he added in exasperation, "But he's got them old f—king ways! He ain't getting out of them, you know what I mean?"[13]

Most of the code was not stated explicitly but can be inferred from the numerous conversations that were recorded by law enforcement agencies over the years. Of central concern was a set of informal rules that defined "unfair" competition. Anyone was allowed to start or expand an illegal business; but he should do so by recruiting his own agents and customers and not by trying to recruit agents or customers already attached to the business of another member or associate.

This was clear, for instance, in a June 1978 conversation in which Charles ("Chickie," or "Noodle," or "Chicken Noodle") Warrington, a respected family associate, spoke with an unidentified numbers banker named Busco. Busco came to Chickie to complain that someone was trying to steal his numbers writers. Chickie's response was that anyone had a right to start a numbers bank: "See, I don't, I don't mind anybody, ah, you know, you can't stop a guy from makin' a livin.'" Busco agreed but added:

Busco: But, . . . don't f— with my books. Now, how many times I come to you. And you tell that motherf—in' Pat . . .
Chick: Yeah.
Busco: To stay away from my f—in' writers. . . . And, ah, I know right, damn right well, if I'm f—in' with your books, you're gonna come, "Hey, Busco, what the f—are you doin'?" You know.[14]

Not only was it wrong to recruit someone's agents but also to entice away customers. Harry Riccobene, who joined the Philadelphia family in 1931 and was regarded by many as a repository of family lore, explained the rules to Louis "Babe" Marchetti in an October 1977 conversation. Using the example of a loan-shark customer, Harry explained: "Knowing that somebody is doing business with somebody else, you shouldn't do business with them. That is all." He elucidated later: "Say I got a customer. 'Joe Blow' is my customer. He comes to you and says, 'Hey, Babe, I'm in a jam, I need a hundred dollars.' Right? Now you know he's my customer. You know he's doing business with me. Not only money, maybe other things. Your place to him is: 'Oh, geez, you're doing business with Harry. Why are you coming to me?' Now he'll give you another cock and bull story. And you say, 'I can't give it to you until . . . unless Harry okays it.' You follow, you understand what I'm saying?"[15]

Among those who accepted the legitimacy of the family—whether members or not—a central principle was that the business of members or their associates were protected from raids by other members or by outsiders. This was, in fact, one of the advantages of membership. Nonmembers frequently sought out members as partners because their illegal businesses would then be protected from unfair competition.

There were, however, obligations, as well as opportunities, for those who chose to do business with a family member. If, for instance, a numbers banker borrowed from a member loan shark who also took edge-off bets, then the numbers banker was also expected to provide his edge-off business to the loan shark. Some persons went beyond being occasional customers and dealt regularly with one or more members. They were regarded as being "with" the member who was their closest associate. Although they were not expected to make payments to the member, they were expected to cooperate in a range of business activities. In 1977, for instance, a Center City bookmaker who was known to be "with" Harry

Riccobene was not giving his edge-off work to Harry. Another associate of Harry's approached the bookmaker and admonished him, in his words: "Everybody around here knows you are with Harry . . . and you are giving f—king edge to somebody else."[16]

On another occasion Harry explained the rules of the relationship to an associate named Babe:

Harry: If you want to work under my wing?
Babe: Right, right, right.
Harry: I want to know what you're doing!
Babe: Okay.
Harry: Now, I don't want nothing! I don't need, I don't want nothing from you. I'm not looking for anybody to give me anything! You understand what I'm saying?
Babe: You're helping me?[17]

At any rate, members, their associates, and their customers constituted a complicated system of mutual obligations and exchange of favors.

Another quasi-governmental function of the family was an informal system for handling a member's businesses if the member died or went to prison. With regard to legal businesses, they remained with the member's partners or relatives, much as the businesses would for any legal small-business man. With regard to an illegal business, the business generally remained with the partners if the business had been operated by partners. If there were no partners, however, the family might redistribute ownership. This was often a complicated process. For a loan-shark operation, for instance, it would be necessary to find the scattered and incomplete records in order to reconstruct a list of loans and payments. There was, furthermore, a responsibility to take care of the member's family and to return the business to the member when the member returned to the street.[18]

Finally, the Philadelphia family was part of a national network of families. This meant that Philadelphia family members had the advantage that they could call upon contacts in other cities in their legal and illegal businesses. There was, furthermore, a complicated protocol by which members from one city could open businesses in another city. If a member of a family from another city wished to open a business in an area where Bruno family members operated, there had to be consultation and generally an offer to share in the profits. Phil Testa, then the underboss in the Bruno family, explained an agreement between New York and Philadelphia with regard to Trenton, New Jersey: "In other words, they have an agreement for card games and crap games. Say like you're from New York and I want to open up this game. I say, 'Look, I want to open up. You've got fifty percent." He went on to state that Carl "Pappy" Ippolito, a Bruno family member in Trenton, had a half interest in a local crap game run by two New Yorkers.[19]

In the late 1970s, several Gambinos opened a series of businesses in the Delaware Valley; these included a restaurant in Cherry Hill, New Jersey, a disco in Atlantic City, and a number of pizza parlors in South Jersey and Philadelphia. (Later it would be learned that the pizza parlors were fronts for the distribution of heroin.) While the Gambinos who were active in these businesses had been born in Sicily and presumably became Mafia members there, they operated in the Delaware Valley under the aegis of the Gambino family of New York. Angelo Bruno was a longtime friend of Carlo Gambino, the head of the New York family; indeed, Bruno's wife, Sue, owned property in Florida jointly with Carlo. Bruno met with the Gambinos at their Cherry Hill restaurant. Out of these contacts evolved a set of mutual favors. The pizza parlor owners sought Bruno's advice concerning cigarette vending companies to service their parlors, used an attorney who was also attorney for John's Vending (in which Bruno had an interest), and bought insurance from Bruno's son-in-law, Ralph Puppo.[20] The opening of the business, in short, involved a fairly elaborate negotiation of mutual favors and assistance.

Members and associates of the Bruno family, then, carried on their legal and illegal businesses within a complicated informal framework of rules and obligations. The quasi-governmental functions of the family constituted the most important way that association with the family impacted upon the business activities of those within the family's influence.

Conclusion

During the 1970s, under the leadership of Bruno, the economic activities of the members exhibited a number of characteristics. Most important, perhaps, each of the active members carried on his money-making activities within a relatively independent cluster of business partners and associates who cooperated in a variety of enterprises. Sometimes only one participant in the cluster was a member of the family. In the group around Scalleat in Hazleton, for instance, only Scalleat was a member; he formed partnerships with various relatives and outside businessmen to run the garment factories and beer distributorship that were a central part of his business operations. Riccobene, similarly, was the only Bruno family member in the cluster of legal and illegal activities operated by him and his stepbrothers in South Philadelphia. In the cluster of businesses coordinated by Sindone from a headquarters in South Philadelphia, by contrast, there were at least half a dozen members, along with a number of associates, who formed shifting partnerships to operate in a variety of illegal activities.

While different participants in each cluster might specialize in particular types of businesses, the central figures in each cluster were involved in a range of legal and illegal ventures. Sometimes an enterprise was owned by one man, but more commonly, enterprises were owned by two or more partners. Typically one of the partners took responsibility for day-to-day oversight of the enterprise, either by becoming the manager or by keeping in regular contact with the manager. If the enterprise was illegal, like a numbers bank or loan-sharking operation, then generally persons working on commission reported to the manager. Examples were the runners who collected from the numbers writers or loan-shark agents who placed loans and oversaw collection. In the case of a legal venture, like a restaurant or bar, the structure would parallel the structure of similar legal businesses owned by legitimate businessmen.

Members carried on their money-making activities chiefly with their partners and associates. Their partners and associates, not the family, were the focus of their daily rounds: discussing a loan-shark deal with an agent, tallying the daily reports from numbers runners, and stopping in at the bar or restaurant in the evening to see how business was going. These were ventures that they had established or purchased and from which they derived their illegal and legal income. At the same time, as members of the Bruno family, they had a number of expectations and informal obligations. Particularly in places like Hazleton, Pennsylvania, or Newark and Trenton, New Jersey, where members of several families were active in the same region, they were expected to observe the protocol that defined the ways that members of different families did mutual favors and avoided disruptive competitive activities. Sometimes members of different families formed partnerships. At other times, they used each other's contacts for mutual advantage.

More important, of course, the Bruno family provided a quasi government within which members and associates operated. Sometimes persons in one cluster of enterprises did business with someone in another cluster. Commonly, for instance, a numbers banker would edge off with the numbers bank of another member. Beyond this, members and their associates were aware that they should carry on their businesses in keeping with the informal rules of the family. In short, members and associates recognized they were part of a larger network of legal and illegal businessmen who were expected to do favors for each other, avoid acts of unfair competition, and not cheat those who ran businesses that were "connected" to other members.

Notes

1. In the fall of 1962, Bruno explained that his success in numbers gambling derived from his honesty in running the business: "If I wanted business, I can get all the business I want. I turn it down every day. They come to me because they know I'm solid. . . . They know if they got $50 going [on a numbers bet], they are going to get paid. They are not sure of a lot of guys. That's why I get all the business I want" (*The F.B.I. Transcripts* on Exhibit in *U.S.A. v. DeCavalcante, Vastola, and Annunziata,* Lemma Publishing Corporation, 1970, Book VI, volume 13:41).

After Bruno's assassination, his old friend and attorney Jacob Kossman reminisced about Bruno for a reporter: "I've known him 40 years. . . . I like his wife's cooking, which is the best and then I have known his children and his grandchildren." Kossman added: "He's a great reader; he's a philosopher. In terms of government, he sees our government sinking with inflation. He sees the government sinking with communism" (Philadelphia *Bulletin,* 23 March 1980).

2. Confidential interview, 27-28 July 1989.

3. Annelise G. Anderson, *The Business of Crime: A Cosa Nostra Family* (Hoover Institution, 1979), 2-3.

4. Mark H. Haller, "Illegal Enterprise: A Theoretical and Historical Interpretation," *Criminology* (May 1990): 207-35.

5. Ibid.; Peter Reuter, *Disorganized Crime: The Economics of the Visible Hand* (Cambridge: MIT Press, 1983), Chap. 4; John M. Siedl, "'Upon the Hip,'—A Study of the Criminal Loan-Shark Industry," Ph.D. dissertation, Harvard University, 1968.

6. Anderson, *Business of Crime,* Chapter 4.

7. Mark H. Haller, "Bootleggers and American Gambling, 1920-1950," in Commission on Review of National Policy Toward Gambling, *Gambling in America* (G.P.O.), Appendix I, 117-21.

8. Another risk was that writers or pickup men would try to cheat the bank by waiting until after the winning number was known and then slip winning numbers into the daily bets. Because of this danger, those operating numbers banks had to maintain a small headquarters and oversee the daily responsibility of collecting a record of all bets each day before the winning number could be known.

9. For a summary of involvement of Bruno family members and associates in various drug trafficking, see Pennsylvania Crime Commission, *A Decade of Organized Crime: 1980 Report,* Chapter 6.

10. Ralph Salerno and John Tompkins, *The Crime Confederation* (Garden City, NY: Doubleday, 1969), 119-20. This development paralleled warfare in the Middle Ages when fighting often involved an attempt to capture the enemy and hold him for ransom. Eventually, there was mutual agreement among nobles to ban the practice. This parallel was pointed out to me by my colleague, Russell F. Wrigley; Wrigley, *The Age of Battles: The Quest for Decisive Warfare from Breitenfeld to Waterloo* (Indiana University, Press, 1991), 18.

11. Interview, 27-28 July 1989.

12. From the federal RICO indictment, 81-00049, 20 February 1981. The rule forbidding betting with member bookmakers did not, of course, protect independent bookmakers. There were examples of members who bet with independents and, when they lost, refused to pay. According to one informant, Nicholas Caramandi once bet with Joseph Mastronardo, former mayor Frank Rizzo's son-in-law, the largest sports book-maker in the Delaware Valley, and then refused to pay after losing. Allegedly Mastronardo was stuck with a $50,000 loss.

13. Referring to Bruno's generation, Sindone added: "Those guys, I don't know. I don't understand them! It's just get the money! Get the money! Get the money! . . . Don't spend it! What the f—good is it?" See FBI transcript, 2 April 1976, at Frank's cabana.

14. FBI transcripts, 2 October 1977, at Tyrone DeNittis Agency.

15. FBI transcripts, 2 October 1978, at Tyrone DeNittis Agency.

16. FBI transcripts, 28 September 1977, at Tyrone DeNittis Agency.

17. FBI transcripts, 28 September 1977, at Tyrone DeNittis Agency.

18. Interview, 27 July 1989.

19. FBI transcript, 4 November 1977, at Tyrone DeNittis Agency, recording conversation among Harry Riccobene, Philip Testa, Frank Narducci, and Nicky Scarfo.

20. Based chiefly on testimony of Angelo Bruno, Emmanuel Gambino, and Domenico Adamita before New Jersey State Commission of Investigation. The

later, highly-publicized Pizza Connection trials concerning heroin smuggling have been chronicled in several books; see Shana Alexander, *The Pizza Connection* (New York: Weidenfeld and Nicolson, 1988).

Chapter 7

Loansharking in Philadelphia: Social Control in an Illegal Enterprise

The modern system of loansharking, in which the loanshark makes loans at illegal rates of interest and uses violence or the threat of violence as the ultimate collection mechanism, became a regular part of underworld activities in New York City during the 1930s and spread to many other large, American cities shortly after World War II. Loansharks often meet their customers in the informal milieu of a streetcorner, bar, or restaurant and conduct their negotiations with little or no paperwork. While many loans are less than $500—and many loansharks specialize in making small loans—other loans may run into the tens of thousands of dollars. There is clearly much at stake in such transactions for both loanshark and borrower. In order to understand the mutual obligations and rule enforcement within loansharking, it is necessary to understand the social context within which both borrower and lender come together.[1]

This chapter will focus on two loansharks, Harry Riccobene and Frank Sindone, who were active in Philadelphia in the 1970s. Riccobene, who operated out of a small office located in a talent agency on South Broad Street, specialized in small loans of $500 to $1,000. Sindone, whose many businesses were run from a lunch counter on a commercial street in South Philadelphia, may have been the most important loanshark in the region and typically made loans in excess of $10,000. While their operations differed in scale and type of loan, both were known within the community as members of the Bruno Crime family of South Philadelphia; and both pursued long careers operating gambling, loansharking, and other rackets in Philadelphia and its region.

The Bruno Family and Loansharking

Part of the social context for the loansharking businesses of Riccobene and Sindone was their membership in the Bruno Family. The Family had been founded by the late 1920s and, after 1959, was run by Angelo Bruno until his assassination in 1980. In 1970, the family had about 58 active members. Of these, a few had no known illegal sources of income; some were known to have only illegal sources of income; and another group—generally those best known to the public and to law enforcement—combined legal and illegal sources of income. By the late 1970s, the number of active members—as estimated by the Pennsylvania Crime Commission in 1980—had declined by about ten.[2]

The members of the Bruno Family were independent businessmen— that is, the various legal and illegal money-making schemes belonged to the individual members and their associates. As owners, they pocketed the profits, when there were profits; they suffered the losses, when there were losses. The Bruno Family can be thought of as a sort of chamber of commerce—a social organization to which various independent and mostly criminal entrepreneurs belonged. On the street corners and in the bars and nightclubs where they hung out, there was prestige that derived from being known as members. But membership in the Family also was part of the social structure within which they carried on their business activities. Within the Family, members made useful contacts, learned about business opportunities, and exchanged mutual favors. The Family was, in addition, a sort of shadow government that provided a set of rules and expectations that facilitated members in their legal and illegal activities. For those who recognized its legitimacy, in short, the Bruno Family constituted an alternate source of legitimate rules.[3]

The major illegal business engaged in by members of the Bruno family was loansharking. Nevertheless, the members were probably a minority of loansharks in the region. Loansharking was significant not only because of the money earned by those who operated as loansharks but also because, as lenders to finance various illegal activities, the loansharks sometimes exercised a broad economic influence upon the underworld of the Delaware Valley. The loans to legal businessmen, at the same time, made them important players in the small businesses of South Philadelphia.

For those involved in loansharking, membership in the family aided in the recruitment of customers, provided leverage for the collection of debts, and protected them from certain forms of competition. The reputation that they enjoyed as members meant that borrowers often recognized that they were dealing with an "important" person, one with influential friends and contacts. Some borrowers sought them out in order to establish a relationship with an important person in the neighborhood or were referred by friends who wished to curry favor. At the same time, delinquent borrowers were often more willing to make repayments because of the general belief that that members of crime families were particularly dangerous when crossed.

The Family, in addition, fostered a set of understandings that forbid "unfair" competition among members. Anyone was free to start or expand an illegal business, but it was expected that he would do so by recruiting his own agents and customers and not by recruiting agents or customers already attached to the business of another member.

Harry Riccobene, who joined the Philadelphia family in 1931 and was a repository of family lore, explained the rules to an associate. Using the example of a loanshark customer, he explained:

Harry: "Knowing that somebody is doing business with somebody else, you shouldn't do business with them. That is all." And he elucidated later:

Harry: "Say I got a customer. 'Joe Blow' is my customer. He comes to you and says, 'Hey, Babe, I'm in a jam, I need a hundred dollars.' Right? Now you know he's my customer. You know he's doing business with me. Not only money, maybe other things. Your place to him is: 'Oh, geez, you're doing business with Harry. Why are you coming to me?' Now he'll give you another cock and bull story. And you say, 'I can't give it to you until, unless Harry okays it.' You follow, you understand what I'm saying?"[4]

Among those who accepted the legitimacy of the family—whether members or not—a central principle was that the businesses of members or their associates were protected from raids by other members or by outsiders. This was, in fact, one of the advantages of membership. Nonmembers frequently sought out members as partners because their illegal businesses would then be protected from unfair competition.

Loansharking as a Business

The chief business problem in running loansharking was, of course, collecting the money owed by borrowers. Often, the borrowers were poor risks—persons who could not secure loans from legitimate sources or had exhausted their legitimate credit and turned to illegal borrowing. The high interest rates charged by loansharks in part reflected the risk of making loans to undependable borrowers. The profitability of the enterprise, nevertheless, depended upon the skill of loansharks in collecting from those same borrowers.

For those who were members of the Bruno family, the fact of their membership sometimes increased the credibility of their threats. Regular borrowers, though, were often aware that threats were seldom followed by actual violence. In Philadelphia, in fact, loansharking was largely non-violent. Violence was, after all, a two-edged sword. On the one hand, violence might persuade a reluctant borrower to repay and discourage other borrowers from missing payments. But violence might also cause a borrower to turn to the police for protection and result in prosecution of the loanshark. And a loanshark's reputation for violence could discourage new borrowers from taking the risk of turning to a loanshark. Thus, while threats of violence were part of loansharking and customers generally were not permitted to believe that they could avoid repayment with impunity, nevertheless, loansharking operated within a system of rules and obligations that seldom led to violence.

The first line of defense was to make loans wisely. This involved an attempt by the lender to determine the reliability of the borrower and to keep the loan within a range that the borrower could manage. For repeat borrowers, this judgment was based upon a borrower's record in repaying previous loans. Some borrowers had good credit ratings; some did not. New borrowers were often referred by other borrowers. In that case, the person making the referral vouched for the new borrower. He was also expected to make payment if the borrower defaulted—but this was true more in theory than in practice.

The lender tried to increase the borrower's sense of obligation by making the loan a personal transaction—that is, the borrower was not receiving the money from an impersonal bureaucracy but, instead, as pledging his honor, man to man, to make repayment. Often the borrower and lender came from the same blue-collar background—even the same neighborhood—and shared a rough and ready set of values which was based on a perception that the world operated through mutual deals and favors and which placed great emphasis upon the notion that a man's word was his bond. Because of the personal, male-bonding relationship involved, loans to women were not part of the culture of loansharking. Instead, loansharking involved an obligation assumed within a male culture of honor.

Despite this, many borrowers were chronically delinquent in their payments and the attempt to collect from those in default was a loanshark's most difficult and time-consuming activity. Unreliable borrowers, of course, lost their access to future loans—a genuine threat for those who regularly relied upon loansharks for money. In general, however, delinquent payments were regarded by loansharks as a normal business risk. Interest rates, of course, reflected the fact that some borrowers would become delinquent. Once a borrower was delinquent, the loanshark made every effort to prevent the borrower from walking away from the loan and, instead, tried to induce the borrower to acknowledge his obligation and agree to a new payment schedule.

Case Studies

Harry Riccobene, born in Sicily in 1910, arrived in Philadelphia when he was three. Because he suffered from a tubercular spine as a child, he developed a hunchbacked appearance and, as an adult, barely reached 5 feet in height. As a result, he tried to get by on his charm and wits. He left school at age 14 and was soon selling numbers in South Philadelphia. By the late 1920s, he was part of a gang that raided bootleg stills in the neighborhood. In 1931 he was inducted as a made member of the Philadelphia family. He pursued a variety of business ventures over the years. After World War II, for instance, he sold mineral water in Philadelphia for a New York firm. In the 1950s, he was arrested for the wholesaling of heroin in Cleveland. For this and other charges, he was in prison during much of the 1960s and 1970s. In March 1975, he returned to the street again.

While widely known by family members and honored by some as the only active member who could recount the early history and procedures of the family, he generally operated independent of other family members. His closest associate and partner was his half-brother Mario (Sonny) Riccobene, along with his other half-brother Robert. Also involved with them was their brother-in-law, who ostensibly ran a transmission company at Second and Snyder in South Philadelphia. Even his step-mother was involved in some of the legal businesses. Because of the complicated relationships among them, it is difficult to untangle which businesses were Harry's and which were shared with other members of the family.

By 1975 a company called Ricco, Inc., owned the Yesteryear Lounge at 9th and Morris Streets, which listed Sonny as manager. The Riccobenes also controlled the Villa DiRoma restaurant on 9th Street near the Italian Market. Harry had an office there when he first got out of prison in 1975. At that time, he and Mario were widely believed to be running a ziginetti game nearby. Harry also became associated with the Tyrone DeNittis Talent Agency. DeNittis, once a rock and roll musician, founded the business to book bands and entertainers into bars and clubs in Philadelphia and South Jersey. When the Agency opened a modest office on South Broad Street, Harry had an small room there from which he ran his varied businesses. By late 1977, unknown to him, the FBI was recording his business conversations.

Harry's main money-making activity was a varied loansharking business. Once, for instance, he made a loan of $20,000 to a sports and numbers bookmaker in West Philadelphia. He not only expected the usual payments on the loan but also insisted that the borrower use Robert Riccobene's numbers operations for his edge-off. [5] Harry also lent to persons running signineti games in South Philadelphia. But the heart of his loansharking business consisted of small loans to hustlers and merchants in and around the Italian Market in South Philadelphia.

Harry had a number of agents who worked with him. Harry provided the money while the agents lent the money and handled routine collections. In return, they received half the profits that resulted from their customers. The standard loan had an interest of 20 percent and the term of the loan was about ten weeks payable in equal weekly installments each week. On a loan of $1,000, then, a customer might pay $120 weekly for ten weeks. Harry periodically kept track of collections, approved new loans, and sometimes dealt directly with customers when payments lagged.[6]

Despite a few large loans, the heart of his business was small loans under $1,000. By late 1977, he generally tried to keep new loans to $500 so that, if a customer failed to pay, the loss would be manageable. This was, of course, more work for the agent, since collecting from four customers who borrowed $500 each was harder than from one who borrowed $2,000. As Harry explained to one agent, "It's more work for you, but it's, it's safe . . . because you don't lose much. You don't lose nothing." Most customers were regulars and saw their loans as a sort of revolving credit. In fact, Harry worried about borrowers who, having borrowed a small amount that they were able to repay, would then "try to, you know, . . . climb, climb and then they get stuck and then you got a problem." As he explained to Frank Primerano, one of his collectors:

> Harry: "Yeah, but, see you . . . when you give a guy, if a guy's only good for a $300 loan. . . ."
> Frank: "Right."
> Harry: "You never bring him up to $1,000 because you're hurting him, you're choking him."

Generally, then, he kept borrowers at their original limit, so that, if someone borrowed $500 and then established his reliability by bringing the amount down to $300, he could borrow $200 more.[7]

Even within this modest business, borrowers continually fell behind in payments. Often Harry became exasperated with what he saw to be the irresponsibility of borrowers. He scolded one delinquent borrower: "All right there, you shouldn't, you shouldn't have borrowed money you can't pay. You had a limited income. Why do you go borrowing that kind of money with a limited income?" Because of the numerous missed payments and partial payments, Harry and his agents repeatedly lost track of how much customers still owed. On one occasion, in frustration, Harry decided that the only way to find out was to have his agent ask the customer:

> Harry: "You ask him, what's your, what is your balance?"
> Agent: "Okay, yeah."
> Harry: "Say, what do you think it is? Say, I didn't see Harry."

There was, then, a continual struggle to keep the loans within the range that customers could afford and to hold customers to a regular payment schedule.[8]

Regular customers understood that, when they fell behind, they should negotiate a new payment schedule. In discussion with one customer, Harry urged: "Just start giving me something."

Customer: "Okay."
Harry: "There's no deal. Just start giving me money."
Customer: "Okay, okay. [I'll] start next week."
Harry: "You're six weeks behind."
Customer: "Yeah. Well, Harry, I'm fightin' to stay alive. All right. So I'll come in and give you something every week. All right. Bear with me knockin' off the bill, we'll get even."

Later, when Harry pointed out how considerate he was being, the customer remarked: "I know that. You tried in every way and I want to be decent enough, too, to show my respect, you know." Here the customer explicitly recognized that honor required his payment of his debt.[9]

At least one of Harry's agents was troubled by his willingness to let payments ride. Joseph Bongiovanni, a former Philadelphia policeman and one of Harry's chief agents, ran pools and a ziginetti game on the side and was fascinated by the mob members and their intrigues.

J.B.: "That's why nobody pays you. They think you've got a lot of money."
Harry: "From what?"
J.B.: "I don't know. You don't cry.... You just take it in stride."

Eventually he sarcastically suggested: "Say, why don't you make a list up of all your f—ing bad money, Harry, and what I collect I can keep."

Harry: "If I want, if I wanted to press these guys, I would do it myself. I don't want to press them."
J.B.: "Why?"
Harry: "It's that way! Why does the sun come out every day?"
J.B.: "Because you're a philanthropist!"[10]

At any rate, Harry and his agents operated a revolving credit system for the hustlers and small businessmen of South Philadelphia. Some were legitimate businessmen—fruit peddlers, grocers, garbage haulers. Others were illegitimate—sports bookmakers, numbers bankers, and operators of ziginetti games. Within their culture, borrowing informally from a loanshark was a normal and accepted business practice.

More important than the network of legal and illegal businesses operated by the Riccobenes were the businesses run from Frank's Cabana, a lunch counter at 10th and Moyamensing Streets in South Philadelphia. This was Frank Sindone's headquarters. Born in South Philadelphia in 1927, he left school early and soon had a juvenile record. In his early twenties, while in the U.S. Army, he was caught dealing heroin and received a dishonorable discharge and a federal prison sentence. Once back on the streets, he quickly won recognition as a talented hustler. Phil Testa, later the Underboss of the Bruno Family, took him on as a loanshark collector, and Angelo Bruno backed him in a numbers bank. Soon he was a made member of the family. Over the years, he picked up numerous arrests for participation in numbers, crap games, and loansharking.[11]

The most important enterprise run from Frank's Cabana was Sindone's extensive loanshark operation. His close associate was Joseph "Chickie" Ciancaglini, a stocky, tough-looking former enforcer for Teamster Local 107. Sindone was the largest loanshark among family members and possibly one of the three or four largest loansharks in the Delaware Valley. Indeed, his loanshark operation was probably the most important illegal business run by any member of the Bruno family. Because he rose to underworld prominence through the backing of Bruno and Testa, they almost certainly continued as partners in his loanshark operation.[12]

Sindone's loansharking operations differed significantly from those of the Riccobenes. He or his agents often made loans of $10,000 to $50,000 or higher. Many of the loans were to legitimate businessmen. Construction contractors were common customers because of their need to meet payrolls. His lending operations were not focused on South Philadelphia but instead were widely spread into Northeast Philadelphia, South Jersey, and the Pennsylvania suburbs. He and his agents, while seldom using actual violence in the collection of delinquent loans, had mastered the orchestrated use of vicious, vulgar, and convincing threats of violence to the borrower and the borrower's family. The purpose of the threats was to compel the borrower to acknowledge the debt and agree to continue payments on a new schedule. Sindone regularly used delinquent payments as an excuse to become a partner in the business or to use the business for frauds that would earn income to pay the debts.

Sindone made some loans himself but frequently worked through relatively independent agents who shared in the profits from the loans that they made. Whatever the economic arrangement between Sindone and the agents, realistically Sindone would not be paid if loans went bad. As a result, Sindone was sometimes involved in approving large loans made by agents and regularly intervened to participate in collecting delinquent loans.

The loans made to William James, a car dealer in the Northeast, demonstrated the pattern of Sindone's loansharking. By 1972, James had multiple credit problems. He was being pursued by the IRS for failure to withhold income tax from his employees, owed $150,000 to a bank, had outstanding loans of $90,000 from the Small Business Administration, and owed customers about $90,000 from the sale of untitled cars. Sometime in late 1972 or early 1973, he borrowed a small amount from Vincent "Tippy" Panetta and, after repayment, asked for a bigger loan. Tippy referred him to Alexander Hartzell, an ex-policeman and owner of a bicycle and bowling center in the Northeast. Hartzell handled large loans for Sindone in the Northeast. In March 1973 James borrowed $10,000 and repaid $11,750 in five weeks. In June he took out a second loan and repaid it, with interest, in eleven weeks. Then in September he took out a third loan of $25,000. He paid about $875 per week interest for twenty-one weeks, plus principle of $4,000. By this time, though, he was no longer able to make payments, and a pattern of threats and negotiations began. James made a series of promises and then failed to meet them. By early April 1974, he was sufficiently desperate that he turned to the FBI and began wearing a body mike.

When James sought Tippy Panetta's advice, Tippy warned him that the money really belonged to "downtown" and that the mob would collect its money or make an example of him. ("You ought to leave or go to Africa or India or go leave the world or something, you know?") Tippy urged him to negotiate a payment schedule. Hartzell's warnings were more direct. He, too, stressed that the money belonged downtown. "That's who I, I work, I work, I work for Phil, Frank, and Ange [Testa, Sindone, and Angelo Bruno], and ah Frank, ah Frank is the f—ing enforcer and Frank, man, I got to tell you, he is a f—ing cold, heartless, mother f—er."). Hartzell increasingly lost patience. On April 16th he warned James: "Hey, f— them stories! What has that [SBA] got to do with me? Now I mean if you want me to go and f—ing bust you, I'll bust you if that is what you want. . . . I mean you are making a f—ing fool out of me. "Two days later, he warned: "If they say to me, 'Al, put him the f— away,' I am going to put you away. . . . This is the f—ing pressure I get." On April 30, Hartzell finally told James: "I know exactly what's happening. You gotta ride downtown with me tomorrow. I gotta take you right to the mob, that's all. I oughta just take you there, and let you talk with Frank yourself. I'm tired of f—ing carrying you."[13]

So on Saturday, May 1st, they rode down to Frank's Cabana. There Hartzell told Sindone that James owed about $25,000 plus five weeks' "juice." Sindone then rounded off the remaining debt to $30,000 and ruled that James should pay $1,000 per week until the total had been repaid. James agreed: "Thank you very much. I appreciate it. "Eight days later, though, James returned to Frank's Cabana for a second conference with Sindone without informing Hartzell. He now tried to persuade Sindone that he had repaid more than Hartzell claimed. Sindone, as a result, agreed to delay the payments for six weeks until James had recovered financially. When James expressed fear that Hartzell would be angry because he had come to Sindone behind Hartzell's back, Sindone reassured him: "You got problems, you come down to me."

James: "All right, sir."
Sindone: "If he threatens you, you come here. Tell him to go f— himself."
James: "OK. Fair enough."[14]

There are several interesting aspects of this transaction. First of all, James was a lousy credit risk, who turned to the illegal lending market to shore up a tottering business. Secondly, he did so in a context in which he shared the culture of the illegal lenders. His conversation suggested that he was raised in South Philly. He boasted that in his youth he had known Frank Sinatra and Joseph Palumbo (the popular restaurateur in South Philadelphia).To represent his car dealership in a civil suit, he employed Robert Simone—an attorney who later represented Sindone in the trial that arose out of the loan to James. Furthermore, one of his car salesmen once borrowed from Hartzell and fell behind in payments; James withheld the payments from the salesman's salary and gave them to Hartzell.

When James fell into financial difficulty in 1973, then, it was not surprising that he turned to the illegal market as a regular and normal source of funds. Finally, the incident demonstrates the way in which Hartzell and Sindone, playing good cop and bad cop, orchestrated threats with the goal of securing a new payment schedule that James might be able to meet.

Conclusion

The rules and obligations that gave structure to loansharking were not, like legal lending, accompanied by the signing of formal documents nor were they determined by state and federal law. Instead, they were embedded within a set of informal social relationships and mutual expectations.

Central to loansharking was a culture largely shared by both lenders and borrowers. Within that culture, the world was seen to be a place of deals and favors, not of formal laws and universalistic principles. Structure was provided by the understanding that men would meet their obligations. In such a world, loansharking, while formally illegal, was a legitimate obligation. For loansharks like Riccobene and Sindone, the world was further shaped by their membership in the Bruno Family. Their membership, however illegitimate from the point of view of those trying to jail them, gave them prestige within their own social world. They were important men—looked up to and also, to some extent, feared. The Family provided an alternate "government" that legitimized the culture of deals and favors. Within this culture, then, borrowers and lenders negotiated loans and settled disputes in a way that generally served both lenders and borrowers.

Notes

1. For the history of loansharking, see Haller and John Alviti, "Loansharking in American Cities: Historical Analysis of a Marginal Enterprise," *American Journal of Legal History*, 21 (1977), 125-156. For the best analysis of loansharking, see John M. Seidl, "'Upon the Hip'—A study of the Criminal Loan-Shark Industry" (Unpublished dissertation, Harvard Univ., 1968); for an insightful analysis from a law enforcement viewpoint, see Ronald Goldstock & Dan T. Coenen, "Controlling the Contemporary Loanshark: The Problem of Witness Fear," Cornell Law Review, 65 (1980): 127-185.

This paper is based upon research at the Pennsylvania Crime Commission, where I was given complete access to the intelligence files. Because of the confidential nature of the files, the footnotes are mostly limited to materials that are publicly available. I wish to thank the staff of the Crime Commission, including Frederick Martens, the Executive Director, for the friendly help they have given me in my research.

2. Annelise G. Anderson, *The Business of Organized Crime: A Cosa Nostra Family*, (Hoover Institution Press, 1979), pp. 2-3.

3. This and succeeding paragraphs are based on Haller, *Life Under Bruno: The Economics of an Organized Crime Family*, monograph published by Pennsylvania Crime Commission (Conshohocken, Pa., 1991).

4. FBI transcripts, Oct. 2, 1977, at Tyrone DeNittis Agency.

5. Confidential interviews.

6. The description of Riccobene's loansharking is taken from FBI transcripts of conversations at the Tyrone DeNittis Agency.

7. FBI transcripts of conversations between Riccobene and Frank Primerano at DeNittis Agency, Oct. 8 & 13, 1977.

8. FBI transcripts of conversations by Riccobene at DeNittis Agency Oct 10, 1977 (with unknown male) and Oct. 1, 1977 (with Thomas Rudi).

9. FBI transcripts of conversation between Riccobene and customer at DeNittis Agency, Oct. 4, 1977.

10. FBI transcripts of conversation between Riccobene and Bongiovanni, Oct. 13, 1977.

11. During part of 1976, the FBI bugged Frank's Cabana and had a tap on the pay telephone across the street. For a biography of Ciancaglini, see *Profile of Organized Crime: Mid-Atlantic Region*: Hearings before the Permanent Subcommittee on Government Affairs, U.S. Senate, 98th Congress, First Session, Feb. 15, 23, & 24, 1983 (Government Printing Office), p. 261.

12. In 1976, in conversation with Salvatore and Lawrence Merlino, Sindone spoke of the previous ten years and described how he once estimated "my end would come to $425,000," and added: "Now he [presumably Bruno] got $225,000 of that." This recognized Bruno as his partner. In the same conversation, he described how he recently informed Bruno that he wanted to retire and told Bruno: "With everything I've got here? You and Phil [Testa] split it up!" See FBI transcripts, Frank's Cabana, April 2, 1976.

13. FBI transcripts from body mike carried by James.

14. FBI transcripts, May 1 & 9. It is possible that at the May 9th meeting Sindone suspected James was in touch with the FBI and was especially accommodating as a result. At the subsequent trial, Hartzell was found guilty, but Sindone's attorney, Robert Simone, apparently created reasonable doubt in the minds of jurors by arguing that Sindone was not the lender but merely a mediator in a dispute.

Part III
Illegal Enterprise Theory

Chapter 8

The Changing Structure of American Gambling in the Twentieth Century

There is a common assumption, found in scholarly literature as well as popular crime histories, that the bootlegging syndicates of the 1920's originated "organized crime" in America. In fact, gambling syndicates, often with city-wide or regional affiliations, arose in many cities during the decades following the Civil War. As early as the Civil War era, policy gambling—a forerunner of modern numbers gambling—was expanding rapidly. Increasingly, policy was coordinated by backers who financed local policy shops and often provided protection from police or political interference. By 1900, a single policy organization in Chicago had more than 200 policy writers scattered in stores, saloons, and barbershops to collect the bets and funnel them to a central headquarters (Asbury, 1938; Comstock, 1967; Johnson, 1977; Chicago Tribune, 1881; Citizens' Assoc. of Chicago Bulletin, 1903). In a parallel development, off-track bookmaking syndicates developed by the 1890's. Syndicate leaders provided financial backing for local bookmakers, coordinated protection, and arranged to channel racing information to bookmaking outlets. Often backers of policy or bookmaking also ran the major gambling houses and played an important role in the political and sporting life of the city (Brolasky, 1911; Flynt, 1907; Haller, Note 1; & Jarman, 1968). The years from the 1880's to about 1905 may, indeed, have been the period when activities that are often called "organized crime" had their greatest impact upon American society. During this period gamblers, and vice entrepreneurs generally, exercised an influence on local politics and law enforcement that has seldom been equaled since that time. In many neighborhoods, it was not so much that gambling syndicates influenced local political organization; rather, gambling syndicates *were* the local political organizations, and had, in addition, a broad impact upon other aspects of urban life. In the cities of the East and Midwest, the Irish dominated gambling enterprises; they were also disproportionately involved in local politics and police. To some extent, then, politics and gambling were tied together by common ethnic bonds, as well as common organizational structures. Gambling entrepreneurs were crucial in the promotion and financing of the professional sports that arose during that period, including horse racing, boxing and baseball (Bradley, 1940; Pilat &; Ranson, 1941; Quinn, 1892). There was, furthermore, a close interrelationship between the extensive and informally approved red-light districts and the commercial nightlife entertainment of the cities. Long before national prohibition and the development of bootlegging, then, there had already been close ties among gambling syndicates, vice activities, politics, sports and entertainment.

The purpose of this chapter is to examine a few factors that altered the organization and control of policy and numbers gambling, bookmaking, and casino gambling during the first half of the twentieth century. The factors were diverse. The emergence of black ghettoes in the cities during and after World War I permitted blacks to introduce numbers gambling and to attain controlling positions in numbers and policy syndicates. The changing ownership of the national race wire—and the changing uses to which it was put—both influenced and reflected the changing structure of bookmaking. Even the telephone, by making it possible for some bookmakers to take bets entirely by phone, and thus contributing to the demise of the old-time horse parlor, has greatly altered the nature of sports betting. Finally, the rise of bootlegging in the 1920's gave wealth, business experience, and political influence to a number of ambitious young men predominantly of Jewish and Italian backgrounds. Many bootleggers and ex-bootleggers invested in gambling enterprises and thereby, in complex ways, affected the control of some kinds of gambling in some regions of the country. Their impact cannot be understood, however, without first understanding the structure of bootlegging.

Structure of Bootlegging

On January 17, 1920, the Volstead Act went into effect. Very rapidly, thereafter, a new and complex economic system came into being: the importation, manufacture, bottling, wholesale distribution and retailing of illegal alcoholic beverages. At first the situation was chaotic, as numerous small, struggling entrepreneurs, on a full-time or part-time basis, sought to cash in on the sudden profits. Indeed, throughout the brief history of national prohibition, bootlegging always remained more chaotic and uncoordinated than standard accounts would indicate. By the mid-1920's; nevertheless, some syndicates were growing in scale and provided an increased level of coordination.

Several aspects of the bootleg business are important for understanding the impact of bootleggers upon gambling. One aspect is the background of the leading bootleggers. Because legitimate liquor dealers largely abandoned the business and because gamblers and other established underworld leaders remained on the sidelines, bootlegging was an illegal enterprise that was seized by newcomers, providing rapid upward mobility for ambitious yet marginal men. Leading bootleggers tended to be young, born between 1892 and 1900, and thus 20 to 28 years old when prohibition began. They had generally grown up in America's urban slums. Prohibition arrived just as the first generation of Jews and Italian young people raised in America was reaching maturity. Data on leading bootleggers in major cities indicate that some 50 percent were of Jewish background, 25 percent of Italian background, and the rest were primarily Irish and Polish. Although their previous experiences, frequently, but not universally, involved some sort of street crime, future bootleggers were by no means prominent in crime prior to prohibition. A number, in fact, graduated from juvenile gangs directly into bootlegging (Haller, 1976).

The relative youthfulness of successful bootleggers had long-run implications for leadership of the American underworld in later years. When Prohibition ended in 1933, many bootleggers were still young men, generally in their thirties, yet with wealth and nationwide contacts that had grown out of their bootlegging enterprises. By simple attrition, as the old gambling leaders died or retired, ex-bootleggers sometimes succeeded to their positions. When academic and public attention turned to "organized crime" during the Kefauver Committee investigations of the early 1950's, it was found that in many cities the leading figures in illegal enterprises had started as bootleggers. Indeed, by the 1950's they were in their fifties and at the height of their careers. Thus, the myth arose that "organized crime" in America originated with the bootlegging gangs, and the syndicate gamblers of the earlier period, now departed, were lost to history. Yet, the importance of ex-bootleggers in the 1950's should not be read back into the 1920's and 1930's. At that time, bootleggers were often upstarts, albeit wealthy and ambitious upstarts.

Before the 1920's, those entrepreneurial activities often classified as "organized crime" were conducted in American cities with relatively little violence; yet the violence of bootlegging created an image of a lawless decade and helped to undermine support for prohibition laws. A major factor in the violence was the role of hijacking. Alcoholic beverages were relatively bulky and, on land, had to be carried from breweries, distilleries, or port cities to warehouses or processing plants and then to speakeasies. At sea, imported liquor was carried from large ships to shore on contact boats. An easy way to make quick profits in bootlegging was to hijack someone else's booze while in transit. Thus, some bootleggers got their start as hijackers, and most groups that put together systematic bootlegging operations had to protect against hijacking. A willingness to use violence was often part of the business, and the cost of hiring gunmen to protect shipments was a routine business expense. As bootleg groups expanded and competed with each other for territory and supplies, they sometimes used violence as a competitive strategy. The weapons that had first fended off hijackers were turned against each other. As a result, violence was institutionalized, and only those willing to counter violence with violence could normally achieve success in the competitive world of bootlegging (Landesco, 1968; Waters, 1971).

Another characteristic of bootlegging was the complex local, regional, national, and international ties that necessarily developed among bootlegging entrepreneurs. After all, a large urban market could absorb not only a large quantity of alcoholic beverages, but also a large variety of types: beer, scotch, bourbon, gin, wines, and champagne. No distributor of illegal booze to speakeasies and roadhouses could possibly manufacture or import all the beverages needed in a complex market. Thus, any large organization necessarily had ties with other organizations and, for good economic reasons, some organizations specialized. Successful bootleggers had complex business relations within a city and with surrounding towns; port cities were linked to their hinterlands; and American bootleggers developed ongoing relations with manufacturers or exporters in Canada, the West Indies, and Europe (Asbury, 1968; Haller, Note 2; Nelli, 1976).

Bootleggers, in short, were businessmen with money to invest in a variety of legal and illegal activities. They were young, ambitious, and disproportionately the products of Jewish and Italian slums. Often they were men who had personally used violence and, in any event, were accustomed to the use of violence in business affairs. Despite their backgrounds, leading bootleggers had experienced the broadening that comes from far-flung business interests and wide travel. By the time of Repeal, they had interests in real estate, night clubs, hotels, race tracks, and legitimate liquor distributorships, as well as gambling.

Both gamblers and bootleggers enjoyed certain advantages that influenced the types of relationships that developed between them. Gamblers, for instance, had the crucial advantage of expertise. Bookmakers understood horse racing and the statistical skills necessary to balance their books. Gambling house operators learned the techniques of running games of chance, limiting employee embezzlement in a cash business, and extending credit to keep customers happy but paying. Many gamblers had a second advantage in that they were already part of a complex social and economic system. Among bookmakers there were established relationships with race wires, with local tracks, and with politicians. Most policy operators already coordinated organizations consisting of 100 to 300 neighborhood policy runners who collected the pennies, nickels, and dimes that underlay the profitability of the enterprise. As a third advantage, gamblers often had an investment in good will—not only the good will of politicians and police, but also of the customers whose loyalty they had won through years of association.

There were, nevertheless, a number of reasons why bootleggers were interested in the profits from gambling. A few had been gamblers before prohibition. Many were sports fans and bettors. With their growing wealth, they purchased ring-side seats at fights, attended race tracks, and bet heavily. While bootlegging was their chief business, sports and betting were often their chief love and the role of gambler was an attractive one. To the extent that they sought to invest in gambling, they had a number of resources. First of all, bootlegging often involved the systematic use of violence and violence could be a convincing persuader when bootleggers turned to other activities. Secondly, major bootleg organizations established regional, national, or international ties. The associations and experiences gained in bootlegging could be transferred to other enterprises, making bootleggers tough rivals or welcome partners. Finally, bootleggers established relationships with police and politicians, so that their influence sometimes equaled or exceeded that of traditional gambling entrepreneurs. In short, if old time gamblers had powerful resources, bootleggers could be powerful competitors.

There were many possible outcomes from attempts by bootlegging groups to assume a role in gambling. One outcome was for bootleggers to supplant the old-time gamblers, but this, at least in the short run, was a rare occurrence. Another outcome was for gamblers to continue their operations relatively uninfluenced by bootleggers. This was a fairly common outcome in some parts of the country. A further possibility was parallel development, in which bootleggers and old-time gamblers ran independent operations.

A final, and relatively common, alternative consisted of partnership arrangements between bootleggers and gamblers. Partnerships allowed a sharing of risks and provided a means for bringing together persons with different resources, including capital, managerial ability, and influence with police or politicians. Gamblers, of course, possessed managerial skills. Thus the question arises: Under what circumstances did they welcome the capital or political influence that bootleggers could provide? Furthermore, to what degree were the partnerships voluntary, entered into because all parties saw mutual benefit? Or were partnerships sometimes, at least in part, a method by which ex-bootleggers, using political influence or the threat of violence, took a share of the profits of enterprises established by others?

The evolving relationships between bootleggers and old-time gamblers were, in short, diverse and complex. The relationships, in addition, were never static, but continued to develop into the 1940's and 1950's. A study of the impact of bootlegging upon gambling must therefore attempt to uncover the factors that underlay different sorts of relationships in different places and at different times. This requires examination of specific types of gambling.

Policy and Numbers Gambling

Two factors, entirely independent of bootlegging, reshaped the structure of policy gambling in the 1920's. The first was the introduction of numbers as a rival gambling game that appealed to the same players. Policy was a relatively complex game. In most cities, policy organizations drew 12 numbers between 1 and 78. Before the drawing, customers placed their bets on 1 to 4 numbers that they hoped would be among the 12 numbers drawn. By contrast, in the new game of numbers, a player generally bet on a single number between 1 and 999. There was 1 chance in 999 of winning, and the numbers syndicates usually paid off at a rate between 450 to 1 and 650 to 1. At first the winning number was based on a figure published each day: for instance, the last three digits of the total stocks traded on the New York Stock Exchange. By the 1930's, however, the number was determined in a complex way from the results of three races at a designated track—the system still in use today.

Apparently, numbers was first played in New York City in the early 1920's. Because West Indian blacks predominated among early entrepreneurs in Harlem, it is possible that they introduced the game. By the end of the 1920's, numbers had replaced policy in cities such as New York and Philadelphia. In Detroit, although numbers was eclipsing policy, both games continued through the 1930's. In Chicago and St. Louis, on the other hand, numbers never gained a foothold, so that policy continues to dominate even now (Carlson, 1941).

A second, more important development was the rise of black-controlled numbers or policy syndicates in the 1920's. This, in turn, was linked to the growth in major northern cities of ghettos dominated by blacks. Before World War I, blacks in northern cities generally constituted a minority of the population. World War I, and the 1920s, however, witnessed a great increased migration of blacks to northern cities and a more rigid residential segregation. Within the ghettos local black political organizations developed to organize voting and political influence (Kusmer, 1976; Osofsky, 1966; Spear, 1967). Concurrently, black entrepreneurs backed policy or numbers syndicates. As had been true earlier among whites, there was often a considerable overlap between local political organizations and policy or numbers syndicates. If bootlegging was a growth enterprise for young Jewish and Italian criminals in the 1920's, policy and numbers served a similar function for young blacks. A study of the impact of bootleggers on policy and numbers, then, must analyze the specific influence upon the newly emerging black syndicates as well as upon the general control of policy and numbers.

In New York, a group of young West Indians built numbers syndicates in Harlem in the 1920's. Among them was Jose Enrique (Henry) Miro, who was born in Puerto Rico about 1902, arrived in New York around 1917, and worked as a laborer until he entered the numbers racket about 1926. Soon he may have been backing games in Philadelphia and Boston, as well as in Harlem. Another entrepreneur was William Brunder, a West Indian immigrant who started in numbers about 1923 and was soon a major backer. The Seabury investigation of New York courts in 1931 revealed the large bank accounts of Miro and Brunder, and thus exposed them to prosecution by the Internal Revenue Service for tax evasion. They took brief vacations in the Caribbean and left their affairs in the hands of "Big Joe" Ison, another West Indian black. Upon their return, Miro and Brunder found that Arthur (Dutch) Schultz, represented by his partner George Weinberg, had assumed a majority interest in their operations, as well as in the operations of some other Harlem numbers bankers (Central Files of the Department of Justice, Note 3; Light, 1974; Sann, 1971).

What leverages explain the takeovers? First of all, Schultz and his associates, who dominated beer distribution to the lower Bronx and upper Manhattan, had expanded their bootlegging, in part by the successful use of violence. The threat of violence against Harlem numbers banks was an important persuader. Beyond this, Dixie Davis was attorney for several Harlem numbers syndicates; he was also Dutch Schultz's attorney. Harlem numbers banks received political protection through Tammany leader Jimmy Hines; so did Schultz. Hence, it is reasonable to assume that the numbers bankers were too weak politically to prevent Hines from giving his blessing to the new arrangements, which were negotiated by Dixie Davis. The original entrepreneurs continued as partners and managed the day-to-day operations. Schultz and Weinberg mediated political and police protection and provided financial backing. Even Harlem newspapers admitted that, after the Schultz takeover, the banks were better managed and more likely to pay off winning numbers (Carlson, 1941; *New York Times,* 1935; Sann, 1971).

Although Schultz's activities represented an example of a bootleg organization forcing partnership arrangements upon reluctant numbers syndicates, it still remains a question whether this was typical of the overall New York experience. In Brooklyn, Albert Anastasia, whose wealth derived from his influence in the longshoremen's unions and the waterfront rackets, apparently exercised crucial influence in numbers along the docks. Elsewhere in Brooklyn it is not clear that bootleg groups played a predominant role. Hence, while popular crime histories emphasize the role of Dutch Schultz, it is possible that the Harlem takeover was only one of several patterns in the city (Amen, 1942; *New York Times,* Feb. 7, 1934).

In Philadelphia, bootleggers more clearly attained early dominance in gambling. By 1930, several bootlegging organizations were already leading numbers operators. In South Philadelphia, the Lanzetti brothers operated numbers as well as bootlegging. Elsewhere in the city, Mickey Duffy, a leading bootlegger in Philadelphia and southern New Jersey, was also a numbers operator with headquarters in Camden. There were also small black-controlled syndicates, some apparently with solid political connections. During the 1930's, however, numbers in the city fell increasingly under the influence of the so-called "69th Street Mob" led by Harry (Nig) Rosen. His partners, predominantly Jewish, were drawn from several old bootlegging groups. Rosen's own background is obscure, but he apparently had some experience in bootlegging, was reputed to represent Dutch Schultz, and in any event, had ties with New York Jewish bootleggers and gamblers. The 69th Street Mob began its activities in 1931 about the time of the shooting death of Mickey Duffy. A couple of years later, the Lanzettis reduced their payoff odds from 600 to 1 to 500 to 1. The 69th Street Mob followed suit. And, when two Negro banks retained the old odds and gained a competitive advantage, they were persuaded by bombs to go along. By 1934, the 69th Street Mob provided backing for heavily played numbers in the city, coordinated protection, and, by maintaining the playoff odds, prevented price wars among the numbers banks (Riggio, 1972; Salus Scrapbooks, Note 4).

In Chicago, where black political organizations were strong by the 1920's, policy wheels were closely tied to politics and remained independent of ex-bootleggers until at least the post-World War II period. Black politicians and gamblers were influential parts of the Republican organizations supporting Mayor William Hale (Big Bill) Thompson during his three terms (1915-1923 and 1927-1931). Oscar DePriest, elected during World War I as the first black alderman since Reconstruction and elected in 1928 as the first black Congressman since Reconstruction, was twice indicted for involvement in gambling in his district. More important, perhaps, in mediating between politics and gambling was Dan Jackson. Serving for a time as Republican Committeemen for the Second Ward, he directed several large policy wheels, owned a major gambling house, and was appointed to the Illinois State Commerce Commission by the Republican governor (Chicago Crime Commission, Note 5; Chicago *Daily News,* 1917).

In 1931, Anton Cermak won the mayoralty in Chicago and became the first of a line of Democratic mayors serving in an unbroken chain to the present. Black policy operators, tied closely to the Republican organization, needed now to make their peace with the Democrats. In the process, the Jones brothers entered the policy racket and rapidly rose to predominance among policy operators controlling perhaps 12 of the 38 wheels on the Southside. Although the brothers were indicted for income tax evasion and Edward served time in Federal prison in the early 1940's, they continued to be among the wealthiest and most influential citizens in the ghetto (Chicago Crime Commission, Note 6; Drake & Clayton, 1945; Irey, 1948).

In the years after World War II, Al Capone's old partner, Jack Guzik, along with Tony Accardo, Sam Giancana, and their associates, began to insist upon substantial interests in the city's policy syndicates. In 1946, Edward Jones was kidnapped, and after being ransomed, he and his brothers took refuge in Mexico, where they continued to receive a share of the profits from their policy operations. By the 1950's Guzik and his associates in all probability had interests in several other white and black controlled policy wheels. Yet, given the political power of Negro Congressman William Dawson, his continued concern with gambling in the Southside ghetto, and the management of the enterprises by blacks, the relationship of blacks and whites in the operation of policy syndicates remained complex and obscure (Brashier, 1977; Demans, 1969; Kefauver, 1951; Chicago Crime Commission Note 7).

In Detroit, black gamblers were perhaps more successful than in Chicago. By World War I, men like John Roxborough and Everett Watson had organized profitable policy wheels. Other blacks entered the field in the 1920's and soon developed numbers syndicates as well. By the 1930's, blacks operated numbers and policy not only in Detroit but also in adjoining cities such as Ypsilanti, Dearborn, Ann Arbor and River Rouge. By then there were 35 numbers or policy syndicates in Detroit, most employing more than 300 writers, plus cashiers and other employees. In 1928, when a Jewish group from Cleveland attempted to enter the policy and numbers racket in Detroit, Detroit bankers formed an organization called the Associated Numbers Bankers. Although its chief purpose was to assure black control, it also regulated the payoff for different types of bets, retained a regular attorney to represent the interests of the banks, and arranged protection agreements with police officials. By the 1930's, black numbers and policy bankers were among the most influential blacks in the city, owning the major black businesses and newspapers, contributing to black churches and civil rights organizations, and exercising strong political influence in the city (Carlson, 1941; Carter, 1970).

The four cities—New York, Philadelphia, Chicago, and Detroit—demonstrated diverse patterns in the timing and degree of penetration of numbers and policy by ex-bootleggers. In all cities, however, if ex-bootleggers became involved, the mechanism was a partnership arrangement, so that the original operators or their associates generally continued as managers and partners. Ex-bootleggers often provided a variety of services to the partnerships. These included political protection, financial backing, regulation of competition, and legal representation in case of arrests.

Bookmakers

When the century opened, horse racing had reached perhaps its high point of popularity in America. At the tracks, bookmakers took bets on the horses, in areas set aside for them in return for a fee paid to the tracks. Although the betting was illegal, it was also crucial to the economics of the sport. Without betting, the tracks would lose the fees paid by bookmakers, as well as the admission charges paid by customers who came to gamble at the tracks. In the first decade of the century, a sporadic, nationwide anti-gambling crusade led to the threat that gambling laws might be enforced at the tracks. In a fifteen year period, some 95 tracks on the national circuit ceased operations. When racing made a gradual comeback from the 1920's on, there was state regulation combined with pari-mutuel betting at the tracks, so that the states now shared in the profits of racetrack gambling. The dominant role of bookmakers at the tracks came to an end (Parmer, 1939; Menke, 1940; Pringle, 1916).

As mentioned earlier, off-track bookmaking also flourished at the turn of the century. Off-track bookmakers usually agreed to make payoffs to their customers at the odds prevailing at the track. The key business risk was that, on a given day, too much money might be bet on a winning horse, and the bookmaker would be unable to pay his customers. The solution to this problem has long been a critical consideration in the structure of bookmaking. But because so little is known about the economics of bookmaking, only tentative hypotheses are possible concerning historical developments.

One solution at the turn of the century was a neighborhood bookmaking syndicate. At bars, barbershops, cigar stores, newspaper kiosks, and other similar outlets, small-time bookmakers accepted bets on the horses. They kept a fixed percent of the money bet with them and passed the rest onto a backer, who often ran a large horse parlor of his own. The small-timer was assured a steady income, and the backer paid the winning bettors, thereby assuming the risks in return for the potential profits (Haller, Note 1; Landesco, 1968).

At that time, off-track bookmaking was based primarily on face-to-face transactions between the bookmaker and the customers. The rapid spread of the telephone in the early twentieth century meant that, especially by the 1920's, some bookmakers accepted bets chiefly or solely by phone. This had the advantage of making an enterprise less vulnerable to law enforcement but introduced the major problem of handling collection of money from customers who were betting on credit. It is also probable that a decline in the level of police corruption—and the entry of federal agencies into gambling enforcement in the 1960's—had a tendency to make the old-time horse parlor less attractive as a locus for sports betting. With the decline of face-to-face sports betting, there was a decline of the neighborhood bookmaking syndicate and therefore the necessity to find other systems for covering risks. This, presumably, was the origin of the layoff system, in which bookmakers with too much bet on a particular horse would call another bookmaker and bet some or all of the money with the second bookmaker (Pledge, 1956).

According to his biographer, Arnold Rothstein was pioneering the layoff in New York before 1914 and soon, by telephone and telegraph, was accepting bets from bookmakers and other bettors as far away as Chicago and Boston. He continued until his assassination in 1928. From the early 1920's, Frank Erickson was a major bookmaker in the New York and New Jersey areas. By 1930, he and Frank Costello, a major New York bootlegger, were partners in a number of gambling enterprises in Florida and New York, and Costello was a silent partner in Erickson's bookmaking. In the early 1930's, Erickson moved his headquarters to Bergen County, New Jersey. There, using a large staff and relying on telephones, he accepted bets from bookmakers when they had too much money wagered on a particular horse and also accepted regular bets from wealthy sports fans who desired the services of a bookmaker with a reputation for honesty. Erickson ran his operations virtually unmolested until 1950, when the Manhattan District Attorney uncovered his bank accounts in New York and successfully prosecuted him under the gambling statutes (Katcher, 1958; Manhattan District Attorney, Note 8; Messick 1971; New York State Crime Commission papers, Note 9; Wolf & DiMona, 1974).

While it has sometimes been suggested that lay-off bookmakers were coordinators of bookmaking, there is little evidence for this. Costello and Erickson were important in New York gambling more because of their political connections than because of any leverage provided by the layoff system. Many bookmakers operated without using the layoff; and many who used the layoff entered into a straight business arrangement without sacrificing their independence (Messick, 1969; Special Crime Study Commission on Organized Crime, California, Note 10). Indeed, when most bookmakers operated by telephone, even the distinction between lay-off bookmakers and regular bookmakers blurred, for bookmakers would often bet back and forth with each other.

Until the 1930's and 1940's—and perhaps longer—the big operations taking bets by telephone remained in the hands of the old-time gambling fraternity. Because major bookmakers operated by telephone and by credit, the business depended upon relationships developed over a long period of time and upon a reputation for honesty. The skills, as well as the investment in good will, were not easily transferred. Also, because they operated by telephone and could easily move their headquarters, they were likely to avoid difficulties with local enforcement officials. Both their skills and their mobility made them relatively safe from being muscled in on, as well. When bookmakers like Erickson entered into partnerships with ex-bootleggers, these were likely to be voluntary and mutually profitable arrangements.

In addition to finding a system for insuring against risk, bookmakers in the first half of the twentieth century needed access to up-to-the-minute information from race tracks across the country. The changing control and functions of the race information system has, therefore, also had an impact upon the structure of bookmaking.

In the late nineteenth century, with the proliferation of off-track horse betting, Western Union was the major provider of race track information. The company placed employees at the tracks to report the races as they occurred and leased telegraph tickers and telegraphers to saloons and horse parlors that desired the wire services. Because Western Union generally provided the service to anyone willing to pay, the wire service did not prevent free entry into bookmaking. In the spring of 1905, however, anti-gambling reformers brought pressure upon Western Union, and the company agreed to cease using its own agents to collect or disseminate racing information *(Literary Digest,* 1904). Thereafter, as others put together race wire systems, the systems were sometimes used to control who might become bookmakers and thus limit entry to bookmaking or impose unwanted partners on existing operations.

After Western Union withdrew, John Payne of Cincinnati, backed by bookmakers from Newport, Kentucky, put together the major national race wire. In Chicago, Mont Tennes, coordinator of an important Northside bookmaking syndicate, became local agent for the Payne News Agency and used his hold on racing information to extend his influence on bookmaking citywide. About 1909, Tennes established a General News Bureau to compete with Payne; soon it was the major race track and sports information service in the nation (Landesco, 1968). He, in turn, was bought out in 1927 by Moses (Moe) Annenberg. Annenberg achieved a new level of monopoly control, so that the rise and fall of Annenberg became a crucial part of the history of American gambling.

Moe and his older brother, Max, were born in East Prussia and arrived in Chicago with their parents while still youngsters. During the 1880's, in their late teen years, they worked as newsboys and then in the circulation department of the *Chicago Tribune*. In 1900 and 1902 they left the *Tribune* to head the circulation department of the two Hearst papers in Chicago. One function of a circulation manager was to hire and direct the sluggers who persuaded owners of newsstands to push certain papers and to hide rival papers. The Annenbergs therefore employed many of the young toughs who later rose to importance in the city's bootlegging gangs. Max eventually returned to the *Tribune* and spent the rest of his life in newspaper circulation. But in 1907, finding the political climate in Chicago unhealthy, Moe moved into the national circulation department of the Hearst organization (Murray, 1965; Myers, 1929).

While working for the Hearst empire, Moe Annenberg built his own news empire. In the early 1920's he retired from the Hearst organization to devote full time to his own interests. Eventually, through a complex system of holding companies, he owned considerable real estate in downtown Milwaukee; had purchased the Milwaukee *Journal*, Miami *Tribune*, and Philadelphia *Inquirer;* published radio and screen guides; controlled newspaper and magazine distribution companies in Toronto, Montreal and most major U.S. cities; and had numerous holdings in the field of racing and sports information (Central Files of the Department of Justice, Note 11; Chicago Crime Commission, Note 12; Irey 1948; Messick, 1969).

Annenberg gained a monopoly in most forms of racing and sports information. In 1922, he and two associates purchased a major interest in the *Daily Racing Form,* the chief racing newspaper. Six years later, they acquired the *Morning Telegraph,* the only serious competitor. Annenberg also bought out numerous tip sheets and scratch sheets. In 1927 he bought from Mont Tennes a half interest in the General News Bureau and installed James Ragen as manager. Ragen had worked for both Moe and Max in Chicago newspaper circulation. After quarreling with his remaining partners in the General News Bureau, Annenberg established a rival Nationwide News Service. Because his own man, Ragen, managed the General News Bureau, Nationwide soon took over the sports information business and established monopoly control beyond what Tennes and his partners had achieved earlier. (Central Files of the Department of Justice, Note 11; Chicago Crime Commission, Note 12; Irey 1948; Messick, 1969).

Annenberg had a complex relationship with bookmakers, including ex-bootleggers involved in bookmaking. He was a figure whose wealth and background made him little subject to intimidation by local crime organizations. Indeed, he and his associates were not above the use of violence in extending their information empire. He clearly used his monopoly of racing information to extract maximum profits from bookmakers who were his customers. He not only charged high prices for information supplied by the national wire, but eventually sent the information by code. The code could be deciphered only by purchasing the daily wall sheets sold by his companies at prices many times higher than in earlier years (Central Files of the Department of Justice, Note 11; Chicago Crime Commission, Note 12; Irey, 1948; Messick, 1969).

In 1939 Moe Annenberg, his son Walter, James Ragen, and other associates were indicted for federal tax evasion. In the aftermath Annenberg agreed to divest control of the race wire, settled his civil tax liabilities by agreeing to pay $8 million, and received a prison sentence. By 1940 a number of entrepreneurs, mostly former Annenberg associates, were attempting to revive the race wire. Among them was Arthur B. (Mickey) McBride, who became president of the new Continental News Service. Like Annenberg, McBride had been active in newspaper circulation in the early part of the century. He later branched out, so that he eventually headed the Yellow Cab Company in Cleveland and owned the Cleveland Browns pro football team. Once James Ragen was released from Federal prison, he took over management of Continental (Chicago *Daily News,* 1940; Messick, 1967; Peterson, Note 13).

Soon Jack Guzik and other associates of the old Capone-Guzik bootlegging group in Chicago demanded that Ragen provide them with a partnership interest in Continental. When Ragen refused, the Guzik group formed a rival Trans-America News Publishing Company. They called upon friends in various parts of the country to establish local distributorships for the news wire. On the West Coast, for instance, Benjamin Siegel coordinated local distribution. After a period of competition between the two wires, the Chicago group resorted to direct action: on June 24, 1946, James Ragen was ambushed in Chicago and died after hospitalization. Soon thereafter an arrangement was reached by Guzik and his associates with Continental. Trans-America was dissolved, and many of those who had worked with Trans-America found jobs with Continental. Thus, Annenberg had used his position to charge monopoly prices to bookmakers; the descendants of the bootleggers finally secured an interest—perhaps a predominant interest—in the national wire and the influence it exercised (Chicago Crime Commission Note 14; Kefauver, 1951; Special Crime Study Commission on Organized Crime, California, Note 15).

Local and Regional Coordination

The overall impact of ex-bootleggers upon gambling can best be understood by examining their role in coordinating local gambling in American cities and in creating regional gambling centers. In the development of regional gambling centers—whether in Florida; Hot Springs, Arkansas; or (eventually) Las Vegas—ex-bootleggers played a crucial entrepreneurial role. In coordination of local gambling, the role of ex-bootleggers was far more diverse. As suggested earlier, ex-bootleggers were important in some cities or neighborhoods but of marginal importance in others.

The Chicago region was a prime example of a center in which ex-bootleggers, over time, exerted a significant and increasing role as coordinators and backers of gambling enterprises. The bootlegging group popularly identified with the name of Al Capone was most important in the long run. By 1924, Capone, Guzik, and their partners had an interest in all gambling houses in suburban Cicero. The houses were generally managed by Cicero gamblers, who were given partnerships in the enterprises. Some became regional gambling houses, no longer servicing only the blue-collar workers of Cicero but also attracting customers from a wider area. Thus, an advantage for some Cicero gamblers was that, while they no longer controlled all the profits, they had a partial share in potentially more profitable enterprises (Chicago Crime Commission, Note 16; Internal Revenue Service, Note 17; Kobler, 1971).

Throughout the 1920's, partners in the so-called Capone organization invested in local gambling. In the downtown Loop area, for instance, Guzik, working with Hymie Levin, gained an interest in a number of handbooks and gambling dens. Nevertheless, through the 1930's William Skidmore, an old-time gambler and Westside Democratic political leader, remained the major coordinator of the city's gambling. With William Johnson, he operated the finest casinos in the city. When Skidmore and Johnson were indicted for income tax evasion in 1939, however, their importance evaporated, and the descendants of the bootleggers emerged as the most important single group (Chicago Crime Commission, Note 18; Irey, 1948; Murray, 965). As mentioned earlier, their movement in the 1940's to control the national race wire and to secure a role in Chicago's policy syndicates further extended their importance within, as well as outside, the Chicago metropolitan region.

Parts of New York City and northern New Jersey constituted another region in which ex-bootleggers became major coordinators of gambling activities. Here, of course, Frank Costello was among the many key figures. By the mid-1920's, Costello was a partner with William Dwyer in the largest liquor import syndicate in the region. He early established reliable relations with Tammany politicians, diversified his economic interests, and became a respected part of the nightlife scene in Manhattan. He had strong ties to Irish and Jewish entrepreneurs and was not, like Charles (Lucky) Luciano, rooted chiefly in the Italian neighborhoods of the city (Kobler, 1973; Wolf & Dimona, 1974).

Slot machines were the most publicized of Costello's early gambling ventures. Games activated by putting a coin in the slot had begun to achieve popularity in the 1880's, and penny arcades were soon a standard feature of entertainment districts such as Coney Island. The modern slot machine, or one-armed bandit, was probably introduced in the 1890's. Chicago became the center for the manufacture of coin machines and, by the 1920's, the Mills Novelty Company was the major manufacturer (Central Files of the Department of Justice, Note 19; Pilat & Ranson, 1941; Quinn, 1969). Many bootleggers in the 1920's went into slot machines as a sideline. Possibly there was a good economic reason: after all, as long as bootleggers sent trucks from speak-easy to speak-easy to deliver booze, it was not too difficult at the same time to place and service the slot machines.

With "Dandy" Phil Kastel, Costello, by 1928 had formed the Tru-Mint Company, which became the sole agent in New York for the Mills Novelty Company. By 1931 Tru-Mint had as many as 5,000 machines installed in New York, a substantial capital investment. Then, in 1934, Mayor Fiorello LaGuardia gained considerable publicity by ordering raids on Costello's machines. With thousands of machines stored in warehouses, Costello and Kastel negotiated with Senator Huey Long to have the machines set up in New Orleans. Kastel went to New Orleans to oversee operations there (Wolf & DiMona, 1974).

Over time, the role of Costello and other ex-bootleggers extended well beyond the well-publicized involvement with slot machines. Through the 1930's and 1940's Costello cultivated friendships among local politicians until he exercised considerable backstage influence among Democratic politicians in Manhattan. His associate, Frank Erickson, provided layoff betting for bookmakers in the region. Furthermore, Costello's cousin, Willie Moretti, became an important figure in New Jersey gambling. (New York State Crime Commission, Note 20; Pledge, 1956; Wolf & DiMona, 1974).

Despite the eventual strong influence of bootleggers upon gambling in such places as New York and Chicago, there are two points that need to be stressed. First of all, even in places like New York and Chicago, ex-bootleggers never controlled all gambling and, even where they exercised influence, they seldom displaced the gamblers already in operation. Rather, they became financial backers and political mediators, receiving a share of the profits in return for services rendered. Sometimes of course they used the threat of violence as a bargaining tool. The partnership arrangements meant that, in the actual operations of gambling, there remained considerable continuity. And many old-time gamblers—Erickson would be a prime example—continued to prosper and exercise influence.

The second point is that, while New York and Chicago have been important cities, crime history has too often been written almost solely from the perspective of those two cities. Those two cities may not be typical. In many cities or regions of the country, ex-bootleggers played, at best, a marginal role. Because little attention has been given to crime history outside New York and Chicago, generalizations carry certain risks. For instance, gambling in cities on the West Coast and in the South (outside of Florida) apparently was relatively little influenced. In San Francisco in the 1930's, the McDonough brothers, who operated a bail bond business, continued as they had for twenty years to be the major coordinators and political protectors for vice and wide-open gambling in the city (Central Files of the Department of Justice, Note 21; San Francisco *Chronicle,* 1937). As late as the 1940's, despite the presence in Los Angeles of such luminaries as Benjamin Siegel, bookmaking was chiefly in the hands of persons with no known background in bootlegging (Special Crime Study Commission on Organized Crime, California, Note 22). In. St. Louis, although some ex-bootleggers were active in bookmaking and other forms of gambling, the dominant bookmakers were the firms of James J. Carroll and John Mooney of C. J. Rich and Company. Their roots were among the old-time gamblers (Kefauver, 1951; St. Louis *Post-Dispatch,* Note 23). There were, in short, cities in which ex-bootleggers had little impact upon gambling and in which, as a result, there was continuity of gambling from the old-time gamblers of pre-bootleg days.

In the development of regional gambling centers, however, ex-bootleggers clearly played a crucial role. Newport and Covington Kentucky, located across the Ohio River from Cincinnati, had a long history of illegal gambling, servicing Cincinnati and, at the same time, reflecting the betting and racing culture of Kentucky. In 1941, a largely Jewish group of ex-bootleggers from Cleveland, including Morris (Moe) Dalitz, began to buy into casinos in the area. In what was now a normal pattern, local gambling entrepreneurs retained partnership interests and continued as managers. Indeed, some gambling houses continued entirely under local control. In later years, as the Cleveland partners invested in Florida and Las Vegas, local gamblers from Covington and Newport received investment opportunities and management posts in the larger and more lucrative enterprises elsewhere (Messick, 1967; Messick, 1969; Special Committee to Investigate Organized Crime in Interstate Commerce, Note 24).

Florida constituted another region in which ex-bootleggers made joint gambling investments, especially in race tracks and casinos. The involvement in Florida was based in part on their earlier activities as bootleggers. After the Coast Guard substantially reduced the importation of liquor along the coast from Boston to Cape May, Florida ports became major import centers, and bootleggers from the Northeast and Midwest established business relationships there. Like many of the newly rich of the 1920's, they made real estate investments in Florida and vacationed there. As Florida became a vacation center for the East Coast, there were obvious opportunities for bootleggers to make money from hotels, nightclubs, and casino gambling. Meyer Lansky, a bootlegger from New York, was a key figure not only in the race track investments of the 1930's, but also in the development of Florida casinos after World War II (Kefauver, 1951; Messick, 1971).

Havana, Cuba, was another city in which ex-bootleggers, led by Meyer Lansky, promoted a regional gambling center. Again, their activities were rooted in a longtime American underworld penetration of Cuba. In the 1920's, Havana was a minor center for American gambling—and a major center for the smuggling of liquor and narcotics into eastern ports. Many bootleggers had investments there and developed friendly relations with Cuban politicians (Coast Guard Intelligence File, Note 25). In the mid-1930's, with the concurrence of Cuban leader Fulgencio Batista, Lansky operated a casino in the Hotel Nacional in Havana and leased a local race track. A major expansion of gambling in Havana occurred with Batista's return to power in 1952, making that city a center for big bettors from America and Europe. Phil Kastel (now from New Orleans), Moe Dalitz and his Cleveland associates, Lansky, and many others promoted lush casinos until Batista's fall from power in 1959 (Messick, 1971).

The major success of the ex-bootleggers and their associates was to turn Las Vegas into a national center for gambling and entertainment. Although air travel after World War II made it possible for Las Vegas to become a national center, there were historical reasons why Las Vegas was available when opportunity knocked. First, Nevada had a long tradition of providing services that were illegal elsewhere. When most states outlawed prize fighting before World War I, Nevada did not, and a number of major fights were staged there, attracting the nation's sporting element to the thinly populated state. Reno, of course, did a thriving business in granting divorces more easily than were legally available in other states. Although gambling was illegal in Nevada for a brief period beginning in 1910, the state legislature legalized licensed gambling in 1931 in a deliberate attempt to rescue state finances and stimulate the state's economy during the Depression (Ashbaugh, 1963; Hulse, 1965; Lillard, 1942; Ostrander, 1966; Skolnick, 1978; Turrano, 1933).

The eventual importance of gambling to the Las Vegas economy can be clarified by a few statistics. In 1928 the city had a stable population of

5,000 which rose in the 1930's to about 8,000 because of construction of Hoover Dam nearby. Reno's population was then nearly 25,000. During World War II, the Army Air Force used the Las Vegas municipal airport as a training base, and the population reached 20,000 by 1944. With the end of the war, however, the city faced a bleak economic future. The Chamber of Commerce saw only one hope: to promote tourism by playing up the city as the "Last Frontier Community." As part of this, local boosters advertised the downtown gaming area as "glitter gulch." Within 20 years, as outside money poured in to build the great hotel-casinos and create the strip with its gambling and entertainment, the city's population swelled to 200,000—the most rapid city growth in the country (Kaufman, Note 26).

If the transformation of Las Vegas was rooted in local history, however, it also depended upon financing by wealthy gambling entrepreneurs. For this Benjamin Siegel, who was a bootlegging associate of Lansky in the 1920's and established himself in Los Angeles in the late 1930's, was an important catalyst. His initial involvement came in the early 1940 s when he was active with Trans-America in its rivalry with the Continental race wire. As West Coast representative for Trans-America, Siegel insisted that he would provide wire service in Las Vegas only to those casinos that offered him a partnership in their bookmaking operations. In this way he became a part of the wide-open, but still relatively small-time, casino gambling of Las Vegas (Jennings, 1967; Skolnick, 1978; Special Crime Study Commission, California, note 15).

With the end of World War II, Siegel had a vision that Las Vegas could support a magnificent hotel-casino complex. The Flamingo, whose estimated cost of $1,000,000 soon experienced massive cost overruns, was financed by mobilizing money from East Coast ex-bootleggers and their business associates. These included Lansky as a key backer, Costello and his partners, Hy Abrams (the old Boston bootlegger), and eventually, many of their friends and more distant associates. Probably, Siegel's unreliability as a financial manager led to his assassination in June 1947; but, after a faltering opening, the Flamingo soon turned a handsome profit. In the succeeding decade, ex-bootleggers from Minneapolis, Chicago, Cleveland, and the East Coast poured their own money and Teamster Union pension funds into additional casinos on the strip. Las Vegas became a successful culmination of the entrepreneurial endeavors of the ex-bootleggers who had made careers and fortunes from the promotion of regional gambling and entertainment centers for America's high rollers (Jennings, 1967; Reid & Demaris, 1963; Turner, 1965).

Summary

Bootleggers and ex-bootleggers exercised more influence over who controlled gambling than over any changes in the structure of gambling. Their success in achieving some measure of control depended upon the experience and wealth that they acquired in the 1920's and upon their relative youthfulness when prohibition ended. In their thirties in 1933, they reached solid middle-age and their peak earning years after World War II.

Long before the 1920's and the rise of bootlegging, however, talented entrepreneurs had built bookmaking and policy syndicates in American cities, operated strings of gambling houses, and engaged in joint investments in race tracks and other sporting activities. Thus, the basic structure already existed before the bootleggers began their investment in gambling. To the extent that the basic structure of gambling changed in the 1920's and 1930's, most changes were the result of social, technological, or legal factors. With the growth of black ghettoes in northern cities, blacks (and West Indians in New York City) pioneered in numbers and, in many cities, gained a predominant role in the operation of policy or numbers gambling. In the field of bookmaking, Annenberg used the race wire to monopolize the information service and squeeze profits from bookmakers in new and effective ways. Concurrently, horse racing made a come-back in the United States under state regulation and with the legalization of pari-mutuel betting, thus gradually eliminating the bookmaker's role at the track. The spread of the telephone meant that local bookmakers operated increasingly from banks of telephones rather than old-time horse parlors. In these and in other developments, bootleggers played, at best, a peripheral role. Only in the introduction of violence and coercion to gambling in some parts of the country did ex-bootleggers significantly influence the way in which gambling operations were carried on in the 1920's and 1930's.

In the coordination of local gambling, the impact of bootleggers varied greatly from city to city and from region to region. Much of the popular crime history has been written from the point of view of New York and Chicago, where bootleggers became heavy investors in gambling. It is, nevertheless, far from clear that New York and Chicago were typical. There were certainly cities, especially on the West Coast and in the South, where bootleggers apparently exercised little significant influence on gambling, especially in the period before World War II. Until there has been research into local gambling history outside the New York and Chicago regions, it is safe to conclude only that the local impact varied greatly from place to place and, overall, was probably far less than has normally been assumed.

There are also a series of conclusions that can be made concerning the background of gamblers in American cities. To begin with, the influence of Italians upon American gambling—and upon illegal enterprise generally—has probably been exaggerated. Certainly this is true for the early years. Among leading bootleggers, persons of Jewish background predominated and after 1933 exercised a disproportionate influence among the ex-bootleggers who went into gambling. The Cleveland group that invested in Newport, Kentucky, in Florida, and in Las Vegas was almost entirely Jewish. The role of Meyer Lansky, along with his Jewish and Italian partners, was crucial in Florida, Havana, and Las Vegas. Even in Chicago Jack Guzik was, in the late 1930's and 1940's, perhaps the most important single figure in the city's gambling.

The background of gambling entrepreneurs is still more varied if one examines the total range of persons involved. Before prohibition, persons of Irish background were disproportionately involved in syndicate gambling. In the South, on the other hand, there was a tradition of WASP involvement, extending back at least to the days of the Mississippi riverboat gambler. And in many cities blacks, who had previously operated on the periphery of the gambling world, became promoters of policy or numbers syndicates by the 1920's. With the rise of bootleggers, the old-time gamblers continued their dominance in some cities and regions; and even in those cities where ex-bootleggers became important gambling coordinators, the normal pattern was that the old-time gamblers remained as partners and managers. Hence, the range of groups involved in the promotion of gambling has remained much broader than many standard accounts might indicate.

Finally, the impact of bootleggers and ex-bootleggers was particularly important in two areas: the coordination of local gambling in some cities and the development of regional gambling centers. In cities like New York, Cleveland, and Chicago, for instance, bootleggers began to invest in gambling enterprises early in their careers. At first they coexisted with traditional gambling entrepreneurs, but because of the relative youthfulness of bootleggers and the willingness of some to employ violence, their influence spread gradually until they and their partners became predominant influences. Often, indeed, their coordination of gambling was only part of their investment in and coordination of the nightlife and commercialized entertainment of a city—nightclubs, bars, juke boxes, legal liquor distribution, and other related enterprises. As bootleggers, many had begun to move into these other areas of entertainment at the same time that they invested in gambling, so that gambling must be seen as part of a larger set of investments.

In the development of regional gambling centers in the 1930's and 1940's, the ex-bootleggers clearly played a crucial role. Las Vegas may be seen as the culmination of their endeavors. The Las Vegas strip came to gaudy fruition through the investment of millions of dollars by ex-bootleggers from Boston, New York, New Jersey, Florida, Cleveland, and Chicago. Their economic activities in Las Vegas were foreshadowed in a variety of earlier joint endeavors in Newport, Kentucky, Florida, and Havana. Their successes in these relatively large-scale joint enterprises were rooted in their experiences as bootleggers. Bootlegging had required cooperation and joint investments. The economic skills learned in the 1920's were transferred to the cooperative investments in race tracks, casinos, and other gambling activities in the period after prohibition. Even there, however, the role of old-time gamblers remained considerable, for development of regional gambling depended upon the recruitment of a skilled management cadre. It was in the promotion of regional gambling centers, at any rate, that ex-bootleggers most clearly placed their stamp upon the history of American gambling.

Notes

1. Haller, M H., *The Rise of Gambling Syndicates*. Chapter 4 of an unpublished book on the history of Chicago crime.
2. Haller, M. H., *Bootlegging in Chicago: The Structure of an Illegal Enterprise*. Paper read at American Historical Association Convention, December 28, 1974.
3. Central Files of the Department of Justice, National Archives, File No. 5-51-476.
4. Salus Scrapbooks (newspaper clippings), Urban Archives, Temple University, Philadelphia, Pennsylvania.

5. Chicago Crime Commission, *File* Nos. 65 and 14877.
6. Chicago Crime Commission, *File* No. 65-2.
7. Chicago Crime Commission, *File* Nos. 65-13 & 65-225.
8. Manhattan District Attorney, Annual Report 1954, 81-86.
9. New York State Crime Commission Papers, Columbia University Library, Folder labeled *Commissioner Osborne,* Box 2.
10. Special Crime Study Commission on Organized Crime, State of California, *Second Progress Report,* Sacramento, California, March 7, 1949, 88.
11. Central Files of Department of Justice, National Archives, Washington, D.C. File No 5-23-1205.
12. Chicago Crime Commission, File No. 34950.
13. Peterson, V. W., *Memorandum for the File.* Chicago Crime Commission, June 22, 1943, File No. 65-13.
14. Chicago Crime Commission, *File* No 65-182.
15. Special Crime Study Commission on Organized Crime, State of California, *Third Progress Report,* Sacramento, California. January 31, 1950, 22-27.
16. Chicago Crime Commission, *File* No. 11654.
17. Internal Revenue Service, File No. S17085-F.
18. Chicago Crime Commission, *File* Nos. 65-1 & 65-2.
19. Central Files of the Department of Justice, National Archives, File No. 5-23-987 on Mills Novelty Co.
20. New York State Crime Commission in New York State Crime Commission papers, Columbia University, mimeographed *Second Report,* Box 1.
21. Central Files of the Department of Justice, Federal Records Center, Suitland, Maryland, File No. 23-11-18.
22. Special Crime Study Commission on Organized Crime, State of California, *Third Progress Report,* Sacramento, California, January 31, 1950, Chapter 3.
23. St. Louis *Post-Dispatch,* gambling file in morgue.
24. Special Committee to Investigate Organized Crime in Interstate Commerce, U.S. Congress, Senate (82nd Congress), *Hearings,* Part VI, 118-23, 132-41, 145-49, 182-83, 368-70, 374-76, 384-85; Part X11, 56-59, 629, 726-39, 755.
25. Coast Guard Intelligence File, National Archives, *General Survey of Cuban Bunco Operations,* Box 64, Folder 1004-5.
26. Kaufman, P., *Public Relations, Men, Images, and the Growth of Las Vegas.* Paper presented at Convention of the Organization of American Historians, April 1973.

References

Amen, J. H., *Report of the Kings County Investigation, 1938-1942.* 1942, 123-24.

Asbury, H., *Sucker's Progress: An Informal History of Gambling in America from the Colonies to Canfield.* New York, 1938, 88-101.

Asbury, H., *The Great Illusion: An Informal History of Prohibition.* New York, 1968, Chaps. 11-13.

Ashbaugh, D., *Nevada's Turbulent Yesterday.* Las Vegas, 1963.

Bradley, H., *Such was Saratoga.* New York, 1940, especially Chapters 6 & 10.

Brashier, W., *The Don: The Life and Death of Sam Giancana.* New York, 1977, 86-87 & Chap. 7.

Brolaski, H., *Easy Money: Being the Experiences of a Reformed Gambler.* Cleveland, 1911.

Carlson, G. G., "Number Gambling: A Study of a Culture Complex, " Ph.D. Dissertation, University of Michigan, 1941, Chap. 2.

Carter, S. D., "Numbers Gambling: The Negro's Illegal Response to Status Discrimination of American Society," M.A. Thesis, Wayne State University, 1970, Chap. 5.

Chicago *Daily News,* Jan. 18 & 23, 1917.

Chicago *Daily News,* April 26, 1940.

Chicago *Tribune,* Dec. 22, 1881.

Citizens' Association of Chicago, *Bulletin,* July 31, 1903, 11.

Comstock, A., *Traps for the Young.* John Harvard Library (Ed.), Cambridge, Massachusetts: 1967, Chapter 6.

Demaris, O., *Captive City: Chicago in Chains.* New York: 1969.

Drake, S. C. & Clayton, H. R., *Black Metropolis: A Study of Negro Life in a Northern City.* New York: 1945, *II,* Chapters 17 & 19.

Flynt, J., "The Pool-Room Vampire and its Money-Mad Victims." *Cosmopolitan Magazine,* February, 1907, XLII, 368-70.

Flynt, J., "The Pool-Room Spider and the Gambling Fly." *Cosmopolitan Magazine,* March, 1907, XLII, 515-16.

Flynt, J., "The Men Behind the Pool Rooms." *Cosmopolitan Magazine,* April, 1907, XLII, 638-39.

Haller, M. H., "Bootleggers and American Gambling, 1920-50" in Commission on the Review of the National Policy Toward Gambling, *Gambling in America,* Appendix I, U.S. Government Printing Office, 1976, 109-114.

Hulse, J., *The Nevada Adventure,* Reno, Nevada, 1965, 250-54.
Irey, E. L., *The Tax Dodgers: The Inside Story of the T-Men's War with America's Political and Underworld Hoodlums,* as told to William J. Slocum, New York: 1948, 187-89.
Jarman, R., "The Great Racetrack Caper." *American Heritage,* August, 1968, XIX, 24-27.
Jennings, D., *We Only Kill Each Other: The Life and Bad Times of Bugsy Siegel,* Englewood Cliffs, N.J.: 1967, 80-82, 139-41.
Johnson, D. R., "A Sinful Business: Origins of Gambling Syndicates in the United States: 1840-1887," in D. Bayley (Ed.), *Police and Society.* Beverly Hills, CA: 1977, Chapter I.
Katcher, L., *The Big Bankroll: The Life and Times of Arnold Rothstein,* New York, 1958, 117-18.
Kefauver, E., *Crime in America,* Garden City, N.Y., 1951, 77-81.
Kobler, J., *Capone: The Life and World of Al Capone.* New York, 1971, Chap. 8.
Kobler, J., *Ardent Spirits.* New York: 261-265, 1973.
Kusmer, K. L., *A Ghetto Takes Shape: Black Cleveland, 1870-1930,* Urbana, Ill., 1976.
Landesco, John, *Organized Crime in Chicago,* new ed., Chicago, 1968, Chap. 5.
Light, I., *Number and Policy Gambling in New York City, 1876-1973.* Council of Planning Libraries, Exchange Bibliography 659-660, Oct., 1974.
Lillard, R. G., *Desert Challenge: An Interpretation of Nevada.* New York, 1942, 81-82.
Literary Digest, Gambling and Western Union, May 28, 1904, *XXVII.* 760-62.
Menke, F. G., *The Story of Churchill Downs and the Kentucky Derby.* New York, 1940.
Messick, H., *The Silent Syndicate.* New York, 1967.
Messick, H., *Secret File.* New York, 1969.
Messick, H., *Lansky.* New York, 1971.
Murray, G., *The Madhouse on Madison Street,* Chicago, 1965, Chap. 4.
Myers, H. B., The Policing of Labor Disputes in Chicago: A Case Study, Ph.D. Dissertation, University of Chicago, 1929, Chap. 12.
Nelli, H. S., *The Business of Crime: Italians in American Syndicate Crime,* New York, 1976, Chap. 6.

New York *Times,* Feb. 7, 1934.
New York *Times,* May 24, 1934.
New York *Times,* March 3, 1935, Sec. IV, 10.
Osofsky, G., *Harlem: The Making of a Ghetto,* New York, 1966.
Ostrander, G. M., *Nevada: The Great Rotten Borough, 1859-1964,* New York, 1966.
Parmer, C. B., *For Gold and Glory: The Story of Thoroughbred Racing in America,* Englewood Cliffs, NJ, 1939.
Pilat, O. and Ranson, J., *Sodom by the Sea: An Affectionate History of Coney Island,* Garden City, NY, 1941.
Pledge, J., *Bombshell: From Boxer to Bookmaker,* New York, 1956.
Pringle, H. N., *The Facts About Race Track Gambling,* Washington, D.C., 1916.
Quinn, J. P., *Fools of Fortune, or Gambling and Gamblers,* Chicago, IL, 1892.
Quinn, J. P., *Gambling and Gambling Devices,* 1912. Reprinted by Patterson, Smith, 1969.
Reid, E. & Demaris, O., *The Green Felt Jungle,* New York, 1963.
Riggio, J., "The Over-the-Hill Mob," *Philadelphia magazine,* November 1972, 190.
San Francisco *Chronicle,* Report of Atherton Investigation, printed in special section, March 17, 1937.
Sann, P., *Kill the Dutchman: The Story of Dutch Schultz,* New Rochelle, NY, 1971.
Skolnick, J. H., *House of Cards: The Legalization and Control of Casino Gambling.* Boston, 1978.
Spear, A. H., *Black Chicago: The Making of a Negro Ghetto, 1890-1920,* Chicago, 1967.
Turner, W., *Gambler's Money: The New Force in American Life,* New York, 1965.
Turrano, A. M., "Nevada's Trial of Licensed Gambling," *American Mercury,* Feb. 1933, *XXVIII,* 190-92.
Waters, H., *Smugglers of Spirits: Prohibition and the Coast Guard,* New York, 1971.
Wolf, G. with DiMona, J., *Frank Costello: Prime Minister of the Underworld,* New York, 1974.

Chapter 9

Loansharking in American Cities: Historical Analysis of a Marginal Enterprise

In the recent past, two distinct types of loansharking have flourished in American cities. The first, which developed in the 1870's or 1880's and probably reached its high point from 1900 to World War I, functioned with an appearance of legality. There is no evidence that these loansharks used violence for collection of debts. Rather, their effectiveness often involved persuading the borrower that the loan represented a legal obligation. Much like a modern, legal lending institution, most such lenders operated out of an office; a prospective borrower was investigated to determine whether he had a steady job; and the borrower signed complicated forms before receiving the loan. Commonly, the loan was treated as a "purchase" of the borrower's future salary. In the event that a borrower failed to meet his payments, collection was attempted by threatening to inform the employer of the debt, by harassment of various sorts, or by filing a law suit. Such loansharks, so far as can be determined, had no connection with gambling syndicates or other "organized crime" activities. They were often referred to as salary lenders.

The second type of loansharking made little or no pretense of legality. Instead, the understanding between lender and borrower was that, while the borrower would be expected to repay because he had promised to do so, the sanction of violence might ultimately be used. Although such loansharks sometimes used a legal lending institution or some other legitimate business as a front, they more often met their customers in saloons, on street corners, in the factory, and at other informal but regular public places. These loansharks often had prior or concurrent careers in bootlegging, gambling, labor racketeering, or other "organized crime" activity. Such an operator, then, might be called a "racketeer loanshark."

Loansharking, for purposes of this study, is defined as the lending of money at an illegal rate of interest and without holding claim to some physical possession of the borrower as collateral. (In short, mortgage lending, pawnbroking, chattel lending, and installment selling, even if done illegally, are not included.) Furthermore, the loan was the personal obligation of the borrower and was typically used to cover special expenses of everyday life. (The complicated subject of business borrowing and banking practices lies outside the scope of this study.) Obviously, the term "loanshark" today evokes images of the racketeer lender—a man who regards the borrower's body as collateral and might resort to mayhem or even murder in a difficult case. What is interesting, though, is how recent such loansharking is. Racketeer loansharking apparently first became extensive in New York City during the early 1930's and received national attention when Thomas E. Dewey undertook a number of highly publicized prosecutions. For many cities, however, such loansharking probably did not become a standard underworld activity until the 1950's.

Thus, the historical problem is to examine the replacement of the old-time salary lenders by modern racketeer loansharks. Although racketeer loansharking developed during the period when salary lending was passing out of existence, there was no direct transition from one to the other. That is, the earlier salary lenders did not become the new racketeer loansharks. Each type nevertheless reflected the legal status of small loans and the economics of the small loan market at different times. Replacement of salary lenders by racketeer loansharks provides an opportunity to examine the ways in which changing laws shaped the market for illegal loans and altered the collection mechanisms available to those who serviced the market.

Because loansharking has always been a relatively secretive and unpublicized activity, researching its history raises problems. Loansharking has received attention during three periods. The first was from 1905 to 1915, when the Russell Sage Foundation and other reform groups focused attention on salary lending. While studies of New York and Chicago were most thorough, there was information on many other cities as well. The second period was 1935 to 1940, as a result of investigations by Dewey and other law enforcement officials. The information was restricted to the boroughs of New York and had the usual weaknesses of information collected and disseminated for law enforcement purposes. The third period was the 1960's, triggered by the "mafia" scare of that period. Like so much "mafiology," the information probably exaggerates the level of violence and hierarchical organization, as well as the degree of Italian control. At any rate, the episodic nature of the evidence means that many of the generalizations should be regarded as tentative.

Salary Lending

Salary lenders operated within a complex system of law and public attitudes toward borrowing. Usury laws of most states in the late nineteenth century set the maximum interest rate so low (about six percent annually) that it was not possible to operate a small loan company profitably within the law. Furthermore, respectable opinion frowned upon consumer borrowing as a sign of poor budget management and moral weakness on the part of the borrower. Established lending institutions, then, avoided the small-loan market both because it was unprofitable and because it was perceived to be a disreputable business activity. Reflecting similar attitudes, employers—because they hoped to protect the morals of their employees, prevent possible employee embezzlement, or avoid the expenses of handling wage assignments—often had a policy of firing employees found to be in debt.

Yet there were many persons with steady jobs who needed to borrow small sums of money and constituted good credit risks. There existed, in short, a substantial market for illegal, yet profitable, small loans. Those lenders who serviced the small borrower necessarily charged higher than the legal rate. But they did so in a context in which the law was sometimes unclear and penalties for usury were minimal. Often usury was not subject to criminal penalties; and, when it was, the crime was classified as a misdemeanor and no official had specific enforcement responsibility. A person making a usurious loan was subject to civil penalties, which ranged from forfeiture of the illegal interest to forfeiture of principal and interest. The penalty could be imposed, however, only if the borrower undertook the expenses of a law suit. Furthermore, lower courts were often hospitable to suits by lenders, and the numerous forms signed by the borrower in taking out the loan created doubt concerning the outcome of suits. The transaction, in short, was illegal, but sometimes only if a judge was willing to look behind the form of the loan to its reality.

Salary lending arose in the post-Civil War period in the context of two legal, small loan institutions. The oldest of these was, of course, the pawnshop—and, in terms of volume of business, it remained by far the most important. Pawnshops began to develop in America's coastal cities even before the Revolution. A second type of enterprise, emerging soon after the Civil War, was the chattel lender, who made small loans secured by a mortgage on personal property such as furniture, a sewing machine, or jewelry. By the 1880's some chattel lenders, as a sideline to their business, were offering small loans without such security. The business proved profitable, expanded in the 1890's, and reached its period of greatest growth, generally independent of chattel lending, during the first decade of the twentieth century.[1]

The expansion was possible because there were reliable customers. Numerous studies of the customers served by salary lenders all reached the same conclusion. Borrowers were generally married men; they held steady jobs; and they had legitimate reasons for seeking a loan. By occupation, borrowers were frequently regular employees of large organizations: government civil servants, railroad workers, streetcar motormen, and clerks in firms such as insurance companies. In describing salary lending companies, for instance, a Chicago study revealed the types of customers: "Near transportation terminal; convenient to railway employees"; or "deals with street car employees"; or "an old telegraph operator; . . . dealing mostly with telegraphers"; or "conveniently located at a street car terminal; specializes with employees." Within those organizations that provided customers for salary lenders, a substantial proportion of the employees borrowed. A New York City study estimated that borrowers included 2,000 policemen, 2,500 firemen, 75,000 railroad clerks, and 75,000 employees of large mercantile houses. In another study, one salary lender alone was found to have 1,500 accounts with city employees. The reasons for borrowing included unexpected illness in the family, the costs of moving or of paying rent in advance, and the need for funds for vacation or Christmas. Only a small minority sought funds because of gambling debts or other reasons that, in terms of the values of the time, represented evidence of moral failure. The high profitability of salary lending stemmed in part from the fact that loans were made to persons who were good credit risks, with regular jobs and family ties that prevented their departure from the city. Borrowers, in a sense, were victims of their own respectability.[2]

Salary lenders attracted their customers by their location, their front as legitimate businesses, and their advertising. In general, the offices of salary lenders clustered in downtown buildings near or within the financial district. In Chicago about 1915, well over half the offices (152 of 263) were located in the Loop, mostly within a block of Madison and Dearborn Streets. Others were located at major transportation terminals and serviced transportation workers. Thus, salary lending offices were not neighborhood centers but attracted their customers by locating near the government and business buildings where the customers worked. By locating near the financial district and assuming legitimate-sounding names, salary lenders appeared to be among the normal financial institutions of the city, serving a respectable clientele.[3] Salary lenders also advertised like other small businesses. They placed ads in newspapers:

> The City Credit Company will advance money to salaried people on their note without security. Lowest rates—strictly confidential.

Indeed, it was not unusual for the New York *Morning World* in 1909 to contain thirty-five such ads. Companies also sent out letters through the mail or distributed circulars from door to door. In addition, they often provided small commissions to those customers who encouraged neighbors or fellow workers to take out loans.[4]

Salary loan offices tended to be relatively small. They were often capitalized at $30,000 or less and generally offered loans from $5 to $50. In city after city, women served in disproportionate numbers as managers, as well as clerks, in salary loan offices. There were probably two reasons for this. One was that competent women could be hired at a lower salary than men. The second was, apparently, that the respectable borrowers, brought up to treat women with courtesy and deference, were more easily manipulated by women than by men. Unfortunately, little is known about the men who stood behind the businesses. Many, in fact, deliberately kept their identities secret; for, as one employee in New York explained:

> My boss don't want anybody to know who he is. You know he lives in a wealthy part of the city and he wouldn't have any of his friends know he was in this business for the world.

On the whole, however, the backers appear to have been old stock Americans with WASP'ish names. Chesterkirk, Graham, Mason, Piermont, Stratton, Tolman, Wells—these were the sorts of names attached to the companies.[5]

When a salary lender found that his business prospered, he was likely to establish a new company rather than expand the old one beyond a modest size. Thus, salary lending companies remained small, but in each city some entrepreneurs backed several companies. A few, in fact, expanded into other cities and controlled nationwide chains. The "King of the Loansharks" in the early years was Daniel H. Tolman, who started in the business in the 1890's and by 1909 had branches in over sixty cities. Indeed, in his advertising he criticized other lenders for keeping their names secret and boasted:

> Salaried people advanced money upon their own names without security, on easy payments. I have the oldest established business in sixty-three principal cities.

Despite his public claims, he was in fact a shadowy figure and, for a while, there was doubt that he existed. In Chicago, his office managers claimed that he lived in Brooklyn; in New York, they claimed that he lived in Chicago. Because his lending companies were among the more exploitative, his offices were frequently subject to suits and prosecutions. When a woman manager was arrested in Cincinnati in 1909, Tolman's son travelled there from New York to assist in the defense and was then himself arrested and convicted. By 1914, D. H. Tolman, the father, was serving a six-month sentence in New York and, reportedly, offered to cancel the usurious interest on 23,000 loans, totaling $500,000, if the governor would pardon him."[6]

Despite differing state laws, procedures for securing a loan from a salary lender varied little from city to city. A prospective borrower first filled out an application form with standard personal information: current and previous addresses; current and previous jobs; frequency of paydays; names of relatives, neighbors, and co-workers; amount and type of property owned; and outstanding debts. The salary lender then checked some of the information to determine the applicant's creditworthiness. Many salary lenders paid commissions to clerks in payroll departments of large firms in return for steering customers to them or for helping to screen applicants by providing information concerning salary and other background information. In Chicago, investigators estimated that forty percent of the paymasters for railroads in the city worked for loansharks on the side. Salary lenders, in short, tried to screen their customers carefully.[7]

When accepted for a loan, an applicant then generally signed a number of complicated forms. In order to appear not to violate usury laws, the transaction was often treated as a purchase of the customer's future salary rather than as a loan. In other words, the customer received money in return for an interest in a portion of his salary at future times, and he signed one or more forms assigning his future salary to the lender. In some cases, in addition, two relatives or friends might be expected to sign forms, which they would later learn were assignments of their wages as well. To the extent that the borrower understood what he was signing, he was assured that his employer need never know and that notice of the assignment would not be given to the employer so long as payments were kept up to date. Normally, too, the borrower signed a document giving a power of attorney to the lender. As a result, the lender could sign additional papers for the borrower without the borrower's knowledge. And, if the lender went to court in order to collect, he often had a power of attorney to appear for the borrower and confess judgment. On top of this, the borrower seldom received copies of the forms that he had signed, and often did not receive receipts for payments. He had, as a result, no written record of the transaction.[8]

Loans were generally small, and repayment was due within a few weeks or, at most, a few months. The size of the loan and the repayment plan were tailored to the borrower's ability to repay. Interest rates varied widely from company to company and also varied with the size of the loan. The smaller the loan, the higher the interest. (Because expenses for investigation and collection were about the same for all loans, a smaller loan involved greater relative expense to the salary lender.) It was not unusual for interest rates to run at more than 1,000 percent when computed on an annual basis.[9]

Why, then, did respectable borrowers enter into such agreements? First of all, the borrower's ignorance of the law and his lack of understanding of what he was signing, combined with the respectable front of the operation, often lulled him into believing that there was nothing exceptional or suspicious about the transaction. Furthermore, most borrowers, like installment buyers today, no doubt focused on the size of the weekly or bi-weekly payments rather than calculating the total to be repaid.

Collection of the debts was, of course, the heart of the salary loan business. Among salary lenders there was a continuum of attitudes and practices. At one end were a minority who were reasonable in making collections and did not use the collection procedure to swell the original debt.

Such lenders were often understanding in granting extensions when a borrower had a legitimate excuse, and they were generally slow in contacting the employer or going to court. In fact, some of these salary lenders welcomed the development of licensing laws for small lenders and would have been satisfied to operate a legal small loan business.[10]

At the other end of the continuum were a far larger group of salary lenders who used various means to swell the original usurious loan and to milk the borrower for as much as could be wrung from him. Most of the ballooning of the debt occurred in handling delinquent accounts. To begin with, many companies immediately assessed penalties for lateness, even of a few minutes or a few hours. The fees—protest fees, collection fees, late fees—might total nearly as much as the principal itself. Often the companies deliberately maneuvered a borrower into a late payment, by falsely suggesting that a late payment would be overlooked or by claiming that a payment sent by mail arrived after the payment deadline. Furthermore, some companies, in the event of default, would attempt to collect the entire debt (principal, interest, and fees) not only from the borrower but also from each of his friends or co-workers who had agreed to make good in case of default. But most important, salary lenders attempted to trap a borrower into a "chain debt," in which the borrower continued to pay interest while never managing to pay off the principal and escaping from the loan.[11]

These techniques, of course, were not unique to salary lenders. Unscrupulous chattel lenders or merchants selling on installment resorted to many of the same tactics.

Borrowers entangled in continuing debt provided the stories that reformers needed to arouse public awareness of the dangers of salary lending. The books of one New York loanshark revealed that, of some 400 borrowers, 163 had been paying off small loans for over two years—suggesting that entanglement was the norm rather than the exception. Individual tragedies were even more effective as reform propaganda. There was, for example, the employee of a New York publishing house who supported a large family on a salary of $22.50 per week and had been paying $5 per week to a salary lender for several years, until he had paid more than ten times the original loan. Or the case of a Chicagoan who borrowed $15, paid back $1.50 per month for three years before fleeing the city to escape the debt. Or the case of a streetcar motorman who, in 1912, had seventeen Chicago loan companies attempting to collect $307 on an original loan of $50 after he had already paid $360. Or the claim of another Chicago borrower that he had borrowed $15, ten years later had repaid $2,153 and still owed the original $15.[12]

There was a range of strategies by which salary lenders persuaded delinquent or resistant borrowers to make payments. The first line of attack was the threat or appeal to honor that the manager used in face to face confrontations with the borrower. D. H. Tolman, for instance, instructed his managers (usually women):

> Bluff the borrower by rattling papers on your desk. Pretend to phone an attorney, but hold the phone closed. Remember, the whole proceeding is more or less a bluff.[13]

Another tactic was to employ a "bawler-out"—usually a woman with a stentorian voice and rich vocabulary. The bawler-out went to the borrower's place of work or neighborhood and, in a loud voice, denounced him for his dishonesty in refusing to repay the loan. To avoid further embarrassment or the possibility of being fired, the borrower might well seek a settlement.[14]

Finally, salary lenders had access to legal institutions. The chief purpose of the complicated legal forms, of course, was to persuade the borrower that the transaction was a moral and legal obligation. Even when the papers were used solely as a threat, the borrower's chief fear, quite often, was that an attempt by the lender to enforce the wage assignment would cause the employer to fire him—even though the wage assignment itself was of doubtful legality. The threat of a suit, in short, could be effective in collecting an illegal obligation.

But beyond this, salary lenders often did, as a last resort, use the judicial process. Much of the success of the salary lender in court resulted from the advantages that he wielded as a legal adversary. The lender produced complicated forms signed by the borrower; he often had a power of attorney, so that he could appear for the borrower and confess judgment; and the borrower, already unable to make payments on a small loan, was seldom able to hire an attorney. Indeed, in those few cases in which a borrower had legal representation, the lender would normally withdraw the suit and negotiate a settlement. Secondly, the success of salary lenders reflected the structure of the lower courts, which were staffed by justices of the peace or magistrates who seldom had legal training and whose incomes derived from fees for handling cases. Justices who found for salary lenders could often attract a good deal of business and thus earn tidy sums, so that it was in the economic interest of justices to look with favor upon suits by lenders. Hence, salary lenders, as regular and experienced users of the courts, often enforced illegal contracts against their customers who, as inexperienced and unrepresented defendants, were unable effectively to assert their legal rights.[15]

The movement against salary lending was spearheaded not by dissatisfied customers but rather by a variety of elite reform groups. There were three primary contexts in which elites became aware of the extent and abuses of salary lenders. One context was when, because of the illness or unemployment of the breadwinner, a family applied to a charity organization for relief. At such times, of course, continued payments to salary lenders were particularly onerous and, if payments were missed, the family might be faced with threat of a law suit. (If the borrowing was from a chattel lender, the lender might also seize the furniture or other goods mortgaged to obtain the loan.) A charitable organization might then find itself in the position that any aid to the family would instead wind up in the hands of the lender. Thus a crucial necessity in providing relief was to free the family from loanshark demands. Each depression was likely to bring renewed concern with the impact of salary lending upon the "worthy poor."[16]

A second occasion in which elites learned of salary lending was when employers were served with court orders in attempts by lenders to collect on wage assignments. In many cities, as a result, elite businessmen led the campaign against illegal salary lending. A third context occurred when, during the first three decades of the twentieth century, city bar associations established legal aid societies to provide free or inexpensive legal services for those unable to afford attorneys. Because, in several cities, a significant proportion of the clients for legal aid societies were borrowers trapped by loanshark debts, local bar associations were sometimes drawn into campaigns against loansharks. In Chicago, for instance, a Legal Aid Society was established in 1905 and, in its first eleven years, received 2,617 complaints against chattel lenders and 4,059 complaints against salary lenders.[17]

Campaigns against loansharks had three goals: to assist those persons already in debt, to drive out the salary lenders, and finally to provide legal sources of small loans so that borrowers would no longer be dependent upon loansharks. In important respects, the campaign against loansharks involved a questioning of previous attitudes toward indebtedness. Opponents of loansharks argued that borrowing by persons of modest means was often necessary to tide a family over temporary crises and that indebtedness was not evidence of moral failure. The reason for usurious salary lending, they maintained, was the existence of a market for small loans. The solution to the problem was to provide legal, adequately regulated sources of small loans at rates that were reasonable for the borrower yet profitable for the lender. Because loanshark opponents stressed the legitimacy of borrowing, their campaigns contributed to the process by which America changed from a society of frugal producers to a society of borrowers and consumers.[18]

Campaigns against loansharks were fought on several fronts. In many cities businessmen attempted to persuade their fellow employers not to fire employees found to be in debt, for such a policy did not prevent employees from borrowing but, ironically, made the employers unintended collectors for loanshark debts. In a number of cities, local district attorneys undertook campaigns to prosecute salary lenders on criminal charges for violation of usury laws.[19] The attempts at prosecution often disclosed the weaknesses of usury laws and thus triggered efforts to strengthen them. Many wrestled with the problem that wage assignments were often used to circumvent usury laws. A few states passed laws to forbid wage assignments. Others tried some form of regulation: for instance, a requirement that a wage assignment not be legal unless approved by the borrower's spouse or employer.[20] In a number of cities, charitable organizations or legal aid societies provided legal representation for borrowers entangled in debts or faced with suits.

Campaigns to combat salary lending were the most exciting and publicized strategy in the short run. In the long run, however, significant change resulted chiefly from laws designed to create alternative lending institutions. In this the Russell Sage Foundation provided crucial national leadership. The Foundation sponsored several careful and scholarly studies of the loanshark problem. Under its auspices, experts drafted a model small-loan act that would permit licensed institutions to offer small loans at rates high enough to earn a profit. The model act provided for a state body to license small lenders, forbade small loans by unlicensed institutions, required that the borrower receive a copy of all documents in the transaction, prohibited all charges other than the stated interest, and set a maximum interest rate. Studies soon suggested that a rate of 3% percent monthly was necessary for a profitable small loan business. Despite opposition from salary lenders, by 1933 twenty-seven states, mostly outside the South, had passed satisfactory small loan acts.[21]

In the 1910's and 1920's, then, a variety of small loan systems emerged in American cities. Corporations and labor unions established credit unions for their employees or members. Ethnic benevolent societies, especially among Jewish and Catholic immigrants, set up loan funds, on a profit-making or self-sustaining basis, to tide persons over temporary financial difficulties. Under the new small loan laws, a variety of licensed small loan companies developed. Chattel loan companies, for instance, often supported passage of model small loan acts and then became licensed lenders. In the same period, Morris Plan Banks—and analogous institutions—appeared in a number of cities. Finally, by the 1920's and 1930's commercial bankers, recognizing both the profitability and respectability of the small loan market, opened small loan departments. Gradually sources of credit became available for middle income groups, especially those with the highest incomes and most stable employment records.[22]

The interrelationships between government action and salary lending can be clarified somewhat by examining developments in New York and Chicago. Under New York's usury law at the turn of the century, the maximum allowable interest was six percent annually. Violation of the law was a misdemeanor. In the winter of 1903-1904, William Travers Jerome, a dynamic and reforming district attorney for Manhattan, brought charges against numerous salary lenders, forcing many to close and some to move their operations across the river to New Jersey. In 1904 the state legislature responded to the loanshark problem by passing a law to regulate wage assignments, chiefly by requiring that a copy of the wage assignment be given to the employer within three days of the signing. With salary lending now regulated, the law removed criminal penalties for salary lending. The unanticipated result was a revival of illegal salary lending in New York. Lenders easily circumvented the requirement that a copy of the wage assignment be filed promptly with the employer by having the borrower sign a power of attorney at the time the loan was negotiated. Then, if the borrower was delinquent, the lender would at that time sign a wage assignment on behalf of the borrower and serve it on the employer. The firm of H. A. Courtright used another system.

After a background investigation, a borrower (and three of his friends) signed powers of attorney, and the firm acted as agent for a loan that was purportedly transacted in Rhode Island and thus subject to Rhode Island rather than New York law. The check for the loan was sent from Providence and repayments were made by mail to Providence. If the borrower was late in making payments, the Coast Cities Collection Company, in New York, then proceeded against the borrower and his endorsers.[23]

New York was headquarters for the Russell Sage Foundation and for a variety of local and national reform groups. Investigations of New York loansharking continued and agitation for reform resulted in a 1914 act licensing and regulating small loan companies, including pawnbrokers, chattel lenders, and salary lenders. The law provided that licensed companies could make loans up to $200, with interest on the unpaid balance not to exceed two percent per month (three percent for pawnbrokers). The law permitted maximum additional charges of $1 on loans under $50 and $2 on loans over $50. The borrower had to be given a copy of the contract, stating the amount of the loan and the rate of interest. No power of attorney or confession of judgment could be taken from the borrower. Violations of the act, including operation as an unlicensed lender, were misdemeanors. The two-percent interest rate was too low, however, and did little to encourage small loan companies. This was not remedied until 1932, when a new law greatly strengthened the provisions of the 1914 law and also allowed three-percent interest per month on the unpaid balance under $300 and 2 1/2 percent on the unpaid balance under $150.[24]

In Illinois, by contrast, there were no criminal penalties for loans above the legal limit of seven percent annually. The only civil penalty, if the borrower went to court, was forfeiture of all interest (but not of the principal). Chicago was a major center for salary lending. By 1904 business leaders were concerned enough to sponsor a number of laws to regulate or forbid wage assignments. In 1905 the legislature passed a law, over fierce opposition of lobbyists for salary lenders, to regulate wage assignments by limiting them to six months from the time of assignment, requiring the concurrence of the borrower's spouse, and specifying that the employer be notified within three days of the agreement. But the law was overturned by the courts. Efforts by the city council to pass a licensing law were frustrated by the lack of legal authority to regulate lending activities. But in 1911 the corporation council announced that the city would no longer recognize wage assignments filed against city employees. Finally, in 1913, the state legislature passed a law to license companies lending money on wage assignments. Licensed companies could make loan loans up to $250 with an interest not to exceed three percent per month and no other charges "upon any pretext whatsoever." The borrower was to receive a copy of the agreement and was to receive receipts for all payments. Then in 1917 the state passed a general law, based on the model small loan act, licensing lenders making loans up to $300. Under this act, interest was not to exceed 3 1/2 percent per month on the unpaid balance; there were to be no other charges; the borrower was to receive copies of the contract and receipts for payments, and the lender was forbidden to receive a power of attorney or confession of judgment. Violations of the act had criminal and civil penalties.[25]

As a result of the small loan acts in New York, Illinois, and other states, salary lenders could no longer threaten court action to collect loans and were easily subject to prosecution as unlicensed lenders. By the late 1930's and 1940's, they remained active chiefly in the southern states, extending from Florida and the Carolinas to Texas, where small loan acts had not yet been passed. Here the relationships of salary lenders and lower courts remained strong, while the movement to pass the model small loan act generally faltered. The interstate chains of salary lenders now located their headquarters in cities like Atlanta, Miami, Memphis, and Dallas. In the South, campaigns against salary lending, completed in other states ten or twenty years earlier, still remained to be fought out.[26]

Although model small loan laws gradually drove out illegal salary lenders, the new legal lending institutions did not, as had been expected, meet the needs of persons desiring small, short-term loans—the group serviced earlier by illegal salary lenders. Despite the fact that in many states lenders were permitted to charge a "profitable" interest rate of 3 1/2 percent monthly, lenders faced declining profits, brought on by the inflationary pressures of the 1920's and by the risks of making loans for personal needs. Licensed small lenders, however, were specifically forbidden to adopt profit-maximizing strategies of earlier salary lenders, such as penalty and service fees, chain debt tactics, or higher interest rates. Instead, an increase in the average size of loans became the chief method by which lending companies could protect profits. As a result, the average size of a legal small loan in Massachusetts rose from $26 in 1915 to $150 in 1931; average loans in New Jersey grew from $55 to

$240 in the same period; and in Illinois average size increased from $89 in 1918 to $149 in 1931. The upward shift was made possible, in part, by servicing a newly-created, somewhat more affluent class of borrowers who desired larger loans and had the financial stability to make repayments. Emergence of the new class of borrowers reflected, in turn, a continued breakdown during the 1920's of traditional moral obstacles against borrowing money for consumer purposes. Because the needs of small borrowers were often unmet by legal lenders, the small loan market remained in major cities; and this market came gradually to be serviced by a new type of illegal lender: the racketeer loanshark.[27]

Racketeer Loansharking

Unfortunately, little is known about the origins of racketeer loansharking, except that it apparently first appeared in New York City in the 1920's. Outside New York's metropolitan region, there is little evidence of systematic racketeer loansharking until the 1950's.[28] It is not clear why such a profitable enterprise should require fifteen years to diffuse. By the late 1950's, however, loan- sharking was a standard part of the profit-making activities of crime syndicates in major cities across the country.

The origins of racketeer loansharking doubtless were rooted in certain informal lending activities that existed during the heyday of salary lending. A few salary lenders, for instance, operated on their own, and provided loans to employees of a particular firm or factory. Instead of the formal system of an office and a background investigation, such lenders often had personal acquaintance with borrowers and relied upon informal connections within the factory or with a local justice for making collections.[29] More important, no doubt, was the sporadic involvement of criminals in lending operations. As early as the turn of the century, Arnold Rothstein, eventually a leading New York gambler and reputedly the fixer of the 1919 baseball World Series, was a source of credit for bettors at crap games. He used the services of Monk Eastman's gang as enforcers for the collection of debts. There is also evidence to suggest that at least one group of Brooklyn bootleggers provided illegal loans for local businessmen, as well as bettors, by the mid-1920's.[30] Such lending, in its informality or its use of violence, foreshadowed the eventual rise of racketeer loansharking.

Not until the early 1930's did racketeer loansharks develop the small loan market to consumers that had been serviced by salary lenders. This development in New York was an important transition from the salary lending of the early twentieth century to the syndicate-controlled operations of present day. During the 1930's[,] significant changes took place in the social background of the loanshark entrepreneurs, the nature of the lending market itself, the method of collecting delinquent accounts, and, finally, the social setting in which illegal lending transactions occurred. While some of these changes reached a considerable degree of maturity, others were still in embryonic stages at the end of the decade. The evidence is not available to write a history of the development of racketeer loansharking in American cities. But an examination of early racketeer loansharking in New York, and of later loansharking in Chicago, can suggest a number of hypotheses concerning the origins and economics of the enterprise.

New York in the 1930's

On January 16, 1935, the *New York Times* reported that, as part of his extensive rackets investigation as special prosecutor, Dewey's office was examining loanshark activity in Manhattan's financial district. The investigation was prompted by an incident two weeks earlier in which a twenty-year-old clerk was beaten near his place of employment by collection agents of loansharks operating in the Wall Street section of the city. The reason for the beating—failure to meet a $6 interest payment on a $10 loan—suggested that an important change had taken place in the practice of illegal lending.[31] As had been true of salary lending, the incident involved a borrower who held a steady, low-salaried position. Also, the loan remained small and the interest charges high. What had changed was the collection mechanism: the use of violence, or the threat of violence, emerged as a standard collection procedure.[32]

For the next nine months the investigation became a nearly forgotten issue. On October 28th, however, Dewey arrested twenty-seven individuals for loansharking activities.[33] Dewey's dramatic raid touched off a wave of arrests by three other law enforcement agencies as well.[34] Also, a growing concern over widespread loansharking among government employees led to special internal investigations within the city's WPA projects, the post office, and city government.[35] By late January 1937, nearly one hundred persons had been arrested. Many were charged with violating the 1932 small-loan act: lending money without a license and charging usurious interest rates. The rest—individuals whom the authorities believed to be collection agents (sluggers) for some of the loansharks—were charged with vagrancy. Finally, a large proportion of both groups also faced charges of extortion and assault.[36]

In commenting on Dewey's arrests, Rolf Nugent, Director of the Remedial Loans Department of the Russell Sage Foundation, offered several observations. Although in the past loansharks were "fearful of the law," recent loanshark enterprises were "carried on in large part by criminals who belong to the worst element in New York gangdom." According to Nugent, "the entrance of criminals into the small loan field has occurred within the last two years and most rapidly within the last six months." He concluded that the repeal of prohibition in 1933 probably made the money lending business an opportune field for investment by former bootleggers.[37]

A study of the 100 persons arrested for involvement in racketeer loansharking shows that Nugent's ideas were suggestive but need some elaboration.[38] A disproportionate number of the racketeer loansharks and their collection agents were of Italian or Eastern European Jewish descent. For the most part, they were relatively young men. Their ages ranged from nineteen to forty-five, with an overwhelming number falling between the ages of twenty-four and thirty-six. Because of their youth, it is difficult to determine their previous occupational career. Yet, for those who held down a legitimate job, a common characteristic was evident. Most of the employed racketeer loansharks were engaged in service-oriented occupations: cigar and candy stand operators, payroll office clerks, and a variety of municipal jobs. Finally, a number exhibited a past history of arrests, especially for such street crimes as burglary, larceny and felonious assault. This was particularly true for those individuals who served as collection agents.

That so many of the loansharks and collectors were young men from the city's Italian and Jewish slums meant that they shared a similar background with those who dominated New York bootlegging in the 1920's and were active in gambling and other criminal enterprises. But it is less clear that the money lent on the streets was invested by ex-bootleggers. Despite Dewey's efforts to link Manhattan loanshark activities to such notable bootleggers as Arthur Flegenheimer (Dutch Schultz) and Charles "Lucky" Luciano, or to labor racketeers such as Louis "Lepke" Buchalter and Jacob "Gurrah Jake" Shapiro, he never produced evidence to prove such a connection.[39]

Law enforcement agencies in the Bronx, and especially in Brooklyn, proved more successful in linking racketeer loansharks to local underworld leaders and to other types of illegal enterprises. The Anti-Racket Bureau of the state Attorney General's office uncovered a loansharking operation in the Bronx in which one of the key figures was a former policy collector for the late Dutch Schultz.[40] In Brooklyn, the District Attorney's office discovered a loanshark racket that not only lent money at usurious rates but also operated race track handbooks and crap games, as well as a protection racket victimizing small businessmen.[41] But more importantly, Brooklyn detectives exposed an illegal lending operation—an enterprise that received $1,500 per week in interest from loans to BMT employees—in which the arrested individuals were all members of the Abe Reles-Bugsy Goldstein ring. The *New York Times* reported that this ring served as agents in the Brownsville and East New York section for the Amberg brothers.[42]

A closer look at the origins of the Reles-Goldstein loansharking suggests that a strong association existed, almost a decade before Dewey's prosecutions, between the illegal lending of money and other illegal enterprises, particularly bootlegging. At age twenty, Reles and Harry Maione, also a leader of a youth gang but in the Ocean Hill district of Brooklyn, were hired as collectors for the Amberg brothers' loanshark operations. According to one source, Louis Amberg employed Reles and Maione to make collections when he began experiencing difficulty in collecting interest payments from delinquent borrowers. The Ambergs were major figures in Brooklyn's underworld during the 1920's and early 1930's. After careers in burglary and robbery, they made bootlegging a new source of income when they forcibly became silent partners with a long established, Brownsville brewery. The Ambergs employed members of the Reles and Maione gangs as beer watchers for the speakeasies they serviced and as guards for their beer trucks, as well as collectors in loansharking. In their roles as sluggers, Reles, Maione, and other members of their gangs acquired a first hand knowledge of loansharking and of the functions of violence in certain illegal enterprises.[43]

Beginning in 1931 and ending some time in 1935, a series of murders helped to elevate Reles and Maione, along with other members of their gang—Phil "Bugsy" Goldstein, "Pittsburgh" Phil Strauss, and Frank Abbandondo—from the status of sluggers to that of entrepreneurs with interests in loansharking, pinball machines, and numbers gambling in the Brownsville district. (Their continued involvement in homicide, though, earned them the name of "Murder, Inc.," when they were finally prosecuted successfully at the end of the decade.) In 1940, Brooklyn's District Attorney, William O'Dwyer, estimated the group's return from loansharking alone at $35,000 per week.[44]

Throughout the 1930's, racketeer loansharks in Manhattan and Brooklyn serviced the traditional small loan market formerly serviced by salary lenders. One survey, reported in the *New York Times* during the Dewey prosecutions, estimated that perhaps 50,000 New Yorkers were borrowing small sums of money from an illegal enterprise that involved over 2,000 loansharks and collectors.[45] As in earlier salary lending operations, the small loan market consisted of upper blue-collar workers and lower white-collar workers—individuals with small salaried positions and a steady source of income. According to another source, many individuals who borrowed from the Brooklyn group "included hundreds of civilian employees at the Navy Yard, transportation and building workers, WPA workers, and housewives."[46] When state laws made salary lending no longer possible, therefore, the market was not entirely absorbed by the new legal lending institutions. The continuation of the market provided the economic basis for new groups to undertake loansharking operations. But, because the small-loan laws made the pretense of legality almost impossible, the new loansharks had to employ the more direct mechanism of violence for collection.

Although in Manhattan prosecutors exposed primarily the traditional, small-loan market, this was not the case in Brooklyn. There prosecutors uncovered two other markets: local businessmen who were unable to secure loans from legitimate sources and bettors in local, floating crap games. The small businessmen market, for example, proved to be an extremely profitable venture; by 1938 over $400,000 had been accumulated from this market.[47] Sam "Dapper" Siegel managed the Brownsville group's local small businessmen's market. Siegel operated from a Brownsville candy store owned by his mother, Rose Gold. While violence was often employed when borrowers became delinquent in their payments, the actual negotiation of the loan and its conditions for repayment were more respectable and legitimate in character. First the loan would be negotiated in the candy store. Then a check for the amount to be lent would be made out to the borrower, drawn on the account of Rose Gold. Before receiving the check, the customer provided Siegel with post-dated checks for six successive weeks, which totaled the amount of the loan plus the illegal interest. Thus, if the borrower missed a payment, he was accused of passing a bad check.[48]

The bettor's market, on the other hand, was managed by Louis "Tiny" Benson. (Predictably, "Tiny" Benson weighed over 400 pounds.) The night before each crap game, Benson would receive $10,000 in cash from Reles to be used for lending purposes. While little else is known about the structure of this market, it should be noted that many of the crap losers included respectable neighborhood businessmen.[49]

Thus, in a number of respects, the Brownsville-Ocean Hill group foreshadowed the type of racketeer loansharking that has become characteristic of American cities. Not only were these individuals closely linked to the syndicate that coordinated much of the gambling and other illegal enterprises in the Brooklyn area, but, equally important, the group developed two distinct markets for their loanshark operations. While some of their agents handled the more traditional small loan market of salaried workers with steady jobs, other agents provided illegal loans, generally larger and at a higher risk, to businessmen and bettors at crap games. The development of the second market was a significant departure from earlier salary lending practices. At the same time, the high-risk market of the Brooklyn group was limited and seldom extended beyond the range of their neighborhood contacts and influence.

Finally, the social setting in which illegal lenders transacted their business was also transformed during the 1930's. For many of the Manhattan loansharks, and even the Brooklyn agents who serviced the traditional small loan market, their work situation proved a strong influence upon their lending operations. Their occupations sometimes involved daily contact with a large number of people—people they would see on a regular basis while providing for their legitimate needs.[50] Such a work situation, at the very least, made potential borrowers regular acquaintances of the loanshark. Also many racketeer loansharks were actual coworkers of their customers.[51] Such a relationship provided the illegal money lender with a personal estimation of his customer's financial status, borrowing needs, and repayment potential. Like the earlier salary lenders, it was common practice for a loanshark to limit his lending to postal employees, the workers on a particular relief work project, or employees of one of the city's municipal institutions. The social environment of the work situation tended to personalize the loansharking operation, making informal networks of communication and social associations important. The informality with which many of the racketeer loansharks conducted their business differed sharply from the salary lender's more formal, semi-respectable, and quasi-legitimate operation.

Chicago in the 1950's

In Chicago in the 1950's, racketeer loansharking—or the juice racket, as it was called—developed in ways that have become characteristic of a number of American cities.[52] To begin with, loansharking enterprises were generally backed or operated by entrepreneurs linked to the syndicate that coordinated various gambling and other illegal enterprises in the metropolitan region. Indeed, the initial financing of Chicago racketeer loansharking was apparently by gambling entrepreneurs. This development, of course, was foreshadowed by the sorts of persons who pioneered much of the racketeer loansharking in New York City twenty years earlier. Secondly, two types of racketeer loanshark specialties prevailed. While some loansharks continued to handle small loans for employees in factories, the garment district, and similar traditional loanshark markets[;] others serviced a market of relatively large loans to persons who were, in general, poor credit risks. This, too, had been foreshadowed, particularly in the Brooklyn loansharking of the 1930's.

The high-risk market for relatively large loans included three major groups. One group consisted of bettors unable to cover their losses in high-stakes games. Decisions concerning credit and collection of debts had long been a problem for gambling entrepreneurs who, because of the illegality of their operations, could not use legal collection methods. In the 1950's some gamblers, especially operators of crap games, solved the problem by referring a debtor to a loanshark. As a result, the gambling operator received his money, and the loanshark specialized in collection in return for normal loanshark profits. To the extent that the gambling operator and loanshark were partners or had the same financial backers, the enterprise now profited both from the gambling and the usurious loan. A second market consisted of thieves, bookmakers, and other criminals, whose occupations were characterized by periods of relative prosperity alternating with periods of need. As money lenders to criminals, loansharks sometimes became underworld coordinators. Loans to thieves not only allowed loansharks to garner part of the profits of theft but sometimes put them in a position to profit further as fences for stolen goods. A third market involved the small- or medium-sized businessman faced with a cash flow crisis and unable or unwilling to secure loans through legitimate channels. Failure to repay such a loan sometimes resulted in the loanshark's becoming an owner or partner in the legitimate business.

The various large loan markets—so different from the safer, small-loan markets serviced earlier by the salary lenders and by most racketeer loansharks in New York in the 1930's—were high-profit, high-risk ventures. Because of the high risks, development of such markets was possible only with the institutionalization of the convincing use of force in loanshark collections. Furthermore, because management of high-risk loans required special knowledge and substantial time devoted to each loan, the lender handling high-risk loans was likely to be different from the lender in the garment district or factory who specialized in large numbers of small loans. Both, however, might sometimes have the same financial backers.

Unfortunately for historians, the juice racket in Chicago did not come to public attention until the early 1960's, so that the early story must be pieced together from later exposés.[53] Nevertheless, an examination of those who were important juice racketeers by the early 1960's and thus were leaders in the pioneering days of the 1950's reveals many shared characteristics. They derived from Italian or Jewish backgrounds and had been raised in the city's lower-class, ethnic neighborhoods. Born generally between 1912 and 1917 and therefore teenagers during the final years of prohibition, they were too young to be bootleggers. In their late teens and twenties, they built impressive police records for burglary, robbery and crimes of violence. While they were no doubt known to syndicate leaders in the 1930's because of their local reputations and their roots in the same neighborhoods, their careers were in street crime rather than syndicate enterprises. At some point in the late 1930's and 1940's, most of the future leaders in the juice racket served long prison terms. When they emerged from prison in the 1940's at a stage in the life cycle when street crime had lost its attractiveness, they moved into "organized crime" activities as members of gambling syndicates and as enforcers. Thus their movement into the juice rackets in the 1950's derived from their background in violence and their emerging connections with syndicate backers.[54]

Sam DeStefano was reputedly the most important figure in developing the juice racket for thieves and businessmen in the 1950's. Born about 1909, he was a member of the famous Forty-Two Gang of youthful criminals on Chicago's near West Side in the 1920's. In 1927 he received a three-year sentence for the gang rape of a seventeen-year-old girl. In 1932 he was shot during an attempted burglary and the next year went to prison until 1944 for the robbery of a Wisconsin bank. In 1947 he was back in federal prison on a one-year sentence for peddling counterfeit sugar rationing stamps. Upon his release, now entering middle age, he settled down in a civil service job (city dump foreman) and pioneered the juice racket on the West Side. He was a major figure in the juice racket until April 1973, when his shotgun slaying was recorded as the city's 1,019th gangland slaying since 1919.[55]

Much of the information concerning the early years derives from Charles Crimaldi. He started working for DeStefano in 1955 after release from the state penitentiary on a burglary charge, left DeStefano's operation in 1968, and turned state's evidence in 1971. As Crimaldi described his position with DeStefano, it was routine: "The thought in your life was to go out, put money out, collect money, catch this guy, give him a beating if he deserves it. You look at everything as a potential score." Even before their association, Crimaldi knew DeStefano's street reputation as "just a well organized hood, a crazy man." Among his associates it was believed that DeStefano killed his own brother (an addict) in a Cicero joint and participated in the killing of William "Action" Jackson in 1961. The Jackson killing was notorious: he was hoisted onto a meat hook, tortured with an ice pick, cattle prod, and blow torch, and killed by being beaten with a baseball bat before being shot.[56]

From the beginning of his juice racket activities, according to Crimaldi, DeStefano had ties with top syndicate figures. In the 1950's, on a social basis, he played gin rummy Sunday mornings with Tony Accardo, Joey Glimco (a labor racketeer), and Jackie Cerone at Accardo's suburban home. Politically, he did favors for the syndicate-dominated First Ward Democratic organization and thus had important political influence. His relations with the police were sufficiently friendly that, Crimaldi claimed, policemen sometimes brought loansharks to DeStefano's house rather than the police station after an arrest. Although it appears that higher syndicate figures, like Accardo, were partners in DeStefano's loansharking and received a percentage of the profits, it is probable that the initial money did not come from Accardo but rather from a West Side gambler with whom DeStefano launched the loansharking operation. What DeStefano demonstrated in the 1950's was that, with sufficient energy and convincing use of force, loans to thieves and small businessmen could yield high profits. Indeed, only someone with DeStefano's street knowledge of Chicago thieves, along with his reputation for violence, could make possible the profitable development of that market.[57]

Concurrently with DeStefano's operations, others developed the loan market among bettors at syndicate gambling games. By the late 1940's or early 1950's, according to later newspaper accounts, Moishe Baer (also known as Morris Saletko) was not only a Loop gambler but was allegedly lending money at usurious interest rates to losers in the games. He continued to develop the operation, so that by the 1960's newspaper stories reported that Baer was running an extensive juice racket for syndicate dice and other gambling games.[58] It is possible, then, that initially the market for loans to bettors developed relatively independent from the market for thieves and businessmen. There was one factor, however, that both had in common: they apparently received their initial financial backing from gambling profits.

Although the juice racket in the 1950's was coordinated by persons with ties to leading syndicate figures, much of the early development depended upon individual initiative by middle level figures. Because of the high profitability of the juice racket, it was characterized by rapid growth and proliferation of a number of relatively independent enterprises. By the early 1960's, however, syndicate leaders began to establish somewhat greater coordination to what they increasingly saw as a profitable line of investment for themselves.

For instance, there apparently was a policy of extending and coordinating the traditional small loan market. One news story in 1964 claimed that in West Side factories, men who formerly had been walking bookmakers were switching to loansharking. The backers of bookmaking, in short, had decided that juice was more profitable and were transferring their investments from horse betting to loansharking.[59] There was also evidence of increasing coordination of the large loan market. A news story, again in 1964, reported that the leading backers of the juice racket had opened a central "credit bureau" to which each loanshark was to report loans made. One purpose was to protect loansharks from customers who attempted to borrow from one shark to pay off another, as well as to provide information on the creditworthiness of prospective borrowers. Furthermore, considerable evidence suggested that top figures in the syndicate increasingly attempted to allocate territories, expand those loansharking operations in which they had directly invested money at the expense of other operations, and in other ways become more actively involved in coordinating what remained a decentralized activity.[60]

Conclusion

Despite crucial differences between salary lenders and the later racketeer loansharks, there were similarities that stemmed from the fact that both groups sought profits by lending money at illegal rates of interest. First of all, both types of loansharking have generally been limited to urban areas. Loansharking apparently requires a minimum population before there will be enough borrowers to make such an enterprise profitable.[61]

Secondly, the attempt to extract maximum profits from an unregulated lending enterprise created a number of common strategies, especially among the more unscrupulous loansharks of the earlier and later periods. Normally loans were for a short period of time and the interest computed on a weekly or bi-weekly basis. Often the lender, preferring that the borrower not repay the principal, manipulated the loan into a "chain debt" in which interest payments continued for months or years while the principal remained outstanding. Furthermore, both salary lenders and racketeer loansharks attempted to milk the borrower through additional charges of various sorts: including fees at the time of the original loan and substantial additional charges whenever the borrower became delinquent. For the salary lender, who hoped to profit while avoiding the ultimate sanction of a lawsuit, and for the racketeer loanshark, who hoped to profit while avoiding the ultimate sanction of violence, techniques for extracting maximum profit from the loan were often quite similar.

Despite similarities, there were important changes that occurred over time. The salary lending business came into existence at a time when the increasing scale of both business and government resulted in large organizations with numerous clerical and skilled blue-collar workers. These employees, with their steady but marginal salaries and their frequent need for extra funds to tide them over life's normal exigencies, constituted the primary market for small loans serviced by salary lenders. They constituted the primary market chiefly because they were good credit risks. In part, this resulted from the scale of the organizations in which they worked. To begin with, such organizations often impersonally promulgated employee rules, such as the rule that an employee would be fired if he was in debt or had his salary attached—and these rules could be known to salary lenders. Such information could not have been available if a salary lender dealt, instead, with employees of hundreds of small concerns. Furthermore, because of job security in large firms and, no doubt, the hope to advance within the ranks of a large organization, borrowers were committed to retaining their jobs and thus would undertake considerable financial sacrifice to avoid being fired. Moreover, the separate payroll departments of large organizations meant, for some salary lenders, that they could find payroll clerks willing to assist in screening applicants for loans and even in collecting the debts. Finally, the set salary scales and regular paydays simplified the scheduling of repayments of loans. There developed, then, a symbiotic relationship between the small-time, illegal salary lender and the employees of the society's most advanced institutions.

This relationship, as noted earlier, was shaped and made possible by contemporary attitudes and laws with regard to consumption borrowing. Because respectable opinion frowned upon borrowing for consumption, borrowers often felt uncomfortable about their loans and would scrimp to make payments in order to avoid having the loan become public knowledge. The same attitudes also served as part of the justification for the policy by employers to fire employees in debt. Ironically, then, the attitudes toward borrowing created a situation in which the salary lender's strongest sanction was a threat to reveal the loan. Beyond this, usury laws in effect outlawed small lending—but did so ineffectively. In many states, neither criminal nor civil penalties for illegal lending were sufficient to provide deterrence, so that illegal lenders operated quite openly.

Yet both law and attitudes eventually changed. Particularly important was the passage in many states of model small loan acts. For reformers, the goal of the model act was to drive out loansharks by providing legal sources of small loans, thereby destroying the loanshark market. But, as the development of racketeer loansharking amply demonstrated, the variety of legitimate lending institutions did not satisfy the market for small loans, so that the model acts did not destroy loansharking but caused it to take on a new form. Paradoxically, the model acts drove out salary lending not by destroying the market but rather by undercutting the legal tools of the salary lender. As unlicensed lenders, they were easily subject to criminal prosecution and could no longer use the courts as a last resort for collecting delinquent debts. By the 1930's, in states that had passed the model small loan act, a market for small loans remained, but loansharking could continue only with new collection mechanisms.

The introduction of violence, then, was a watershed in the history of illegal lending. It meant that persons from different backgrounds and with different relations to customers would emerge. Nevertheless, racketeer loansharking in New York in the mid-1930's represented an initial stage in such developments. The social backgrounds of racketeer loansharks differed from salary lenders in ethnicity, as well as the ties that some racketeer loansharks had to various sorts of crime. The social environment in which transactions took place became more informal and personalized, both for the small loans to employees and the new high-risk loans to businessmen and bettors.

The earlier salary lender had the advantage over the racketeer loanshark in that the salary lender could front as a legitimate businessman, could publicly advertise, and could even use the courts for collection. But there were also advantages to the informality of the racketeer loanshark, especially in competing with legal, small-loan institutions that came into existence as salary lending declined. From the racketeer loanshark a borrower could receive the loan without the hassles of filling out forms, waiting for a credit check, and confronting a perhaps formidable bureaucracy. Despite the ultimate sanction of violence, the racketeer loanshark offered his customers immediate cash, in a secret transaction, right in the local bar or on the job.

To the extent that Chicago was typical, it appears that racketeer loansharking reached maturity in the early 1960's. Two characteristics, both of which had their beginnings in New York of the 1930's, had reached fuller development by the 1960's. First, the distinction between the traditional small-loan market and the high-risk market, already apparent in the operations of the Reles-Goldstein ring in Brooklyn, became more systematized. Although there was considerable continuity in the small-loan market in the transition from salary lenders to racketeer loansharks, the high-risk markets were not available to salary lenders. Thieves, as well as high rollers in gambling games and small businessmen, were not likely to fear being fired if their debts were revealed, nor were they likely to be intimidated by the legal forms used in salary lending. But once loansharks had institutionalized violence as the ultimate collection tool, such new markets could be developed systematically.

The second sign of maturity was a movement toward increased coordination of loansharking within the city. As the profitability of loansharking became clear, major syndicate figures invested their own money in the various loansharking enterprises. With their growing investments went a growing involvement in approving large loans, participating in decisions about the use of violence, and, by other means, providing some coordination to the enterprises. By the 1960's, the scale and coordination surpassed that of the relatively freelance racketeer loansharking of the 1930's in New York or of the 1950's in Chicago. As lenders to the underworld and to certain types of small business, racketeer loansharks played a role in the economics of the city that little resembled that of salary lenders in the early twentieth century.

Notes

1. Louis N. Robinson and Rolf Nugent, *Regulation of the Small Loan Business* (1935), pp. 28-52; William R. Patterson, "Pawnbroking in Europe and the United States" in *Bulletin of the Department of Labor, No.* 21 (Government Printing Office: Washington, D.C., March 1899), pp. 173-310; Chicago *Tribune,* Feb. 5, 1885, p. 8. For arguments favoring usury laws, see John Whipple, *Stringent Usury Laws, the Best Defense against "Hard Times"* (1880; reprinted often since original printing in 1836).

2. Quotations from Earle Edward Eubank, "Loan Shark Number," *Bulletin of the Department of Public Welfare, City of Chicago,* Department Serial no. 5, v. 1, no. 4 (1916), pp. 44, 49, 52, 60. On New York see "Crowding Shylock out of Business," *The Outlook,* v. 109 (Feb. 24, 1916), 416; James H. Collins, "Divorcing Your Uncle," *McClure's,* v. 47 (July 1916), 8; Frank M. White, "The Story of a Debt," *World's Work,* v. 23 (Jan. 1912), 349-51. On Boston, see " 'Licensed Extortion' by the Loansharks," *The Survey,* v. 36 (April 8, 1916), 49; on Washington, see "Loan Sharks Crossing the Potomac," *The Survey,* v. 21 (Oct. 11, 1913), 43. On reasons for borrowing, see Clarence W. Wassam's excellent study, *The Salary Loan Business in New York City* (1908), ch. 3; also Clarence Hodson, *Money Lenders, License Laws and the Business of Making Small Loans on Unsecured Notes, Chattel Mortgages, Salary Assignments: A Handbook* (1919), pp. 53-76.

3. Eubank, *op. cit. supra* note 2, at pp. 12-13. For locations in New York City, see "The Loan Shark, the Scourge of the Deep Waters of City Life," *Harper's Weekly,* v. 52 (May 2, 1908), 22.

4. Quotation from Baxter Ware, "The Lure of the Loan Shark," *Harper's Weekly,* v. 52 (July 11, 1908), 32; see also J. M. Oskinson, "John Smith Borrows $20," *Collier's,* v. 43 (Sept. 4, 1909), 14 and 34; and esp. Wassam, *op. cit. supra* note 2, at ch. 7.

5. Quotation from Roswell C. McCrea, "Small Finance and the Wage-Earner," 107 *Yale Law Rev.* 434 (Feb. 1909). On women as managers, see *op. cit. supra* note 3, at p. 14; Oskinson, *op. cit. supra* note 4, at p. 14. On general finances of a salary loan office, see Wassam, *op. cit. supra* note 2, at ch. 6; also Robinson & Nugent, *op. cit. supra* note 1, at pp. 61-62.

6. Quotation from Oskinson, *op. cit. supra* note 4. On Tolman, see Robinson and Nugent, *op. cit. supra* note 1, at p. 47; Eubank, *op. cit. supra* note 2, at p. 18; "Salary Loans in Cincinnati," *Charities and Commons,* v. 21 (Jan. 2, 1909), 500; J. M. Oskinson, "Exploiters of the Needy," *Collier's* v. 44 (Oct. 2, 1909), 17-18, 38; Chicago *Record-Herald,* Sept. 26, 1909, p. 3; "Jail and Exemplary Damages for Loan Sharks," *The Survey,* v. 21 (Jan. 31, 1914), 512.

7. Ware, *op. cit. supra* note 4, at p. 32; Wassam, *op. cit. supra* note 2, at p. 59; Chicago *Record-Herald,* Nov. 12, 1908, p. 7, Nov. 13, 1908, p. 7, and Jan. 25, 1911, p. 7. In Chicago, probably by the 1890's, the city's loansharks funded a central credit bureau to keep records on all borrowers; see Chicago *Record-Herald,* Nov. 11, 1908, p. 9; Eubank, *op. cit. supra* note 2, at p. 21.

8. Wassam, *op. cit. supra* note 2, at pp. 14, 52-54, & *passim;* Ware, *op. cit. supra* note 4, at p. 32.

9. Robinson and Nugent, *op. cit. supra* note 1, at pp. 57-58; Wassam, *op. cit. supra* note 2, at p. 32.

10. Wassam, *op. cit. supra* note 2, at p. 59; Chicago *Record-Herald,* June 6, 1904.

11. For instance, Wassam, *op. cit. supra* note 2, at pp. 55-56; "Salary Loan Business in New York," *Charities and Commons,* v. 21 (Nov. 14, 1908), 274.

12. Frank Marshall White, "The Fine Art of Borrowing," *Harper's Weekly,* v. 54 (April 2, 1910), 16; Chicago *Record-Herald,* June 6, 1904, p. 3, and Feb. 4, 1912, p. 6; White, *op. cit. supra* note 2, at p. 349.

13. Eubank, *op. cit. supra* note 2, at p. 18.

14. See a novel by Forest Halsey, *The Bawlerout* (1912); also White, *op. cit. supra* note 2, at p. 346.

15. For instance, "Courts Coming to See Real Guilt," *The Survey,* v. 27 (Feb. 10, 1912), 1729-30; Chicago *Record-Herald,* June 6, 1904, p. 3, and Aug. 14, 1910, p. 3. For a later period, see Lawrence Dumas, Jr., *Two Anti-Loan Shark Drives* (Junior Bar Conference of the American Bar Assoc., 1945), esp. pp. 41-42; John A. Johnson, A *Survey of Personal Finance Conditions in Oklahoma* (Junior Bar Conference of the American Bar Assoc., 1942-43), p. 16.

16. For example, Eubank, *op. cit. supra* note 2, at p. 6; *Report* of the Operations of the Citizens Permanent Relief Committee of Philadelphia in Relieving Distress in the City during the Winter of 1893-94, cited in Robinson and Nugent, *op. cit. supra* note 1, at pp. 48-53.

17. Eubank, *op. cit. supra* note 2, at pp. 12 and 24; see also Dumas, *op. cit. supra* note 15, at pp. 11-14.

18. For statements of the philosophy, see Arthur H. Ham, *The Campaign against the Loan Shark* (Pamphlet: Russell Sage Foundation, n.d.); Arthur M. Murphy, "Small Loan Usury," in Ernest D. MacDougall, ed., *Crime for Profit: A Symposium on Mercenary Crime* (1933), pp. 205-226; William Trufant Foster, *Loan Sharks and their Victims,* Public Affairs Pamphlet, No. 39 (1940).

An excellent history of the movement for reform is an unpublished book, Herbert J. Bass and Robert P. Shay, "Arthur Morris and the Consumer Credit Revolution."

19. Robinson and Nugent, *op. cit. supra* note 1, at pp. 43-54; Walter Prichard Eaton, "A Poor Man's Bank," *American Magazine,* v. 77 (Feb. 1914), 71; Arthur H. Ham, "Remedial Loan Movement," *The Survey,* v. 24 (Aug. 27, 1910), 734-35; "Millionaire Loan Shark Behind Bars," *The Survey,* v. 27 (Feb. 10, 1912), 1728-29.

20. For summary of laws by 1908, see Wassam, *op. cit. supra* note 2, at ch. 8. Also "To Control Loan Sharks in Illinois," *Charities and Commons,* v. 21 (Dec. 12, 1908), 407-408; "New York Sharks under Brooks Law," *The Survey,* v. 27 (Oct. 7, 1911), 920-921; Arthur H. Ham, "Proposed Remedial Loan Legislation for 1915," *The Survey,* v. 33 (Feb. 27, 1915), 574.

21. John M. Glenn, Lilian Brandt, and F. Emerson Andrews, *Russell Sage Foundation, 1907-1946* (1947), v. 1, ch. 12, and v. 2, ch. 36; Hodson, *op. cit. supra* note 2, at pp. 20ff; Robinson and Nugent, *op. cit. supra* note 1 at chs. 5-7.

22. See esp. Bass and Shay, *op. cit. supra* note 18; also Chicago *Record-Herald,* Sept. 24, 1911, p. 8; Sept. 29, 1911, p. 8; and Feb. 28, 1912, p. 3; Collins, *op. cit. supra* note 2, at p. 55; Eaton, *op. cit. supra* note 19, at pp. 72-74; Eubank, *op. cit. supra* note 2, at pp. 36-38; "To Pull the Loan Shark's Teeth," *Literary Digest,* v. 48 (Jan. 17, 1914), 94.

23. *New York Laws,* 1879, ch. 538; *Laws of New York,* 1904, sec. 77; Wassam, *op. cit. supra* note 2, at pp. 52-56, 73-76; White, *op. cit. supra* note 2, at v. 23 (Jan. 1912), 352.

24. *New York Laws,* 1914, ch. 369; *Laws of New York,* 1932, ch. 399; *McKinney's Consolidated Laws of New York, Annotated,* Book 4 (Banking Laws), pp. 305-350. For later developments, see "Syndicate Loan Shark Activities and New York's Usury Law," 66 *Columbia Law Review* 167-177 (1966).

25. B. J. Schneider, "Usury as Related to Illinois Law," 4 *John Marshall Law Quarterly* 492-493, 502 (June 1939); Eubank, *op. cit. supra* note 2, at pp. 9, 34-35; *Laws of Illinois,* 1905, pp. 79-80; Chicago *Record-Herald,* Oct. 4, 1904, p. 6, Nov. 19, 1904, p. 8, Jan. 9, 1905, p. 2, Jan. 10, 1905, p. 3, Apr. 25, 1905, p. 8, Apr. 29, 1905, p. 4, Nov. 20, 1908, p. 9, Nov. 21, 1908, p. 10, Dec. 6, 1908, p. 4, Apr. 27, 1909, p. 8; *Laws of Illinois,* 1913, pp. 199-203; *Illinois Laws,* 1917, pp. 553-556; *Laws of Illinois,* 1933, pp. 674-677.

26. On salary lending in the 1930's and 1940's, see Committee in Aid of the Small Litigant, *A Survey of Personal Finance Conditions in Kansas* (Junior Bar Conference of the American Bar Assoc., 1943-44); Dumas, *op. cit. supra* note 15 (concerning Alabama); Johnson, *op. cit. supra* note 15; and Victor K. Meador, *Loan Sharks in Georgia* (Junior Bar Conference of the American Bar Assoc., 1947-48).

27. Robinson and Nugent, *op. cit. supra* note 1, at pp. 177-180.

28. Obviously, it is difficult to collect evidence that an activity did *not* exist, and this generalization is made with considerable trepidation.

29. Eubank, *op. cit. supra* note 2, at p. 17; Dumas, *op. cit. supra* note 15, at p. 26.

30. Leo Katcher, *The Big Bankroll: The Life and Times of Arnold Rothstein* (1958), pp. 22-23; Leo Katcher and Malcolm Logan, "The Story of a Gang. Part II: The Apprentice Stage," *New York Post,* April 9, 1940, p. 5.

31. *New York Times,* Jan. 16, 1935, p. 38; also Jan. 12, 1935, p. 15.

32. There is some evidence that loansharks shared the collection services of certain sluggers; see *New York Times,* Oct. 25, 1935, p. 17; Oct. 29, 1935, p. 2.

33. *New York Times,* Oct. 29, 1935, pp. 1-2; Nov. 3, 1935, p. 3; Dec. 3, 1935, p. 11; Dec. 4, 1935, p. 48; Dec. 5, 1935, p. 5; and Dec. 6, 1935, p. 8; Thomas E. Dewey, *Twenty against the Underworld,* ed. Rodney Campbell (1974), pp. 180-183.

34. *New York Times,* Feb. 2, 1935, p. 30; Nov. 1, 1935, p. 6; Nov. 10, 1935, p. 10; Nov. 16, 1935, p. 32; Nov. 22, 1935, p. 48; Nov. 24, 1935, p. 35; and Nov. 28, 1935, p. 35.

35. *New York Times,* Oct. 22, 1935, p. 4; Nov. 23, 1935, p. 2; Dec. 2, 1935, p. 3; Jan. 9, 1937, p. 19; Jan. 20, 1937, p. 6; March 11, 1937, pp. 1-2; June 7, 1938, p. 4; and Oct. 15, 1938, p. 19.

36. *New York Times,* Oct. 29, 1935, p. 2; Feb. 2, 1935, p. 30; Sep. 1, 1935, p. 6; Oct. 30, 1935, p. 4; Nov. 1, 1935, p. 6; Nov. 2, 1935, p. 34; Nov. 9, 1935, p. 32; Nov. 13, 1935, pp. 1 and 10; Nov. 15, 1935, p. 48; Nov. 16, 1935, p. 32; Nov. 22, 1935, p. 48; Nov. 23, 1935, p. 3; Nov. 24, 1935, p. 35; Nov. 30, 1935, p. 32; Dec. 3, 1935, p. 11; Jan. 11, 1936, p. 4; Jan. 31, 1936, p. 40; Feb. 12, 1936, p. 44; and March 6, 1936, p. 5.

37. *New York Times,* Oct. 29, 1935, p. 2.

38. Information on each of the individuals arrested for involvement in loansharking was obtained from the newspaper stories in the *New York Times* beginning January 12, 1935, and ending December 6, 1939. Also the 1932 city telephone directories for Manhattan-Bronx and Brooklyn were checked for address and occupation. For each individual, the following information was sought: ethnicity, age, alias, residence, occupation, career experiences and criminal record, association with alleged racketeers, and previous involvement in other types of illegal enterprises. With regard to loansharking, the information included: location of operation, function or position in the operation, type of borrower serviced, conditions of loan, method of collection, and source of capital to carry out lending transactions. It is important to note that the profiles are incomplete and the conclusions therefore tentative. Unfortunately, it was generally not possible to distinguish lenders and enforcers, so both are grouped together in the generalizations.

39. On October 25, 1935, the *New York Times* suggested that the killing of Dutch Schultz and Martin Krompier could be related to the recent growth of the usury racket as an investment outlet for major underworld figures. While Dewey was unable to link Manhattan loansharking to Schultz and Krompier, he continued to believe that those arrested were being financed by more important racketeers; see *New York Times,* Oct. 29, 1935, pp. 1-2; Nov. 3, 1935, p. 10; Dec. 4, 1935, p. 48; and Dec. 27, 1935, pp. 1-2.

40. *New York Times,* Nov. 27, 1935, p. 44.

41. *New York Times,* March 9, 1939, p. 3.

42. *New York Times,* Nov. 24, 1935, p. 35.

43. Katcher and Logan, *op. cit. supra* note 30; also a series of 14 articles by Edward P. Flynn which appeared in the *New York Post* from April 15, 1940, to April 29, 1940.

44. Burton B. Turkus and Sid Feder, *Murder, Inc.: The Story of the Syndicate* (1951), *passim; New York Post,* April 8, 1940, p. 16.

45. *New York Times,* Nov. 10, 1935, p. 10.

46. See references in footnote 43 above.

47. John Harlan Amen, *Report of the Kings County Investigation, 1938-1942,* pp. 123-125 and 178-181; Turkus and Feder, *op. cit. supra* note 44, at pp. 121-122; Alan A. Block, "Lepke, Kid Twist and the Combination: Organized Crime in New York City, 1930-1944" (Unpublished Ph.D. dissertation, University of California at Los Angeles, 1975), p. 166.

48. See references in footnote 43 above.

49. Turkus, *op. cit. supra* note 44, at pp. 123-124; Block, *op. cit. supra* note 47, at p. 167.

50. *New York Times,* Oct. 29, 1935, p. 2; Nov. 19, 1935, p. 45; Nov. 20, 1935, p. 48; Nov. 22, 1935, p. 48; Nov. 23, 1935, p. 3; Nov. 24, 1935, p. 35; Nov. 26, 1935, p. 52; Nov. 27, 1935, p. 44; Nov. 29, 1935, p. 40; Dec. 5, 1935, p. 5; and Feb. 22, 1936, p. 5.

51. *New York Times,* Oct. 22, 1935, p. 4; Oct. 29, 1935, pp. 1-2; Oct. 30, 1935, p. 4; Nov. 10, 1935, p. 10; Nov. 23, 1935, p. 2; Nov. 26, 1935, p. 52; Nov. 30, 1935, p. 32; Dec. 6, 1935, p. 8; Dec. 18, 1935, p. 52; Jan. 17, 1936, p. 40; March 6, 1936, p. 5; March 17, 1936, p. 9; Oct. 22, 1936, p. 13; and Nov. 18, 1936, p. 28.

52. The major scholarly study of current loansharking structure is John Michael Seidl, "'Upon the Hip'—A Study of the Criminal Loan-Shark Industry" (Unpublished Ph.D. dissertation, Harvard Univ., 1968). For Philadelphia, see Annelise G. Anderson, "The Economics of Organized Crime: A Case Study of an Organized Crime Group in a Major U.S. City" (Unpublished Ph.D. dissertation, Columbia Univ., 1974), pp. 127-138; for New York, see *An Investigation of the Loan-Shark Racket:* A Report by the New York State Commission of Investigation (1965). Less helpful is Lawrence J. Kaplan and Salvatore

Matteis, "The Economics of Loansharking," *American Journal of Economics and Sociology,* v.27 (1968), 239-252.

53. That the juice racket originated in Chicago in the late 1940's or early 1950's rests on a good deal of indirect evidence. In an interview, a man who worked in a number of Chicago gambling houses in the late 1930's reported that he knew of no loansharking in that period. By the late 1960's, Chicago newspapers and detectives traced the racket to the late 1940's or early 1950's. The *Chicago Daily News,* Nov. 24, 1961, claimed that the racket began in Chicago in the past decade, perhaps in 1956, when Leonard Patrick (also known as Leonard Levine and Joseph Cohen) controlled juice among Jewish workers in the garment district. The Chicago *American,* March 2, 1964, stated: "Sam DeStefano, reputed kingpin of underworld loan operations, showed hoodlums that big money could be made by lending at usurious rates and collecting by muscle, a business he has been in for at least 15 years." The *Sun-Times,* Aug. 19, 1965, quoted the director of police intelligence as stating that the juice racket began "many years ago" in Chicago in the 6 for 5 operation, in which tavern owners or shop foremen would lend $5.00 and expect $6.00 on payday." On March 11, 1967, a *Daily News* article stated vaguely that "juice is a post-World War racket."

54. Based on biographical sketches of eight juice racketeers listed in a memo dated Jan. 28, 1964, in Chicago Crime Commission (hereafter cited as CCC), File No. 60-325; plus biographical information on Sam DeStefano in CCC, No. 70-64; and on Joseph (Big Joe Arnold in Chicago *Tribune,* July 28, 1964, in CCC, No. 60-325. Illinois Crime Investigating Commission, *Juice Racketeers: Report on Criminal Usury in the Chicago Area* (1970), has biographical sketches of 93 minor and 23 major juice racketeers as of 1970.

55. On Forty-Two Gang, see unpublished book manuscript by John Landesco, "The Forty-Two Gang: A Study of a Neighborhood Criminal Group," Landesco papers, Univ. of Chicago Library; DeStefano mentioned ch. 1, pp. 6-7, 9, 10. For biographical information, see Chicago *Tribune,* April 6 and 2, 1973, and other materials in CCC, No. 70-64; also *Daily News,* March 28, 1952, in CCC, No. 60-182.

56. Crimaldi's story was told in a series of articles in the Chicago *Tribune,* July 4-15, 1973, in CCC, No. 70-64.

57. CCC, No. 70-64.

58. Chicago *American,* July 12, 1962; *Tribune,* Dec. 30, 1962; memo "Re: Juice Racket in the Chicago Area," Sep. 29, 1965; all in CCC, No. 60-325; Mike Royko, *I May Be Wrong, But I Doubt It* (1968), pp. 48-51.

59. Chicago *Tribune,* June 8, 1964, in CCC, No. 60-325.

60. On credit bureau, see Chicago *Tribune,* Jan. 15, 1964, in CCC, No. 60-325. On increasing coordination of structure of Chicago juice rackets, see Seidl, *op. cit. supra* note 52, at pp. 81-83; series of articles in Chicago *Tribune,* July 26-28, 1964, in CCC, No. 60-325; and memo "Re: Juice Racket."

61. See Seidl, *op. cit. supra* note 52, at pp. 97-100; Baxter Ware, "Parasites of the Poor: Further Light on the Devious Ways of the Loan Shark," *Harper's Weekly,* v. 52 (Aug. 8, 1908), 32.

Chapter 10

Bootleggers as Businessmen: From City Slums to City Builders

Shortly after World War II, a group of entrepreneurs began construction of a large hotel-casino in the desert several miles outside the moribund town of Las Vegas, Nevada. Improbably, they named their gaudy structure the Flamingo. When the Flamingo succeeded, the same entrepreneurs and their associates built other huge structures in the desert, thereby initiating the transformation of Las Vegas into a national center of entertainment as well as the most rapidly growing city in the United States. Modern Las Vegas might not have been possible without the vision and resources of men who, forty years earlier, had been raised in the ethnic slums of American cities and then struggled to success as bootleggers during the prohibition era of the 1920s. Las Vegas, then, can be seen as their crowning achievement. And by exploring their careers from slum youths to city builders, we can learn much about the business of bootlegging and the impact of bootleggers upon American life after prohibition.

If ex-bootleggers were improbable agents for transforming a dying desert town into a booming city, it was equally improbable that the same men would rise to dominate bootlegging in the 1920s. Their backgrounds provided little that marked them for future business success. When national prohibition began in 1920, most of those who became leading bootleggers in the major cities were still young men, often in their teens or early twenties. Their formative years were spent in the ethnic slums of the cities. About half were of Eastern European Jewish background, a quarter were Italian, and the final quarter were largely Irish and Polish.

Typically, they had left school by age fourteen and then had spent time on the streets—as newsboys, gang members, petty crooks. With the coming of prohibition, they found, like many Americans, that they could hustle some money by small-time bootlegging. With luck, skill, and (sometimes) violence, successful bootleggers rapidly expanded into extensive importing, manufacturing, or wholesaling activities. When prohibition ended in 1933, they were relatively young, generally in their early to mid thirties. Their adult careers still lay ahead of them.[1]

Newspapers of the day—as well as subsequent histories—have stressed the violence that often accompanied the rise of bootlegging. Indeed, Chicago (and Al Capone) gained worldwide notoriety because of the hundreds of deaths in that city in the 1920s. At sea and on land, bootleggers had to protect their booze from hijackers, so that successful bootleggers were often those most able to use gunmen to safeguard their shipments and warehouses. The gunmen, initially used to protect against hijacking, were sometimes then employed in competition with rival entrepreneurs. In all probability, the young men from the slums rose to prominence as bootleggers precisely because they were willing to operate in the sometimes violent world of bootlegging.

The emphasis on gang rivalries, however important, has nevertheless obscured what was far more significant about the structure of bootlegging: the systematic and ongoing cooperation among bootleggers that was necessary to supply alcohol to major metropolitan markets. In a metropolitan market, diverse tastes required a broad range of alcoholic beverages. The beverages derived from importation, diversion of industrial alcohol, large but clandestine distilleries, beer breweries, and many other sources. The alcohol often needed processing (caramel, creosote, and prune juice could be added, for instance, to give the taste and color of scotch). Once processed, the beverages were bottled and labeled. Only then would wholesalers truck the booze to warehouses and deliver it to retail outlets. (See Figure 10.1)[2]

Leading bootleggers and their partners, then, tended to specialize either in importation, in various forms of manufacture, or in wholesaling. By the late 1920s a wholesaling group in Chicago, such as that associated with Al Capone and Jack Guzick, might have ongoing arrangements with importers in Detroit, New York, New Orleans, and Florida; with brewers in Joliet, Illinois, and Racine, Wisconsin; with Philadelphia entrepreneurs who diverted industrial alcohol; and with illegal distillers throughout the Midwest. Similarly, successful importers

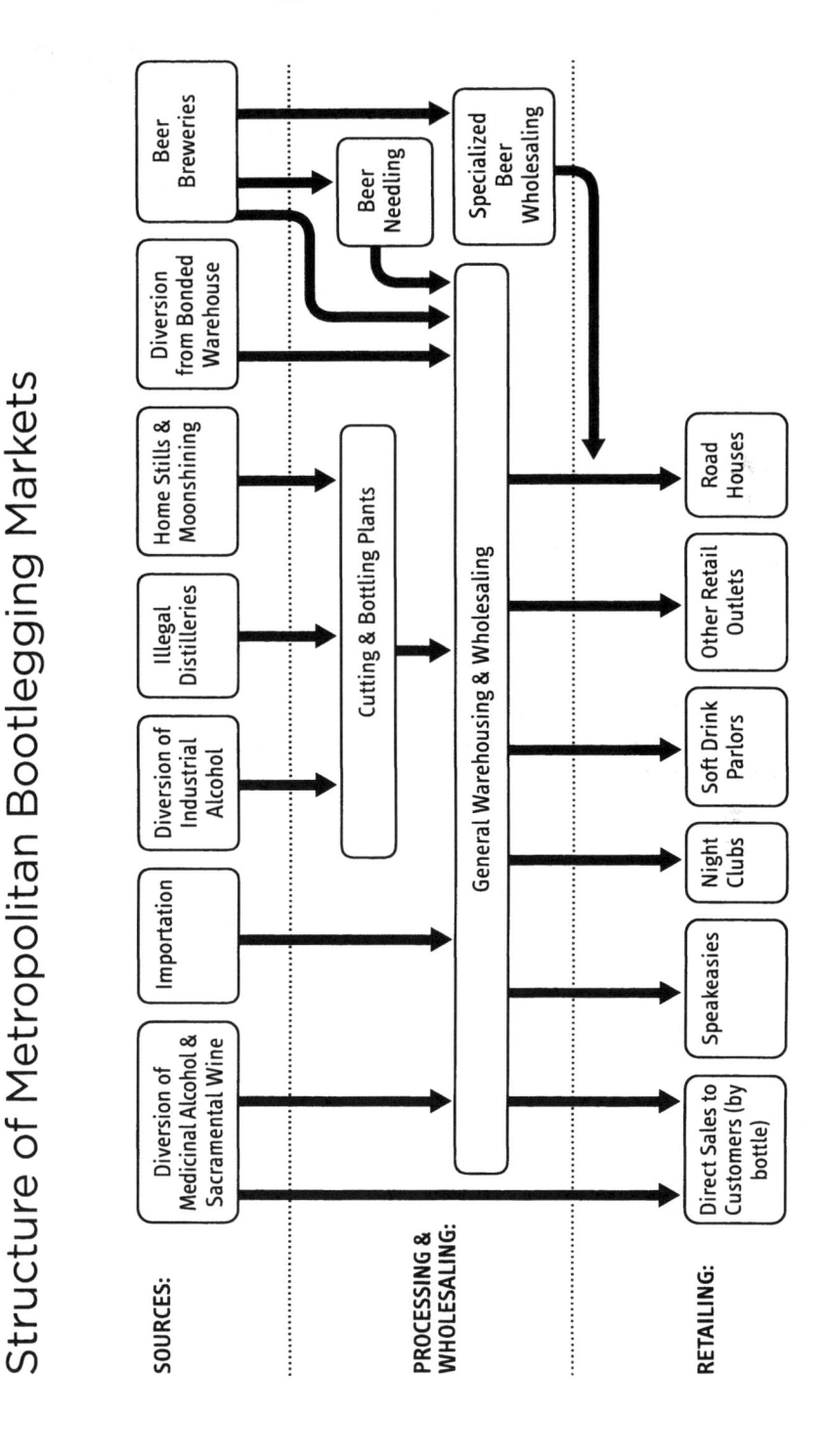

Figure 10.1

Structure of Metropolitan Bootlegging Markets

SOURCES:
- Diversion of Medicinal Alcohol & Sacramental Wine
- Importation
- Diversion of Industrial Alcohol
- Illegal Distilleries
- Home Stills & Moonshining
- Diversion from Bonded Warehouse
- Beer Breweries

PROCESSING & WHOLESALING:
- Cutting & Bottling Plants
- General Warehousing & Wholesaling
- Beer Needling
- Specialized Beer Wholesaling

RETAILING:
- Direct Sales to Customers (by bottle)
- Speakeasies
- Night Clubs
- Soft Drink Parlors
- Other Retail Outlets
- Road Houses

Bootleggers as Businessmen 201

or manufacturers cut deals with a variety of wholesalers to ensure a market for their often fluctuating businesses.

For the young men from the slums who climbed to success in the 1920s, coordination of bootlegging activities was a crash course in a number of business skills. Partly because of the brief thirteen years that prohibition lasted, few if any became managers of large-scale bureaucratic structures. To the extent that they needed ships' captains, warehouse foremen, distillers, or brewers to manage enterprises, bootleggers normally secured their cooperation by offering them a piece of the profits or a set amount for completing a project. As compared to the so-called Whiskey Trust of earlier years or the giant distributors who rose after repeal, bootleggers were relatively small-time operators. Leading bootleggers had interests in varied short-term and long-term operations of limited scale; they were primarily hustlers, makers of deals, partners in businesses, coordinators of markets—not executives presiding over bureaucratic organizations.

In that capacity, bootleggers confronted a variety of business challenges. (1) They were forced, by the process of building bootlegging operations, to think in terms of regional, national, and even international markets. Importers, in fact, had to plan their activities around Atlantic or Pacific trade routes and to negotiate deals with foreign manufacturers and shippers. To do this often required meetings of exporters, importers, and shippers: in Nova Scotia in the spring to plan the summer import business on the Atlantic, or in Florida, where many bootleggers wintered by the late 1920s. (2) Bootleggers learned to use partnerships in order to pool resources and share risks in setting up a variety of legal and illegal enterprises. Whether establishing a liquor exporting company in Havana, a brewery in Reading, Pennsylvania, or a bottling plant in New Jersey; they brought together persons with investment capital, managerial skills, political influence, and other needed resources. (3) As illegal entrepreneurs, they also had to learn to use legal institutions to service their illegal enterprises: they had to learn banking to handle money, insurance to protect their ships, and the methods of incorporation to gain control of chemical and cosmetics companies from which they diverted industrial alcohol. They also dealt with varied legitimate companies to purchase trucks, boats, copper tubing, corn sugar, bottles, and labels. (4) Finally, bootleggers early began to diversify their business activities in directions that were predictable given their backgrounds and interests. Importers not only smuggled booze but sometimes smuggled opium, French perfume, or illegal aliens. Because they were often sports fans and high rollers, successful bootleggers invested in gambling houses, numbers syndicates, and slot machine distributorships, as well as race tracks and dog tracks. Many, attracted to the city's nightlife, invested in nightclubs and speakeasies.

By the time of repeal in 1933, then, many leading bootleggers, essentially wheeler-dealers, had nevertheless gained a variety of entrepreneurial skills and business interests. They were still young men. And while some would be killed, jailed, or bankrupted, others found successful business careers in enterprises that reflected the skills and interests they demonstrated in the 1920s. Two of their business activities were of particular importance: first, their role in moving from the illegal to the legal liquor business; and second, their role in promoting regional gambling centers, culminating with the founding of modern Las Vegas.

The Liquor Business after Repeal

The history of the liquor business, especially in the years since repeal, has been little explored. On the whole, however, the manufacture of alcoholic beverages appears to have recovered from prohibition without, at first, undergoing major transformation. California wine growers, although they anticipated disaster from prohibition, did quite well in the 1920s by selling wine grapes to those Americans who wished to make home wine. As a result, they kept their vineyards and wineries intact and were ready to return to wine making as repeal approached. The major beer brewers had less success in the 1920s. Although some struggled to stay in business by making near beer, malt syrups, or soft drinks, many turned their breweries into parking lots, warehouses, or factories. But the major brewers, such as Anheuser-Busch, Schlitz, and Pabst, as well as many regional brewers, returned to the brewing of beer in the 1930s. The Kentucky bourbon business, too, rebounded in the 1930s despite a thirteen-year halt in production.[3]

While production of alcoholic beverages emerged reasonably unscathed given the potentially devastating impact of the 1920s, prohibition destroyed the earlier system of national and local distribution. Many bootleggers involved in the export, import, and distribution systems of the 1920s built upon the skills and ties of that period and achieved a central role as distributors after repeal. This was particularly clear among the handful of companies that now dominate national distribution of alcoholic beverages in the United States.[4]

Seagram, now the major national manufacturer and distributor of alcoholic beverages, provides the most obvious example. By the 1890s, the Bronfman family, after fleeing the pograms of Russia, operated small hotels in the prairie provinces of Canada. When most of the provinces went dry before World War I, Samuel Bronfman and his brothers started a mail-order business for sale of liquor across provincial borders. When prohibition came to the United States, the Bronfmans quickly became major sellers to American bootleggers who sneaked booze across the border into Montana, North Dakota, and Minnesota. Recognizing that the prairie provinces had no access to the primary U.S. markets, the Bronfmans established headquarters in Nova Scotia in 1924 to participate in the lucrative Atlantic trade. Eventually they joined with other Canadian exporters to set up a shipping company in Vancouver, British Columbia, for smuggling to California ports. Soon they also had outposts in Nassau, Havana, and Belize to coordinate smuggling activities into Florida and Gulf Coast ports. In 1928, as part of their expansion, they purchased the distilling company of Joseph E. Seagram and Sons, Ltd., in Ontario. By this time, the Bronfman interests were the major coordinators of liquor importation into U.S. Pacific, Atlantic, and Gulf Coast cities. After repeal Samuel Bronfman moved Seagram's headquarters to the Chrysler Building in New York. In 1936 Seagram paid the U.S. government $1.5 million in a negotiated settlement of the claims against the company from prohibition violations. Within a few years, Bronfman had purchased major American distilleries and wineries, as well as founding distilleries of his own, so that Seagram became the dominant distributor. By 1980 Seagram sold some 600 brands in 175 countries at a total annual value of nearly $3 billion.

In 1926 Harry C. Hatch purchased Hiram Walker and Sons. This prestigious company, founded by Boston-born Hiram Walker on the Canadian side of the Detroit River in 1858, manufactured the famous Canadian Club brand. Earlier Hatch had purchased Gooderham and Worts, Canada's oldest distillery. In 1928, Hatch and his many Canadian and American associates were indicted by the U.S. government for their extensive smuggling into various American cities through the Detroit and Buffalo areas across Lake Erie. With repeal, Hatch's company built an American distillery in Peoria, Illinois, as well as expanding into European and South American markets. Like Seagram, the company negotiated a settlement of U.S. government claims. Hiram Walker became one of the three biggest American distributors.

By contrast, Schenley's success had American origins. Lewis Rosensteil, whose family had been important in the Cincinnati distilling business, branched out in the 1920s by acquiring distilleries whose warehouses were particularly well stocked. Ostensibly his business was the sale of alcoholic beverages for medicinal purposes. He purchased Schenley Products Company of Schenley, Pennsylvania, around 1924. He also imported liquor from Canada and Bermuda and, in the process, dealt extensively with Samuel Bronfman. By the time of repeal, he and his associates were important owners of American distilleries and had one of the largest stocks of liquor available in the United States. At first Rosensteil and Bronfman planned to jointly develop the American market, but they soon quarreled bitterly. Until 1937 Schenley was the largest legal distributor of alcoholic beverages in the United States, but in that year it was overtaken by Seagram.

The major national distributors of hard liquor, in short, descended directly from companies that first rose to prominence by servicing the American market during prohibition. Because prohibition destroyed the old distribution system, a few of the more capable and ambitious distributors from the 1920s enjoyed crucial advantages in seizing the opportunities opened by repeal. They owned distilleries that had been in active production in the 1920s, they had contacts in major cities through which to distribute their beverages, and, in the depression years of the early 1930s, they had capital to invest in the expansion of their holdings. While bootlegging of the 1920s had been highly competitive and characterized by numerous firms, the legal system was more easily dominated by a handful of national distributors. With the resources that stemmed from national distribution, they purchased American distilleries and wineries, as well as European and Latin American brands, and thus created forms of vertical monopoly.

Not only was national distribution dominated by firms that rose during prohibition, but many bootleggers also became local distributors. Sometimes, no doubt, local distributors continued the ties with suppliers forged during prohibition. Abner ("Longie") Zwillman, for instance, had been a sixteen-year-old hustler on the streets of Newark, New Jersey, when prohibition began. By the late 1920s he was a partner in the so-called Reinfeld Syndicate, the largest illegal liquor importers in northern New Jersey. The syndicate's Canadian contacts were with the Bronfman interests. After repeal Zwillman and his partners formed Browne Vintners to distribute liquor in the New York region. In 1940, Zwillman sold the company to Seagram for $7.5 million.[5]

There were many other examples. A 1937 investigation by the Internal Revenue Service uncovered evidence that a New York firm, Alliance Distributors, Inc., with sole rights to sell certain selected Scotch whiskeys in the United States, was apparently backed by Frank Costello, perhaps the most important New York importer during prohibition, and Irving Haim, an ex-bootlegger with interests in New York and Philadelphia. John Torrio put together a bootleg conglomerate in Chicago in the early 1920s but, finding Chicago violence unsettling, departed in 1924, leaving his enterprises to Jack Guzik, Al Capone, and Frank Nitti. In New York, Torrio continued a variety of bootleg activities until repeal. Afterwards, he was the major entrepreneur in establishing Prendergast and Davies, which became an important liquor distributor. In Kansas City, as Humbert Nelli has noted in his book on Italian crime, Midwest Distributing Company was by 1934 the exclusive distributor for Seagram, while Superior Wines and Liquor Company handled Schenley brands. Both had ex-bootleggers as major investors.[6]

In short, the pattern was similar in many cities: ex-bootleggers continued as liquor distributors at the local level. In that business they could use the expertise gained during bootlegging days, as well as their political contacts and their ties with national and foreign distributors. Except for the brewing of beer, the long-range effect of prohibition may have been to reorganize the control of the American liquor business. For many bootleggers, the liquor business was not an interlude of the 1920s but a means by which they gained the resources to control the legal liquor business and thereby achieve success and respectability.

Regional Gambling and the Founding of Las Vegas

If reshaping the liquor industry was a major accomplishment of ex-bootleggers, a close rival in importance was the creation of Las Vegas as a national entertainment center. Like their impact on the liquor business, Las Vegas represented the ex-bootleggers' ability to think in terms of regional and national markets, to pool resources in joint ventures, and to recruit able managers to run the enterprises for which they provided the entrepreneurial skills. To understand the creation of modern Las Vegas after World War II, one must understand both the special environment of Nevada and the prior experience of ex-bootleggers from many cities in the cooperative formation of regional gambling centers in the fifteen years following repeal. In this brief space it is possible merely to sketch the activities of ex-bootleggers as developers of regional gambling.[7]

Frank Costello, a partner in the 1920s in what was probably the largest New York importing syndicate, also became an important figure in the city's nightlife and politics. Even before prohibition ended, he and "Dandy" Phil Kastel established the Tru-Mint Company to install slot machines in the city. When Mayor Fiorello LaGuardia created headlines in 1934 with his campaign against Costello's machines, Costello made arrangements with Senator Huey Long to install the machines in New Orleans. Kastel went there to oversee their joint venture. After World War II, Kastel, with Costello as partner, operated the Beverly Club near New Orleans, the major illegal casino for the Costello group. Later, Kastel went to Hot Springs, Arkansas, in the 1930s to revitalize casino gambling in that southern resort city. He was almost certainly backed by Costello, and perhaps by Meyer Lansky as well.

In Cleveland, five partners, led by Morris B. ("Moe") Dalitz, engaged in smuggling across Lake Erie into Buffalo, Erie, and Cleveland during the 1920s. Ranging in age from seventeen to twenty-four when prohibition began, they became major investors in a variety of enterprises, legitimate and illegitimate. In addition to investment in various Cleveland gambling enterprises, the partners in 1941 bought into the gambling houses of Newport and Covington, Kentucky, across the Ohio River from Cincinnati. These blue-collar towns had long provided gambling and vice for the big city across the river, but the Cleveland investors made their Beverly Hills Club and Lookout House renowned midwestern centers for gambling. The Cleveland group also invested in a variety of enterprises in Florida and Cuba. Dalitz was second only to Lansky in the importance of his contribution to the development of Las Vegas.

Jack Guzik—a partner with Al Capone, Ralph Capone, and Frank Nitti in Chicago's largest wholesale bootlegging operation—was a key figure afterwards among a number of Chicago gambling entrepreneurs. His chief partner was Nitti until Nitti's suicide in the early 1940s; thereafter, his closest associate, with whom he often filed joint tax returns, was Tony Accardo. In the 1920s, Guzik's associates had already made

Cicero, a blue-collar suburb west of Chicago, an important gambling center. Guzik by 1930 had his hand in much of the gambling in Chicago's downtown Loop. The Chicago group, often acting through their good friend Johnny Patton (once the teenage mayor of Burnham, Illinois), were eager investors in Florida dog and horse tracks. During World War II, Guzik and his partners established a national race wire, Trans-America Publishing and News Service, in order to bankrupt the dominant Continental Press and give the Chicago group a monopoly in providing sports information to bookmakers, newspapers, and radio news. By the post-World War II period, Guzik and associates had also begun investing in gambling in downstate Illinois.

There were other entrepreneurs as well. In Boston, Hy Abrams and his partners, successful but largely unpublicized bootleggers, invested in a Boston dog track in the 1930s and joined other bootleggers in a variety of ventures. In northern New Jersey, Abner ("Longie") Zwillman, partner in the Reinfeld Syndicate of bootleggers, became a major force in the gambling of Newark and surrounding cities. In the 1930s and 1940s, he invested in race tracks in New Jersey, Kentucky, and California. Harry Rosen (ne Stromberg), born in Russia and raised on the Lower East Side of New York, was a mere seventeen when prohibition began. During the 1920s he became involved in numerous vice and bootlegging activities in the New York—Philadelphia region. After repeal he put together a group of ex-bootleggers to coordinate numbers gambling in Philadelphia. In the mid-1930s, he also took over the Maryland Athletic Club, an important gambling house servicing the Washington, D.C., area. By the 1940s Rosen and his associates developed various gambling and other investments in Florida.

The leading figure among those ex-bootleggers involved in gambling was Meyer Lansky. Indeed, he is perhaps the most important gambling entrepreneur in American history. Only eighteen when prohibition began (his partner, Benjamin Siegel, was fourteen). he gradually achieved importance as a New York bootleg importer by the end of the 1920s. Then, in the 1930s, as he pioneered gambling and race track investments in Florida and Cuba, his planning and judgment proved so profitable that he attracted a range of investors eager to have a share in his enterprises. In a move that would be important later in the founding of modern Las Vegas, Siegel went to Los Angeles in the late 1930s, where he became a notorious figure in Hollywood social life while scouting various investment opportunities on the West Coast.

Florida was the crucial arena in which ex-bootleggers developed their cooperative ventures in gambling and entertainment and built the ties that would later be seen in Las Vegas. By the late 1920s, after the Coast Guard effectively reduced smuggling in the North Atlantic, Florida ports were major entry points for imported liquor. East Coast and midwestern bootleggers came to Florida on business, and like other wealthy Americans, many wintered in Florida by the late 1920s and invested in Florida real estate. They were aware, therefore, of Florida's potential as a resort and entertainment center. In 1931, after Florida legalized parimutuel betting at the track, Canadian liquor interests contributed funds to convert Tropical Park near Coral Gables into a horse track and selected Bill Dwyer, Costello's former bootleg partner, as manager. When the track needed additional backing in 1934, Lansky and Erickson purchased the park, while Johnny Patton, probably representing Chicago money, was also involved. Sometimes under Lansky's leadership and sometimes independently, a variety of investors placed money in other Florida tracks, gambling houses, bookmaking operations, hotels, and other ventures. In 1946 Lansky assembled a group of New York, Chicago, and Detroit investors to establish the Colonial Inn near Miami, perhaps the largest illegal casino-nightclub in the United States at that time.

Lansky also provided leadership for the penetration of Cuba. Even in the 1920s, Havana had provided gambling for vacationing Americans and was an important center for smuggling from Europe into the United States. A number of bootleggers, as a result, developed close times with Cuban politicians. By the mid-1930s, through agreements with Fulgencio Batista, Lansky operated a casino in the Hotel Nacional and had an interest in race tracks. After Batista lost power in 1944, American investments declined but made a remarkable recovery after Batista returned to power in 1952. Lansky, Dalitz, Kastel, and others associated with ex-bootleggers turned Havana into an important center of gambling, vice, and entertainment until Fidel Castro drove them out.

By the end of World War II, ex-bootleggers were approaching their fifties and the height of their careers. Their youth had been spent in the dangerous but exciting ventures that provided bootleg liquor to a thirsty nation. Since that time, some had engaged in joint investments to develop recreational centers of gambling, racing, and night-life entertainment. (See Figure 10.2 for a diagram of their relationships.) In this context, they discovered the opportunities in Las Vegas.

Figure 10.2
Ex-Bootleggers and Regional Gambling: 1935-1950

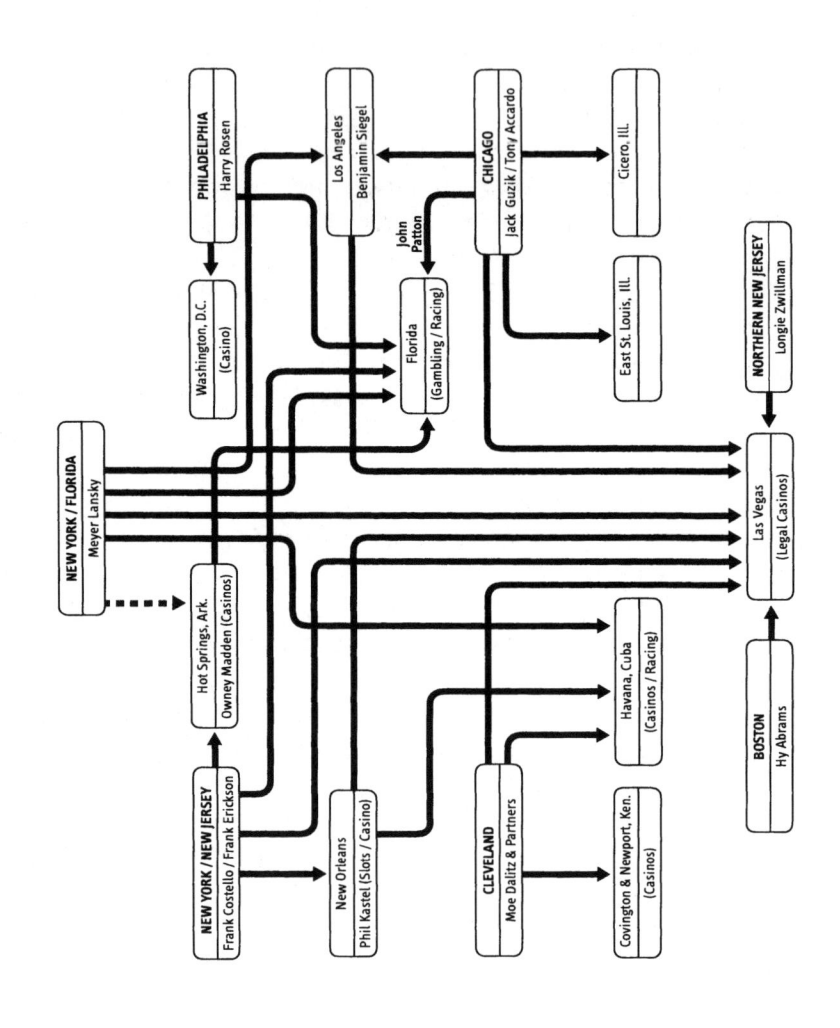

Nevada offered a special environment: a sparsely populated state, still proud of its wide-open frontier ethos and also cynically aware that there was profit to be made by providing services not legally available elsewhere. The Reno divorce, after all, was an important prop for that city's economy. Many wealthy Americans, otherwise unlikely to spend time and money in a desert state, lived in Reno for six weeks to establish residency for divorce purposes. In the late nineteenth and early twentieth centuries, when most states banned or restricted prizefighting, Nevada had no restrictions. Thus, in 1910, when Jim Jeffries, the Great White Hope, emerged from retirement in a vain attempt to wrest the heavyweight title from Jack Johnson, the fight was moved to Reno when the California governor banned it in San Francisco. Crowds of sportsmen and bettors from as far as New York came to see the fight.

Traditionally a wide-open mining and gambling state, Nevada legally banned gambling in 1909 but established licensed gambling in 1931. In that depression year the state legislature hoped to gain tax revenues and tourist business through a policy of legalization. Reno, by far the largest city in the state, was at first the main beneficiary.

Las Vegas in 1928 was a desert town and county seat with a population of about 5,000. That population swelled slightly in the next few years because of construction of the nearby Hoover Dam. During World War II, when the Army Air Force turned the municipal airport into a training base, the population may have boomed to 20,000, and there was even some new construction of small nightclubs and gambling houses. But with the war over and the dam long since completed, the town faced a bleak future. A desperate chamber of commerce saw but one hope: to attract tourists by advertising the city as a frontier town, including promotion of the downtown main street as a frontier "Glitter Gulch." Las Vegas leaders would welcome investors and not inquire too closely concerning their backgrounds.[8]

Toward the end of the war, Benjamin Siegel (assisted by Mickey Cohen) became the West Coast distributor for the sports information service established in Chicago by the Guzik-Accardo group. Siegel traveled to Las Vegas to peddle his services to the bookmakers operating from the small casinos there. Often, in return for racing information, Siegel expected a partnership interest in the bookmaking operations. On one trip he may have brought Lansky with him. At any rate, Siegel soon believed that he could build a magnificent hotel-casino-nightclub in the desert outside Las Vegas, offering legal gambling for the sporting element of southern California. This was, of course, a wild and unproven scheme for which there could be no adequate sources of legitimate credit.[9]

Siegel estimated the cost of the Flamingo at something over $1 million, but massive overruns sent the cost to at least $6 million. Siegel, Lansky, Hy Abrams, and the other original partners not only invested their own money but eventually may have accepted money from a wide variety of additional investors ranging from Longie Zwillman to Moe Dalitz to Frank Costello. In December 1946, although the hotel was not yet completed, Siegel attempted to open the casino. With Jimmy Durante there to entertain, Xavier Cugat's band to play, and George Raft as host, the casino nevertheless flopped. The Flamingo reopened in March and was soon making a handsome profit. Then, in June, Siegel was shot inside the Beverly Hills mansion of his mistress. He died having proven that his dream was profitable.

Over the next few years, of course, there rose from the desert in quick succession a number of hotel casinos. The Thunderbird, for which Lansky and his associates appear to have been major backers, opened in 1948. Construction began on the Desert Inn in 1947, with Wilbur Clark, who had operated gambling ships off the southern coast of California, as the major sponsor. When his group ran out of funds, Moe Dalitz and his partners purchased a 74 percent interest and thus made possible its opening in 1950. Dalitz moved to Las Vegas and soon was numbered among its most respected citizens. The Sands, completed in 1952, was sponsored chiefly by New Jersey backers such as Longie Zwillman. Frank Sinatra, who was, after all, a Hoboken boy, had a minority interest. The Riviera, opening in 1955, seems to have represented chiefly Chicago investors such as Guzik and Accardo. The Tropicana, ready two years later, had backers such as Costello and Kastel. The Stardust had a somewhat more complex origin. Tony Cornero had been a California bootleg importer in the 1920s. Among his ventures in the next two decades, he occasionally operated a gambling ship in Santa Monica Bay. When the Coast Guard seized his ship, he became a bettor and investor along the Strip. He planned the Stardust but died of a heart attack in 1955. Accardo and other Chicago investors attempted to rescue it but soon sold out to Dalitz and his partners.

The impact of the ex-bootleggers went beyond capital and planning. From their hotels, casinos, and nightclubs in Cleveland, Covington, Miami, Hot Springs, and Havana, they recruited hotel men, casino managers, card dealers, bouncers, and other staff required for the entertainment centers along the Strip. Many men, often with long records of illicit activities, found in Las Vegas an opportunity to use their skills in a new environment.

Without the ex-bootleggers to found and staff the first generation of hotel-casinos, Las Vegas might not have been possible. They were the major entrepreneurs with experience in building entertainment centers based on gambling. For such large-scale yet risky ventures, for which legitimate credit was not available, they had the capital and a long history of pooling resources in order to launch high-risk enterprises. As men accustomed to thinking in terms of regional markets, they could see possibilities where others might not. And with the development of transcontinental air travel, Las Vegas became an entertainment center not simply for the West Coast but for the nation. The dying desert town, chosen as a gamblers' paradise by Siegel in 1945, was a booming growth city of 200,000 twenty years later, and reached a population of 464,000 by the census of 1980.

Despite the crucial role of ex-bootleggers in developing the first generation of hotel-casinos, their impact on the future economic growth of Las Vegas was ambiguous. In 1950-51 the Senate Special Committee to Investigate Organized Crime (known popularly as the Kefauver Committee after its chairman, Senator Estes Kefauver of Tennessee) charged that "organized crime" controlled casino development in the city. Subsequent newspaper exposés not only reinforced the charges of mob control but claimed that profits from casinos were skimmed to evade taxes and finance underworld activities throughout the nation. By the mid-l950s, the entertainment industry in Las Vegas required new capital to expand earlier casinos and construct new ones; but the many charges of underworld control meant that the casinos, although profitable, continued to be viewed as doubtful investments by legitimate credit institutions. Several Las Vegas investors, though, had ties with the Teamsters Union and its Central States Pension Fund. By 1977 the fund had sunk some $240 million into Nevada. Although access to Teamster funds brought needed capital at favorable terms, it did not enhance the respectability of the Nevada gaming industry. On the contrary, numerous congressional investigations and newspaper stories highlighted the corruption and underworld friendships of the Teamster leadership—indeed, the investments in Las Vegas were taken as evidence for such charges.[10]

Then, in 1967, Howard Hughes purchased the Desert Inn from Dalitz and subsequently gained ownership of approximately seventeen casinos in Nevada. For the state's politicians, Hughes, despite his outlandish behavior, was perceived as a saviour who could free the casinos from their reputation as underworld investments. A more important factor in refinancing the casinos, however, was that the Nevada legislature passed laws in 1967 and 1969 permitting publicly-held corporations to obtain casino licenses. Soon corporations such as Metro-Goldwyn Mayer, Hyatt Corporation, and Del E. Webb purchased old casinos and built new ones in Las Vegas, Reno, and Lake Tahoe. (In 1971 the Flamingo became a Hilton hotel.) The continued remarkable expansion of Las Vegas in the 1970s was made possible largely by such corporations. By 1980 the twenty largest corporations owned casinos that generated half the gross gambling revenue and provided half the gaming employment in the state. Clearly, the casino industry had been reorganized.

During the fifteen years following the mid-1950s, the bootleg generation reached the age when death and retirement caused them to cease active casino development. By that time, in any event, neither their capital nor their skills as casino and entertainment entrepreneurs were necessary for the continued success of Las Vegas. But, for good or ill, they had shaped the growth of a city. And they had attracted to the city ambitious followers and partners. Despite changes in casino ownership, their influence remains. Even as this essay is being written in October 1983, the federal government, after a five-year investigation, has indicted criminal entrepreneurs from Chicago, Milwaukee, and Kansas City for secret ownership and skimming from two Las Vegas casinos.[11] It has been easier for the casinos to achieve business success than to gain respectability.

In Conclusion

The story told here has implications for understanding the history of what some, rather inaccurately, call organized crime. Remember that in 1950-51, just as Las Vegas was coming to fruition, Senator Kefauver and his Senate committee announced that a mysterious "mafia" controlled "organized crime" in America. Such a view of the coordination of criminal enterprise is historically untenable.[12] Among leading bootleggers, as mentioned earlier, those of Jewish background constituted one-half; they outnumbered Italians two to one. As these same men developed cooperative ventures, criminal and legitimate, in Miami, Hot Springs, Havana, or Las Vegas, the Jewish predominance continued. Furthermore, the brief history provided here gives a clearer model of the structure of cooperation within which these men made their deals and financed their ventures. They were independent businessmen who had learned to pool their resources because this minimized risks and maximized their ability to mobilize capital, influence, and managerial skills. They operated regionally and nationally through a complex set of interlocking partnerships. If men such as Lansky, Dalitz, or Costello sometimes exercised special leadership, it was not because they were crime "bosses" directing hierarchical organizations of master criminals. Rather, they had proven track records as businessmen in legal and illegal enterprises, so that other entrepreneurs competed for the opportunity to participate in their schemes.

Prohibition, by bringing to the fore a group of particularly energetic criminal entrepreneurs, created a general phenomenon in American business history. Approximately twenty years old in 1920, the leading bootleggers gained success during prohibition at an unusually early age. In 1933, still only in their thirties and with careers ahead of them, they put their energies into a variety of business activities. Some restructured the distribution of liquor and achieved both wealth and respectability. The control of the American liquor industry has largely escaped careful scrutiny. Other ex-bootleggers specialized in gambling and entertainment; for them, Las Vegas would finally be their opportunity, also, to hope that they might become legal and therefore respectable. But the many congressional investigations and newspaper exposés have meant that respectability was elusive for those entrepreneurs who made Las Vegas possible.

In 1976, during a deposition in a libel suit that he had brought against Penthouse magazine, Dalitz protested his failure to achieve respectability:

> For 30 years now I have lived in Nevada. I am considered a good citizen of Nevada. I have done all the things a good citizen should do. I have been charitable. I have been honest. I have raised a family. My life has been just as good as anyone's in this room. . . . I have very candidly told you that I was in the liquor business when it was considered to be illegal. I told you that I was in the casino business. . . . In none of these businesses is moral turpitude involved. These are things that if people didn't patronize a casino we couldn't have one. If people didn't drink liquor it wouldn't have been necessary to bring it over. I did nothing more than the head of Seagram's, than the head of G & W [Gooderham and Worts], the head of Canadian Club. They assembled all this merchandise for runners to bring it across. . . . We didn't

regard this as a hideous affair. I don't think you do either in your heart.[13]

Whatever one may think of Dalitz's self-justification, one thing at least is clear: he and other young men who learned business skills as bootleggers had their greatest impact on American society in the years after repeal.

Notes

1. For a presentation of the evidence about the social backgrounds of bootleggers, see Mark H. Haller, "Bootleggers and American Gambling 1920-1950," in Commission on the Review of National Policy toward Gambling, Gambling in America, Appendix I (Washington, D.C.: GPO, 1976), especially pp. 109-15.

2. Discussion of the economics of bootlegging here and in subsequent paragraphs is based on a variety of investigative sources: the extensive Coast Guard Intelligence Files, National Archives, Washington, D.C.; the prosecution files involving cases against bootleggers for prohibition violations and income tax evasion, Central Files of the Department of Justice, National Archives; investigative files of the Internal Revenue Service, Treasury Department, Washington, D.C.; and the many drawers of files on Chicago bootlegging from the Chicago Crime Commission, Chicago, Illinois. There is some discussion of bootlegging as a business in Humbert S. Nelli, The Business of Crime: Italians in American Syndicate Crime (New York: Oxford, 1976), chap. 6.

3. John R. Meers, "The California Wine and Grape Industry and Prohibition," Calfornia Historical Society Quarterly 46 (1967): 19-32; Thomas C. Cochran, The Pabst Brewing Company: The History of an American Business (New York: New York University Press. 1948): William L. Downard, The Cincinnati Brewing Industry: A Social and Economic History (Athens: Ohio University Press, 1973); Robert F. Sexton, "Kentucky Distillers React to Prohibition," paper delivered to American Historical Association, 1974.

4. The basic facts concerning national distributors can be found in William L. Downard, Dictionary of the History of the American Brewing and Distilling Industries (Westport, Conn.: Greenwood, 1980); for a popular history of Seagram and the Bronfmans, see Peter C. Newman, King of the Castle, The Making of a Dynasty: Seagram's and the Bronfman Empire (New York: Atheneum, 1979); also James H. Gray, Booze: The Impact of Whisky on the Prairie West (Toronto: Macmillan of Canada, 1972); on bootlegging by Hatch, see Coast Guard Intelligence File, Box 56.

5. Hank Messick, Secret File (New York: G. P. Putnam's Sons, 1969), chap. 16.

6. Messick, Secret File, chap. 14; Jack McPhaul, Johnny Torrio: First of the Gang Lords (New Rochelle, N.Y.: Arlington House, 1970), pp. 274 et. seq.; Nelli, Business of Crime, pp. 220-22.

7. The following discussion of regional gambling is based on a number of sources. The best single source is the nineteen volumes of testimony before the Kefauver Committee in 1950-51; see U.S. Senate, Special Committee to Investigate Organized Crime in Interstate Commerce, Hearings, 81st and 82nd Cong. (Washington, D.C.: GPO, 1950-51). Much material, particularly on entrepreneurs with Chicago ties, can be found in various files of the Chicago Crime Commission. In addition, there are dozens of popular crime histories and biographies with useful, but not always reliable, information: Estes Kefauver, Crime in America (New York: Doubleday, 1951); Hank Messick, Lansky (New York: G. P. Putnam's Sons, 1971); Messick, Secret File; Messick, The Silent Syndicate (New York: Macmillan, 1967); Dennis Eisenberg, Uri Dan, and Eli Landau, Meyer Lansky: Mogul of the Mob (New York: Paddington Press, 1979); Dean Jennings, We Only Kill Each Other: The Life and Bad Times of Bugsy Siegel (Englewood Cliffs, N.J.: Prentice-Hall, 1967); George Wolf with Joseph DiMona, Frank Costello: Prime Minister of the Underworld (New York: William Morrow, 1974); Andrew Tully, Treasury Agent: The Inside Story (New York: Simon and Schuster, 1958); and Albert Fried, The Rise and Fall of the Jewish Gangster in America (New York: Holt, Rinehart and Winston, 1980), chap. 6.

8. For discussion of the background in Nevada and Las Vegas, see Donald Ashbaugh, Nevada's Turbulent Yesterday (Las Vegas: Western Lore Press, 1963); Gilman M. Ostrander, Nevada: The Great Rotten Borough, 1859-1964 (New York: Knopf, 1964); Perry Kaufman, "Public Relations Men, Images, and the Growth of Las Vegas," paper presented at convention of Organization of American Historians, April 1973.

9. This and the next two paragraphs are based on sources in note 7. See also Ed Reid and Ovid Demaris, The Green Felt Jungle (New York: Pocket Books, 1964); Wallace Turner, Gamblers' Money: The New Force in American Life (Boston: Houghton Mifflin, 1965); and Ralph Pearl, Las Vegas Is My Beat (Secaucus, N.J.: Lyle Stuart, 1973). On Tony Comero's gambling ships, see G. Edward White, Earl Warren: A Public Life (New York: Oxford, 1982), pp. 50-51.

10. The economic history of the casino industry in this paragraph and the next is based primarily on a series of fine articles by William R. Eadington, including: "The Evolution of Corporate Gambling in Nevada," Nevada Review of Business & Economics 6 (Spring 1982): 13-22; "Regulatory Objectives and the Expansion of Casino Gambling," in ibid. 6 (Fall 1982): 4-13. See also Howard J. Klein, "The F.B.I. and the Gaming Industry: Annals of Myth and Reality," Gaming Business Magazine 3 (1982): 214-24. There are many books

on the Teamsters, including Ralph and Estelle James, Hoffa and the Teamsters: A Study of Union Power (Princeton, N.J.: D. Van Nostrand Co., 1965), especially part IV and app. II; and Steven Brill, The Teamsters (New York: Simon and Schuster, 1978). For an insightful analysis of casinos and their regulation in Nevada, see Jerome H. Skolnick, House of Cards: The Legalization and Control of Casino Gambling (Boston: Little, Brown, 1978).

11. *New York Times*, October 12, 1983, p. A1; *Philadelphia Inquirer*, October 16, 1983, p. F1.

12. For an excellent analysis of the process by which the committee reached conclusions not supported by its evidence, see William Howard Moore, The Kefauver Committee and the Politics of Crime, 1950-1952 (Columbia: University of Missouri Press, 1974).

13. "Deposition of Morris B. Dalitz," in case of Rancho LaCosta, Inc., v. Penthouse International, Ltd., Superior Court of the State of California for the County of Los Angeles (August 1976), p. 133.

Chapter 11

Illegal Enterprise: A Theoretical and Historical Interpretation

Illegal enterprise—defined as the sale of illegal goods and services to customers who know that the goods or services are illegal—has long been a central part of the American underworld, but it has received little attention as a separate criminological category. Although such activities are often relatively short term and small scale when compared with legal businesses, three major factors explain the cooperation that sometimes emerges among illegal entrepreneurs. The first factor is systematic corruption, which often permits police or politicians to bring order to illegal activities within a political subdivision. A second factor is overlapping partnerships by which entrepreneurs often launch and maintain illegal businesses. A third factor is the internal economic characteristics of illegal businesses, which shape the manner in which they operate. This chapter explores the implications of each factor through historical examples and suggests hypotheses concerning the changing structure of illegal enterprises in American cities.

A broad range of criminal activities might logically be called "illegal enterprise." Such activities ultimately entail the sale of illegal goods or services to customers who know that the goods or services are illegal. In recent American history, examples of illegal goods have included bootleg liquor in the 1920s, pornography, and a variety of forbidden drugs. Without much thought, however, the list might be considerably expanded: quack medicines like "laetrile," unlicensed weapons, even bald eagle feathers or illegally imported exotic pets. Examples of illegal services include prostitution, loansharking, and; most important, various forms of gambling. Again, the list can be greatly expanded. Less than 20 years ago, illegal abortions were common. Other examples range from murder for hire to the operation of gypsy cabs in the ghettoes of many American cities.

In much of the standard criminological literature, those involved in gambling, narcotics, or loan-sharking are classified as part of "organized crime." As a result, discussion of illegal enterprise has often been subsumed under "organized crime" and has not, in itself, been a central concern of criminological theory and research.[1] Yet illegal enterprises shaped the underworld of American cities long before the rise of Italian-American crime families. Even with the emergence of crime families in a number of cities, most illegal enterprises continue to operate independently of them. It is important, then, that illegal enterprise be made a subject of study in its own right. One purpose of this chapter is to provide a theoretical and historical framework for the analysis of illegal enterprise in American cities.

The advantage of recognizing illegal enterprise as a criminological category is that such activities have common characteristics that provide a basis for analysis. Because they ultimately involve the retailing of goods or services, they can be studied as businesses, and the same questions can be asked that would be asked of analogous legal businesses. What are the sources of capital for starting or expanding the operations? What factors influence locational decisions? How are the goods or services advertised to customers? How are prices set? What financial arrangements exist between the entrepreneur and others who participate in the enterprise? One can, in short, ask all the questions that would be asked of a legal enterprise. But, for enterprises that are illegal, there is an additional question: What difference does it make that the enterprise is illegal? More specifically, how do various law enforcement strategies shape the operations of illegal businesses? How, for instance, do enforcement policies influence sources of capital, recruitment of personnel, location of retail outlets, advertising, pricing, and the internal structure of the enterprise?

Most of those involved in illegal enterprises have operated on a small scale. In American cities, there have been free-lance prostitutes, street-corner drug dealers, and neighborhood bookmakers. As Peter Reuter (1983: ch. 5) has argued convincingly, illegal enterprises are likely to have lower capitalization, fewer personnel, and less formal management than comparable legal enterprises. Nevertheless, illegal enterprises do sometimes bring together a number of entrepreneurs for cooperative ventures that involve some degree of coordination. Such cooperation is worth exploring because it reveals crucial aspects of illegal enterprise.

Historically, three important factors have underlain cooperation among those involved in illegal enterprise. The most important factor has been the oversight of illegal activities by local politicians or police. In a political ward or even in an entire city, corrupt relations between criminals and politicians (or police) have often resulted in informal licensing and coordination. A second factor is the use of partnership arrangements in promoting illegal enterprises. Through participation in overlapping partnerships, some entrepreneurs have exerted influence over a range of activities. A third factor leading to cooperation has been the internal economics of some types of criminal enterprise. Such enterprises—numbers banks would be an example—require coordination for economic success and, as a result, have traditionally been operated as syndicates in various cities over many years. The paper examines each of the three factors in turn.

Police and Political Corruption

American cities have a long history of corrupt relations between some illegal enterprises and local police or politicians. For criminal entrepreneurs, payments to politicians or police can be viewed either as normal business expenses in return for services to the enterprise or as extortionate demands that eat into the profits of the enterprise. For police and politicians, levying regular assessments on illegal entrepreneurs has provided a source of extra income as well as a way to oversee neighborhood enterprises that could not be legally controlled. Historically, oversight by local political organizations (or the police) has been the most important source of coordination for illegal enterprises in American cities.

The process of regularizing payoffs, whether to politicians or to the police, almost inevitably results in some level of coordination or regulation. Indeed, restraint of competition may be in the interest of both the entrepreneurs and political (or police) officials. Those involved in illegal enterprise are often interested in moderating competition, and this can be one of the advantages that they hope to gain through payments to officials. But, to the extent that payments by criminals are regularized, officials have a stake in the economic success of the enterprises and may also see advantages in limiting competition. Furthermore, by arresting outsiders, officials can present the appearance of serious enforcement and reduce the probability that corruption will become a public issue (see, e.g., Chambliss, 1978: 91-92; Whyte, 1955: 123-46).

Similarly, both sides may be interested in regulation. For obvious reasons, public officials hope to avoid scandals that call attention to tolerated underworld activities. Likewise, those who regard themselves as "honest" criminal entrepreneurs may desire regulation. If a fly-by-night numbers bank fails to pay winners, for instance, this can lessen the popularity of betting on the numbers. If some houses of prostitution rob customers, this may discourage customers from patronizing other prostitutes. Regularized corruption, then, has sometimes created a social structure within which the police, often guided by local politicians, use the law as a lever for enforcing informal regulations. Although corrupt relations between politicians and the underworld have been the subject of a number of scholarly studies (Chambliss, 1978; Fox, 1989: Ch. 6; Gardiner, 1970; Haller, 1988; Landesco, 1968: Ch. 8; Reuter, 1984), little attention has been given to historical trends in the impact of corruption on criminal enterprise. In American cities at the turn of the century, a number of factors combined to facilitate corruption. First was the general expectation that urban political organizations (called political "machines" by their opponents) would accept payments to do favors for various interests within a fragmented metropolis (Merton, 1957: 71-82; Tarr, 1967). Second, certain structural characteristics of city government enhanced the role of local politicians. In the nineteenth century, wards were not simply electoral units but also administrative units. It was common for ward boundaries and police precincts to overlap and also for each ward to have its own police court. Because ward politicians often selected the local police captain and because police justices were cogs in the ward's political machine, the criminal justice system was a major resource available to politicians for doing favors that might strengthen the political organization (Fogelson, 1977: Ch. 1; Haller, 1976b; Reppetto, 1978; Richardson, 1970: Ch. 8).

With the passage of time, control by local politicians, particularly in large cities, has weakened, so that regularized corruption has declined as a factor in coordination of illegal activities. To understand the decline, it is first necessary to understand the use of corruption to limit competition and regulate enterprise at the turn of the century.

Politics and Gambling

An example of the use of corruption to limit competition was the role of Chicago ward politicians in allocating bookmaking and other gambling rights during the mayoralty of Carter H. Harrison II from 1897 to 1905.[2] By that time Irish-Americans dominated gambling in the city and were disproportionately represented among local politicians and police. Within this Irish gambling/politics complex, a number of patterns existed by which politicians oversaw and, in effect, licensed important gambling activity.

One pattern was for a local gambler to become the ward leader and thereby combine his political and economic interests. On the West Side, for example, William (Billy) Skidmore started selling racing programs at tracks around the city while still a teenager in the 1890s. Soon he opened a saloon with gambling in the back room, entered politics, and became ward committeeman of the Thirteenth Ward. In 1912 he was sergeant at arms at the Democratic National Convention and later assisted in the presidential campaign of Woodrow Wilson (Murray, 1965: 366-374). By 1905, in partnership with Patrick J. (Patsy) King, he operated a horse parlor at 189 West Madison Street, as well as a major policy gambling syndicate. For nearly four decades, until his conviction in 1939 for income tax evasion, he was a Democratic power and leading gambler in Chicago.

Another pattern was for close relations to develop between an important gambler and local political figures. James O'Leary—just two years old in 1871 when the Chicago fire started in his mother's barn—bore a famous Chicago name. In the 1890s he built a saloon and gambling emporium across from the business headquarters of the thriving Chicago stockyards. His three-story building housed bowling alleys, a barbershop, restaurant, turkish bath, gambling rooms, and a horse parlor—everything that might fulfill the dreams of a cattleman who wanted to celebrate after selling his stock for slaughter. From his gambling house, O'Leary also backed the bookmakers who serviced the stockyard workers in saloons west of the stockyards. He maintained his gambling interests through close connections with ward politicians and with Police Inspector Nicholas Hunt, reputed to be the city's wealthiest cop and a political power in his own right. (His son served as a Democratic member of the state legislature from 1901 to 1904.) Inspector Hunt enjoyed horse racing and frequented the tracks, where, standing by the betting ring, he assured reporters that he saw no gambling.

A final pattern was for local ward leaders, although not themselves major gamblers, to license and oversee a range of gambling activities by political supporters. Those two famous Chicago aldermen, Michael (Hinky Dink) Kenna and "Bathhouse" John Coughlin, were prime examples. Large, gregarious, and a gaudy dresser, Bathhouse was well known in gambling circles before entering politics. Hinky Dink, by contrast, was small and quiet and operated a famous saloon in the First Ward. From 1892 until the early 1940s, either Bathhouse John, Hinky Dink, or both served on the city council and oversaw vice and entertainment in the Loop and the Lively Levee entertainment district south of the Loop (Wendt and Kogan, 1943). In the early twentieth century, Tom McGinnis, a saloonkeeper and gambler, coordinated gambling for the two aldermen. He received a cut from poker games in the downtown hotels and accepted payoffs from bookmakers and gambling house owners. Among his associates was John (Mushmouth) Johnson, a black who owned one of the largest gambling houses in the Levee, supported Democratic candidates among black voters, and collected payments from Chinese gambling house operators in Chicago's Chinatown (Haller, 1988; Wooldridge, 1901: 191-195). In addition, Johnson and McGinnis were partners in the largest policy gambling syndicate in the ward.

Regulating the Red-Light Districts

If gambling in Chicago displayed the patterns by which politicians informally licensed illegal enterprise, the red-light districts of American cities exemplified the role of politicians and police in the regulation of vice. The red-light districts, which emerged in American cities between the 1870s and World War I and were located on the edge of the central business districts, contained the disreputable nightlife entertainment of the city. Crammed together with houses of prostitution were burlesque theaters, concert saloons (night clubs), dance halls, and gambling houses. Within the districts, drug dealers hawked morphine and cocaine, thieves fenced stolen goods, and pimps and other outcasts carried on their social life and hustling activities.[3]

Often the districts abutted skid row and the local Chinatown (Blumberg et al., 1978: Ch. 1-3; Light, 1974, 1977; Rosen, 1982: Ch. 5, 6; Woolston, 1969: Ch. 4, 5).

By 1900 the red-light districts—San Francisco's Barbary Coast, New Orleans' French Quarter, Chicago's Levee, or the Tenderloins of Philadelphia and New York—were integrated within the local political machines. Those who participated in local politics expected to be allowed to operate a saloon, gambling house, or parlor house in the district. Often the local political club was a social center where pimps and politicians hung out, gambled, and plotted political strategy. There was, in short, an overlap between the political organizations and the economic activities of the districts.

In this context, local officials instituted informal and formal regulation. Regulation had a variety of goals: to minimize the spread of venereal diseases, to prevent scandals that often erupted from the forcible recruitment of prostitutes or the employment of young girls, or to shield respectable citizens from the shock of observing the city's sinful underside (see, for instance, Best, 1987). In Chicago in 1910, although prostitution was illegal, written police regulations prescribed that "no house of ill-fame shall be permitted outside of certain restricted districts, or to be established within two blocks of any school, church, hospital, or public institution, or upon any street car line." No "under age" girls were to work in the houses, and no woman was to be detained against her will. Even decorum within the houses was ostensibly regulated by rules that "short skirts, transparent gowns or other improper attire shall not be permitted in the parlors, or public rooms," and "obscene exhibitions or pictures shall not be permitted" (Vice Commission of Chicago, 1911: 329-330). In Houston, where city leaders attempted to establish regulated prostitution in 1907, a major issue was whether to require racially segregated bordellos (Mackey, 1987: Ch. 6).

Illegal Enterprise

A few cities, to stem the spread of venereal diseases, tried medical regulation, modeled on the European system (Flexner, 1969). An early attempt was a "Social Evil Ordinance," which was backed by the St. Louis Board of Health and passed by the city council in 1870. The ordinance required that prostitutes register with the city, that they undergo weekly examination by a city physician, and that women diagnosed to have a venereal disease be hospitalized until cured. Although the ordinance lasted just four years before outraged opponents persuaded the state legislature to nullify it, health officials in other cities looked favorably on the St.

Louis experiment (Burnham, 1971a, 1971b). In 1911, some 40 years later, San Francisco established through its Board of Public Health a system requiring all prostitutes in the city to undergo a medical examination twice weekly at the municipal clinic. Women free of venereal disease received a card that permitted them to practice prostitution in the prescribed red-light district. Despite charges of corruption, the system lasted two years before being abandoned (Shumsky, 1980).

The regulation of red-light districts can, of course, be regarded with cynicism. Generally the regulations were only haphazardly enforced; often they were intended, in part, to assure the public that the problem was under control in order to head off demands that the laws against prostitution be seriously enforced. But the rules also reflected what police leaders and many politicians believed to be sensible public policy. Convinced that prostitution was inevitable, they argued that it was better to regulate it in recognized sections of the city than to have it dispersed throughout the city. In Milwaukee, for instance, although there was no evidence of police corruption, police policies mirrored the policies in other cities. Any woman intending to practice prostitution had to register with the police, listing her age and place of previous work. This was to prevent "white slavery" and the recruitment of underage girls. Milwaukee police also banned the sale of alcoholic beverages in houses of prostitution in the belief that alcohol and sex were a volatile mixture.[4]

The regulation of prostitution within a system of corruption, then, represented an attempt by local authorities to deal with vice activities that, while illegal, were also regarded as inevitable. Systematic corruption had multiple functions: to organize politics and voting within the entertainment district, to supplement the income of police and local politicians, but also to introduce regulations that dominant groups favored as strategies to deal with the shadier entertainment activities of the city.

Discussion of Corruption

To the extent that politicians or the police coordinate illegal enterprise, the coordination generally reflects the structure of local politics and law enforcement. Because law enforcement at the turn of the century was highly decentralized, coordination was decentralized; each ward (and police district) tended to coordinate gambling and vice within its area. On the other hand, to the extent that law enforcement was sometimes centralized, coordination might be centralized. The formation of a citywide gambling squad, for instance, introduced the possibility of citywide coordination of gambling activities and the potential breakdown of local arrangements.

During the twentieth century, the role of institutionalized corruption in the control of illegal enterprise has undergone two important changes. One change has been a relative decline in the importance of corruption as a factor underlying coordination (Haller, 1976b). To the extent that corruption continues to coordinate illegal activities, however, a second change is that the police are now more likely to act on their own rather than under the control of local politicians.

Many factors have reduced systematic corruption and undercut the control of local politicians over the police. These factors include civil service reform, police unionization, centralization of police communication and command functions, and the redrawing of local police districts so that they no longer correspond with political wards (Fogelson, 1977: Ch. 6-9; Walker, 1980: Ch. 9). Particularly since the 1960s, in addition, new laws and policies have empowered state and especially federal law enforcement agencies to investigate local corruption and prosecute criminal entrepreneurs (see, e.g., Carlisle, 1976; Johnson, 1981: Ch. 10, 11; Mollenhoff, 1972).

Local politicians, as a result, have less ability to set local police policy or to protect criminal activities within their bailiwicks. This can be seen, for instance, in the Knapp Commission investigation of the New York City police in the early 1970s. Unlike earlier studies of police corruption in New York, the Knapp Commission found that police acted independently of politicians in establishing corrupt relations for the regulation of gambling or prostitution.[5]

Business Partnerships

Partnership arrangements have long been a common method for launching various illegal enterprises. Partnerships have the same advantages for illegal entrepreneurs as for legal entrepreneurs. First, partnerships allow several entrepreneurs to share risks, particularly the risk of business failure. Second, partnerships enable persons with different resources to pool their resources in a single enterprise. For those involved in illegal businesses, partnerships permit persons with political influence, capital, and managerial skills to cooperate so that each has a direct economic stake in the enterprise. The possibility of coordination arises when some partners, through participation in multiple and overlapping partnerships, can ensure that the different enterprises act cooperatively. The best way to clarify the use of partnerships is by examples.

Colonial Inn

The Colonial Inn, a posh illegal casino that opened in December 1945 in Hallandale, Florida, near Miami, was an example of a partnership that brought together a variety of entrepreneurs in a complex joint venture. Meyer Lansky was the chief entrepreneur. He arranged political protection, oversaw the remodeling of a mansion into a casino with a fine restaurant and elegant gaming rooms, and called on long-time business associates in New York and Florida to provide the necessary capital. Investors included Frank Erickson and Frank Costello (already cooperating in numerous New York and Florida gambling enterprises), Vincent "Jimmy Blue Eyes" Alo, and Joe Adonis. To ensure success, however, the casino needed an expert manager (see Figure 11.1).[6]

Mert Wertheimer had run gambling enterprises in Detroit since the 1920s. Within the American gambling fraternity, he enjoyed a reputation as a skilled operator with important contacts in the world of sports and entertainment. In 1944, after he and his partners—Reuben Mathis, Danny Sullivan, and Lincoln Fitzgerald—were indicted for gambling, they left Michigan to evade prosecution. In October 1945, while attending the World Series in Chicago, Wertheimer ran into Jake Lansky, Meyer's brother. Jake asked Wertheimer to manage the casino in the Colonial Inn. Indeed, so eager was Jake to secure Wertheimer's services that he offered him a 50% partnership. Although Wertheimer was not required to invest money in the casino, he was expected to cover 50% of any losses that might occur. Wertheimer agreed, but insisted that his partners also participate. As a result, Sullivan and Fitzgerald each invested $50,000, and Mathis became the assistant manager.

As opening day approached, however, Wertheimer was troubled by his commitment to cover half the casino's losses. He therefore approached Jack Guzik, once Al Capone's bootlegging partner and now a partner with Tony Accardo in various gambling enterprises in Chicago, downstate Illinois, and Florida. Over the years, Guzik had invested in several Wertheimer ventures. Wertheimer now offered Guzik 50% of his profits from the Colonial Inn if Guzik would agree to cover 50% of his losses.

Figure 11.1

Casino Partnership, 1945-1946

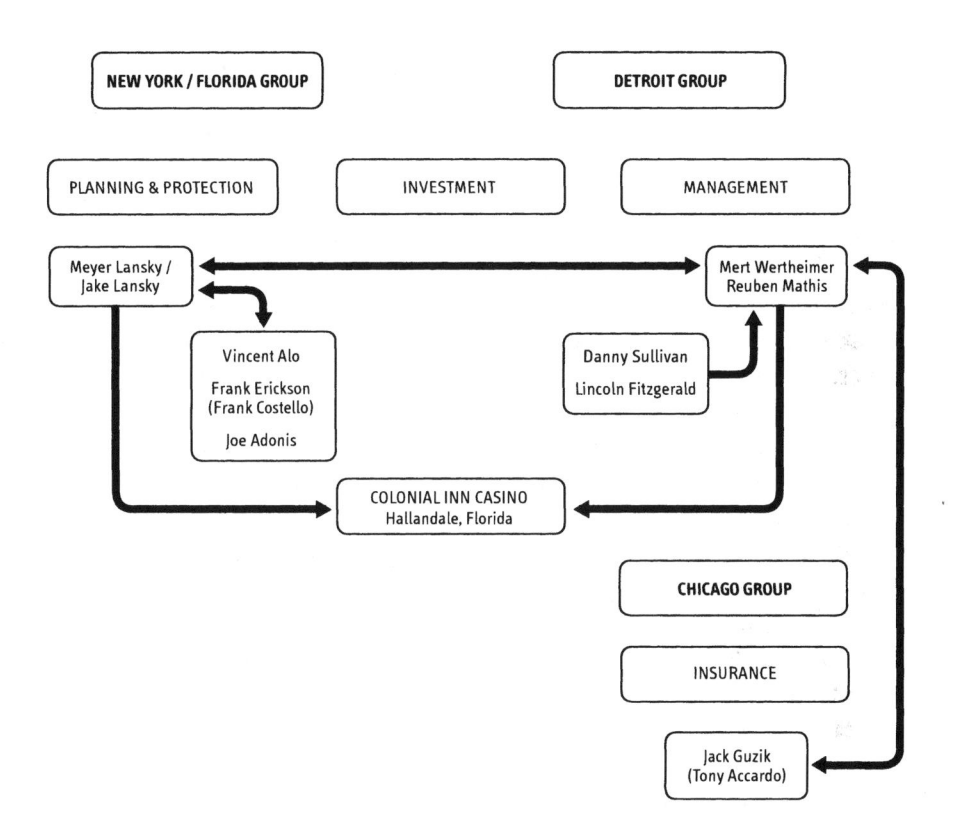

```
         NEW YORK / FLORIDA GROUP                    DETROIT GROUP

    PLANNING & PROTECTION     INVESTMENT           MANAGEMENT

    Meyer Lansky /  ←——————————————————————→   Mert Wertheimer   ←——
    Jake Lansky                                   Reuben Mathis       |
         |   ↓                                         ↑              |
         |   Vincent Alo                     Danny Sullivan           |
         |   Frank Erickson                  Lincoln Fitzgerald       |
         |   (Frank Costello)                                         |
         |   Joe Adonis                                               |
         |                                                            |
         └——→  COLONIAL INN CASINO  ←————————————————————————         |
               Hallandale, Florida                                    |
                                                                      |
                                             CHICAGO GROUP            |
                                                                      |
                                               INSURANCE              |
                                                                      |
                                              Jack Guzik   ←——————————
                                             (Tony Accardo)
```

Guzik (and Accardo) agreed and thereby assumed a 25% interest in the casino.

The Colonial Inn opened on schedule, with Xavier Cugat's band on hand to entertain and deputy sheriffs as attendants to park customers' cars. It was probably the largest and most successful illegal casino in the country. In March 1946 Wertheimer, having earned nearly a quarter of a million dollars, quit as partner. He gave Guzik some $92,000.

The Colonial Inn, then, was a complex partnership that united the skills and resources of diverse entrepreneurs. Geographically, the partners came from Detroit, Chicago, New York, and Florida. In ethnic background, they were Jewish, Italian, and Irish. Together they provided planning, capital, political protection, managerial ability, and insurance against financial loss. Lansky, by combining his entrepreneurial skills and political influence with Wertheimer's managerial competence, ensured the casino's success.

Cicero Enterprises

If the Colonial Inn demonstrated the use of partnerships to pool resources, Cicero, Illinois, in the late 1920s revealed, in exaggerated form, the use of partnerships to provide the structure for coordinating diverse enterprises. Before prohibition, Cicero was a respectable blue-collar town, just five miles west of downtown Chicago. The major employer was Bell Telephone's Western Electric Company. Like many blue-collar towns, Cicero had long been a place where small gambling houses and saloons operated openly.

By 1923 the bootlegging organizations of John Torrio and Dion O'Banion peddled liquor to the speakeasies there, and the two men became jointly involved in local gambling houses. Louis Alterie represented the O'Banion group in the gambling ventures. During the elections in spring 1924, Torrio sent Al (Snorky) Capone and his gunmen into Cicero to seize the polling places and ensure the victory of a friendly slate. Although Chicago police entered the city late in the day and drove the gunmen out, the Torrio slate won, and his group thereafter exercised significant political influence. Then a series of events upset relationships in Cicero. Torrio was arrested at one of his Chicago breweries and soon afterwards was shot and wounded by an O'Banion gunman. In the ensuing gang warfare, O'Banion himself was assassinated, and his allies were ousted from Cicero. A further result of the warfare was that Torrio, after serving a brief jail term, decided that Chicago was dangerous to his health and returned to New York. His associates, including Capone, inherited his business interests. Because Capone was a media celebrity who fascinated both investigative reporters and law enforcement agencies, it is possible to reconstruct the coordination of illegal activities in Cicero from 1925 to 1930 (see Figure 11.2).[7]

The group known to history as the Capone gang is best understood not as a hierarchy directed by Al Capone but as a complex set of partnerships. Four men might be called "senior partners"—Al and his older brother Ralph Capone, their cousin Frank Nitti, and Jack Guzik. They shared more or less equally in their joint income and acted as equals in looking after their varied business interests.[8] The senior partners, in turn, formed partnerships with others to launch numerous bootlegging, gambling, and vice activities in the Chicago Loop, South Side, and several suburbs. Cicero, because of their political influence there, was an important arena for their operations.

The senior partners had an interest in several of the gambling houses in Cicero. Because of periodic police raids or newspaper exposés, gambling houses often closed, moved, merged, or changed their names, and the history of the various houses is too complicated for this paper. By 1925, however, the largest of the gambling houses was the Hawthorne Smoke Shop. To manage bookmaking at the Smoke Shop, the senior partners entered into partnership with Frankie Pope; to run gambling games, they entered into partnership with Pete Penovich.[9] Each of their other gambling houses in Cicero was a separate, relatively small operation, in which the senior partners and a local manager had partnership interests. Another person with a stake in Cicero gambling houses was Louis LaCava, who claimed as much as 20% of the profits and served as an important gambling coordinator until 1927. In all probability, he represented the absent Torrio and was on the scene to look after Torrio's remaining interests. In the early 1930s, at any rate, he followed Torrio to New York and served as an officer in a major Torrio company there.[10]

Other enterprises in Cicero and nearby suburbs were similarly linked to the senior partners. For beer distribution the senior partners negotiated a partnership with Louis Lipschultz, Jack Guzik's brother-in-law. Already a truck dealer in the western suburbs, Lipschultz oversaw the purchase of beer in downstate cities, like Joliet, and the wholesale distribution to the many small speakeasies in Cicero and adjacent towns. Eventually the senior partners decided to expand into slot machines. For this business, they formed a partnership with Sam Guzik, Jack's younger brother. Finally, because Cicero voters opposed prostitution in their community, the senior partners developed a line of vice resorts and roadhouses in the small town of Stickney, just south of Cicero. Here, in partnership with Louis Consentino, they backed the Harlem Inn, a two-story building housing one of the Midwest's notable bordellos.[11]

Another important Cicero enterprise was the Hawthorne Kennel Club, a dog racing track, which opened for business in May 1927. At that time, a St. Louis lawyer appropriately named Edward J. O'Hare held the patent on the mechanical rabbit used for dog racing. (The Chicago airport is named after his son, who died a hero in World War II.) Because dog

Illegal Enterprise

Figure 11.2

Cicero Enterprises, 1925-1929

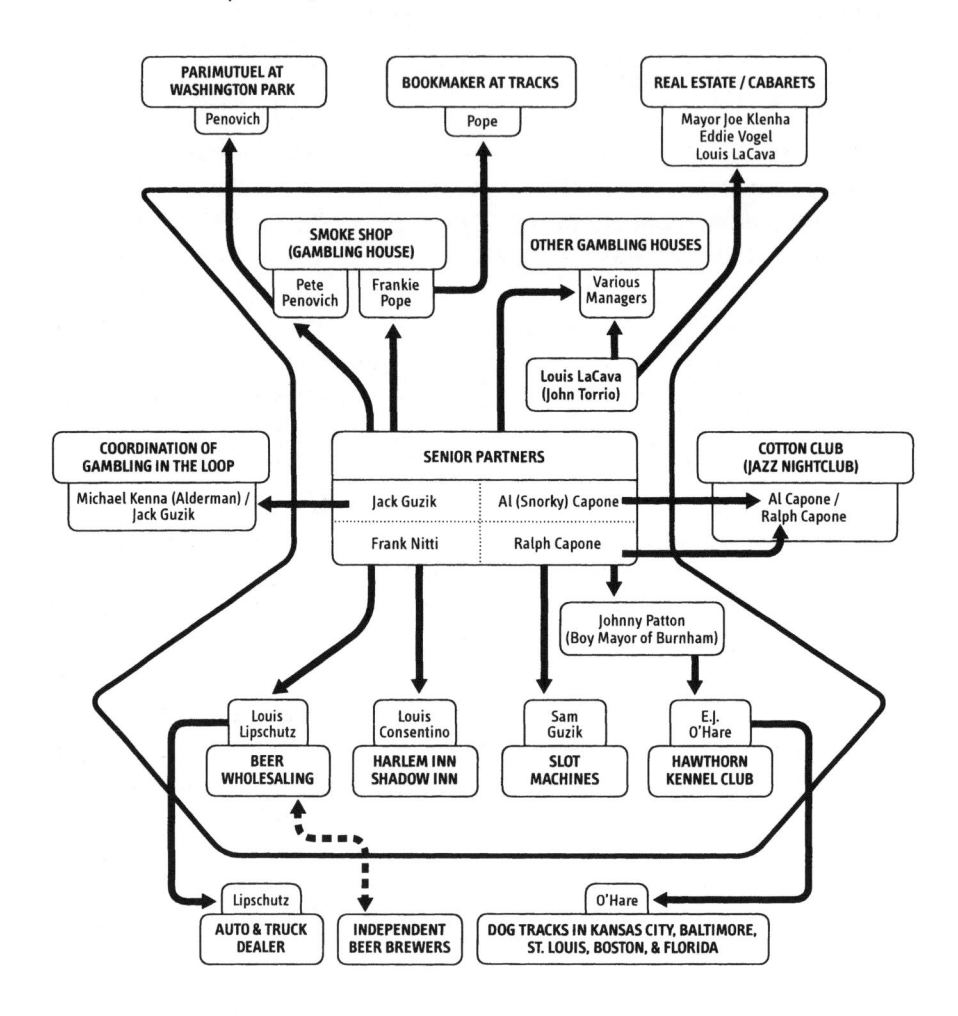

tracks derived their profits from illegal betting, O'Hare searched in various cities for local partners with political connections and a willingness to risk money in an enterprise of questionable legitimacy. Often he turned to bootleggers, because they were likely to have both capital and political influence. In Chicago he entered into an agreement with the senior partners, under which they probably held a 49% interest in the Kennel Club. For this enterprise, the senior partners were joined by Johnny Patton, known as the "Boy Mayor of Burnham." Elected mayor of that small Illinois town while still a teenager before World War I, Patton encouraged Chicago vice entrepreneurs to open resorts there and, in the process, met Torrio and Guzik. Because O'Hare had dog tracks in other states and was often out of town, Patton took on important management responsibilities at the Kennel Club.[12]

In short, the various enterprises of the so-called "Capone gang" were not controlled bureaucratically. Each, instead, was a separate enterprise of small or relatively small scale. Most had managers who were also partners. Coordination was possible because the senior partners, with an interest in each of the enterprises, exerted influence across a range of activities.

The partnerships in Cicero were not a disguise for an essentially hierarchical structure. Many of the partners were themselves businessmen who carried on other business activities, legal and illegal, independently of the senior partners. Penovich and Pope, for instance, in addition to their partnership in the Smoke Shop, were illegal bookmakers at several Chicago dog or horse tracks and pursued other gambling interests around the city. Lipschultz, as already mentioned, was not only a partner in beer distribution with the senior partners but also a truck dealer in the Chicago suburbs. LaCava, in addition to his share in the various gambling houses of Cicero, conducted a real estate business with Cicero Mayor Joe Klenha and two other local politicians. As realtors, they owned picnic grounds and cabarets. Finally, O'Hare not only joined with Patton and the senior partners in the Hawthorne Kennel Club, but also promoted dog tracks in St. Louis, Baltimore, Pennsylvania, and Florida.[13]

Cicero was unusual in terms of the degree of coordination exercised by the senior partners. Nevertheless, the coordination was exerted through a series of deals with relatively independent businessmen to operate separate, small-scale enterprises.

Partnerships: A Discussion

The structure of criminal partnerships differs from that often imputed to those involved in such activities-especially if the activities are thought of as "organized crime." Yet the structure makes sense theoretically. The "organized crime" model stresses hierarchy and centralized control, but a partnership model posits that each enterprise is a separate enterprise that pools resources and provides local management. Such decentralization, of course, renders a business less vulnerable to law enforcement. By spreading the risks among separate partnerships, entrepreneurs minimize losses from bankruptcy or police raids of any single enterprise. But decentralization also makes sense for another important reason: Criminal entrepreneurs generally have had neither the skills nor the personalities for the detailed, bureaucratic oversight of large organizations. They are, instead, hustlers and dealers, for whom partnership arrangements are ideally suited. They enjoy the give and take of personal negotiations, risk-taking, and moving from deal to deal. Adler (1985: 148), in her study of drug dealers, captured this well: "In contrast to the bureaucratization of most conventional forms of work, drug dealing and smuggling were flexible, creative, exciting, and personal enterprises."

An emphasis on decentralization through partnerships is not, however, an argument that all participants are equal. An analysis of partnerships permits, instead, clearer understanding of the mechanisms by which some persons exert more influence than others. Those with political influence, for instance, will be attractive partners because they can supply a critical need. Indeed, they can often insist on being given a share of the profits. Similarly, since enterprises often require capital, wealthy entrepreneurs can invest in a range of enterprises and thereby extend their influence. Partnerships, then, constitute a structure within which some entrepreneurs exercise more influence than others because they have political or economic resources to participate in a number of partnerships simultaneously.

The study of partnerships, therefore, should be given greater attention within criminology. How, for instance, do partners enforce partnership arrangements? One factor is that reliability as a partner (or, at least, the appearance of reliability) is important for career success. Smart entrepreneurs fulfill their obligations in order to be offered future opportunities. Johnny Patton, by being a reliable partner with the Capone/Guzik group in the Hawthorne Kennel Club and other enterprises, established his credentials. In the 1930s and into the 1940s, he was an important figure in several Florida racing ventures. His successful early cooperation was the key to more lucrative opportunities in subsequent years.

Violence or the threat of violence, of course, can also shape partnership behavior. But the importance of violence can easily be exaggerated. Violence is destabilizing and not an effective method for partnership enforcement. A person with a reputation for violence is less likely to be accepted as a partner by successful entrepreneurs. Who, after all, would wish to jeopardize his life or health if he could pursue a successful career without doing so? Furthermore, violence can be used to cheat a partner as easily as it can be used to ensure honesty. A person who is violent can, and often does, take money from an enterprise and dare the partners to do something about it. Although many criminal entrepreneurs, especially since the 1920s, have had reputations for violence, factors other than violence better explain the enforcement of partnership agreements.

Internal Economic Factors

Numerous economic factors also shape the structure of illegal enterprise, some working to bring about forms of cooperation and others tending to reduce the scale of cooperation. This chapter focuses on two quite different types of economic relationships that have been important in providing structure to illegal enterprises. One relationship is that between buyers and sellers in moving illegal goods from manufacture or import to the ultimate consumer. The other relationship is that which develops within gambling syndicates to handle the problem of economic risk that gamblers face when bettors have lucky streaks.

Enterprises that involve illegal goods often have at least three levels of operation. First, the goods must be manufactured or imported; then they may be processed and wholesaled; and finally, they are peddled to consumers. Both the distribution of bootleg liquor in the 1920s and the distribution of illegal drugs in more recent years have generally involved entrepreneurs who specialize at different levels; rarely has a single group been engaged at all three levels. Indeed, recent heroin or cocaine networks have often involved several levels of wholesalers between importation and the final sale, so that the price to the user may be 10 times the price at import (Adler, 1985; Lasswell and McKenna, n.d.: Ch. 3, 4; Moore, 1977; Reuter and Kleiman, 1986). The fact that entrepreneurs have generally operated at separate levels, then, has necessarily required continued business dealings among persons with different specializations.

In the 1920s bootleg liquor importers in the New York region sold their goods not only in the Northeast corridor but also to Midwestern cities. By the late 1920s, when the Coast Guard had considerably reduced smuggling into the Northeast, Florida and New Orleans became major centers of importation, selling to wholesalers in as far away as New York and Chicago. Similarly, wholesalers who serviced a metropolitan market required a broad range of products for sale to the speakeasies and other retail outlets. A group specializing in wholesale activities, such as the Capone/Guzik partnership in Chicago, purchased imported liquor from Detroit, New York, and Florida; obtained alcohol from Midwest distilleries; sometimes secured industrial alcohol from Philadelphia; and trucked beer from Racine, Wisconsin, or from blue-collar cities in downstate Illinois. The fact that liquor was a bulky product and that it often required fairly complicated manufacture or processing forced bootleggers, depending on their position in the network of distribution, to invest in ships, trucks, breweries, distilleries, and bottling companies. Nevertheless, although the range of regional and even international cooperation in bootlegging was impressive, the scale of individual firms was relatively small when compared with the legal liquor industry in the period before or after Prohibition. Crucially important were the sometimes temporary and sometimes regular deals among numerous firms, rather than the creation of large, bureaucratic organizations for trafficking in bootleg liquor.[14]

Among illegal services, the history of policy gambling syndicates in American cities, dating from at least the 1860s, and the history of numbers syndicates, dating from the 1920s, indicate that certain inherent economic factors lead to syndication. (A syndicate is here defined as a system of cooperation so that many retailers are backed by the same group of entrepreneurs.) The primary reason for the 120-year history of policy and numbers syndicates is the desire of small-time operators to limit economic risk.

Policy gambling, which has existed in American cities from at least the late eighteenth century, is a betting game using the numbers 1 to 78. Those operating the game draw 12 numbers, and the bettors normally choose 1 to 5 numbers that they hope will be among the 12 drawn. In the 1920s, numbers gambling replaced policy in most cities, in part because it was a simpler game. In numbers, bettors normally select a single three-digit number between 000 and 999. The odds are 1 in 1,000 of winning, but the payoff has traditionally ranged from 500: 1 to 650: 1. Both policy and numbers have the same crucial characteristic: because the customers select the numbers, there is the risk that, on any given day, a heavily played number may win and the entrepreneur will be unable to cover the losses. For someone selling policy or numbers as an adjunct to operating a barbershop, saloon, or newspaper kiosk, failure to pay will not only lose bettors but legitimate customers as well. What the retailer needs, then, is for someone to assume the risks (Asbury, 1938: Ch. 6; Carlson, 1940: Pt. II; Haller, 1976a: 104-105, 117-121).

As a result, policy and numbers have typically been coordinated by syndicates in which there is a division of function. Retailers cultivate customers in the neighborhoods and take the bets. They keep a set percentage of the money bet with them (typically 15 to 20%) and pass on the rest of the money, along with the betting slips, to syndicate backers. The important economic function of the syndicate is to assume the risk by paying the winners. Syndicate backers often furnish other services: they arrange for the daily collection of money and slips, provide notification of the winning numbers, and, when possible, negotiate political and police protection (Haller, 1976a; Lasswell and McKenna, n.d.: Ch. 3, 4; Reuter, 1983: Ch. 3).[15]

Both retailers and backers benefit from syndication. Retailers enjoy a steady income, based on the amount bet each day by their customers, without assuming the risk of paying winning bettors. Syndicate backers, in turn, receive money from a large number of retailers. Because retailers keep a percentage of the money and because there are the expenses of collecting from retailers, making payments to winners, administering a headquarters, and providing protection, backers may have a small profit margin. Their hope is that the syndicate can clear a small percentage from a large gross income and thus earn a profit commensurate with the investment in the enterprise. Syndication of policy or numbers gambling has meant that dozens or even hundreds of retailers may have the same backers, offer similar odds, and pay off on the same winning numbers. Syndication obviously involves a significant degree of coordination. The hierarchical or bureaucratic nature of that coordination should not be exaggerated, however. To a considerable extent, retailers have remained independent sellers working on a commission. If they operate a barbershop or bar, the numbers or policy selling is a service provided to customers within the context of a legitimate business. The· daily contact of retailers with customers is as important to the syndicate backers as the syndicate backers' assumption of risk is to the sellers. In Chicago in the 1930s, the major retailers (or "policy stations," as they were called) advertised that they sold policy slips for all of the major policy wheels. Like independent insurance agents who represent several companies, the policy stations were commission agents for a number of policy syndicates (Caldwell, 1940). In New York in the early 1930s, when a group of partners including Arthur ("Dutch") Schultz muscled in on many of the Harlem numbers syndicates and then reduced the retailers' commission, retailers ceased writing numbers until the previous commission was restored (Block, 1983: Ch. 6). An important recent study of numbers in New York City found that retailers (collectors) sometimes retained small bets (keeping the full profits and paying the losses), that some collectors made payoffs on winning numbers at a rate lower or higher than that of the syndicate, and that individual collectors, on occasion, moved their business from one syndicate to another (Reuter, 1983: C3). Thus, although syndicate backers typically enjoy greater economic and political resources than retailers, retailers nevertheless may act as relatively independent operators in their dealings with both customers and backers.

Because so much of the research dealing with illegal enterprise uses an "organized crime" model, too little attention has been given to the impact of economics in determining the structure and methods of cooperation within illegal enterprise. Yet, as Reuter (1983) has shown, the internal economics of numbers gambling, sports bookmaking, and loansharking are similar whether or not the entrepreneurs are members of an Italian-American crime family. Even in New York, with its five families, the families have little measurable impact in shaping the structure of an enterprise or in limiting competition among enterprises. Furthermore, an understanding of the economics of illegal enterprise has important implications for understanding the intended and unintended consequences of various law enforcement strategies (see, e.g., Ekland-Olson et al., 1984; Kleiman, 1985). Because the economic decisions of criminal entrepreneurs occur within an environment formed by diverse law enforcement policies, an analysis of the interaction between the legal environment and entrepreneurial decisions provides the most promising strategy for understanding the economic relationships within illegal enterprise.

Discussion and Conclusion

This analysis has implications for understanding the relationship of illegal enterprise to the Cosa Nostra outfits formed by Italian-American criminals and emerging in some American cities during the past 40 to 60 years. If the underworld of illegal enterprise consists typically of entrepreneurs involved in numerous short-term and long-term legal and illegal money-making activities, then one way to understand the functions and durability of Cosa Nostra groups is to examine how they serve their members' business interests.[16]

Such an analysis would recognize the separation between the Cosa Nostra family, on the one hand, and the members' independent business activities, on the other.[17] Like the Chamber of Commerce or Rotary Club for legal businessmen, a Cosa Nostra group would be seen, not as an organization that operates illegal (or legal) businesses, but as an association that businessmen join partly to further their business careers. This notion was captured in a conversation in 1962 between Angelo Bruno, then leader of the Philadelphia outfit, and Sam DeCavalcante, soon-to-be head of a northern New Jersey mob. Bruno complained: "Look, Sam, I got people, they want to go partners with me. I don't want to go partners with them. When a man is hard to get along with, Sam, you should not go partners with him."[18] The statement recognized that he and other individuals within his outfit were independent businessmen whose business relations with each other were mediated chiefly through independent partnerships.

As with legal businessmen in a Rotary club, a major reason to join a Costa Nostra group is to cultivate business contacts. Those who are beginners hope that more experienced entrepreneurs will throw opportunities their way and perhaps offer attractive partnership opportunities. More successful businessmen will wish to wheel and deal among their equals, make selective investments in the enterprises of younger men, and have access to information that will aid their business decision making. Members may also be aided by other members who can provide specific services. Bookmakers, who cannot borrow from legitimate lenders when they suffer loses, can gain access to a loan shark. Or, at a more general level, members who encounter problems with law enforcement anticipate that politically influential members will come to their assistance.

Another function of Cosa Nostra outfits is to provide norms of behavior and a system for resolving business disputes. Those who pursue careers in illegal activities have a need for understood rules for interacting with others in the same culture (Anderson, 1979: 44-47; Best and Luckenbill, 1982: Ch.10) but often lack groups that can define the rules. Beyond this, as many scholars have noted, those in illegal operations generally cannot turn to the legal system to settle disputes that arise out of violations of norms in their business dealings. In earlier years, politicians and police, in order to avoid violence and the attendant scandal, often mediated disputes within the underworld, but their ability to resolve disputes has been weakened in recent years. Under these circumstances, dispute settlement can be a significant activity by Cosa Nostra leaders (Abadinsky, 1983: Ch. 11; Reuter, 1983: Ch. 7).

Although the perspective outlined here offers insight into the relationship of Italian-American outfits to the illegal enterprises of the city, the chief purpose is to explore illegal enterprise as a criminal activity in its own right. In this respect, a number of generalizations can be made.

First, of course, although illegal enterprises may sometimes develop stability through corruption of officials or through skillful and clandestine management, most such activities are relatively small scale and short term. Even activities involving large sums of money and substantial profits are often carried out by relatively small and informally structured groups. A major drug deal, for instance, may involve a few persons who pool resources to purchase drugs from an importer and then sell at a considerable markup to one or more buyers. Although the individuals may remain active in drug trafficking, the particular group may never deal with each other again. And, if groups do develop regular relations, buying or selling on credit, they will generally operate in an informal and unstructured manner. (See, e.g., Adler, 1985: Ch. 4; Reuter, 1988; Reuter and Haaga, 1989: Ch. 3; for an earlier period, see Block, 1979, and Vyhnanek, 1981.)

Careers in illegal enterprise vary considerably. Some operators may specialize and stick to a single illegal activity. A few bookmakers, with a love of sports and sports gambling, will attempt to make a career in bookmaking. Even when a bookmaker goes bankrupt, his next step may be to work for another bookmaker (Pledge, 1956; Reuter, 1983: Ch. 2). Other entrepreneurs, though, may spend their time looking for varied opportunities to turn a profit. Street-level entrepreneurs—the blue-collar workers of illegal enterprise—seek ventures that require street smarts and muscle: selling a van of stolen televisions, bringing in a truckload of untaxed cigarettes from the Carolinas, or helping to collect a delinquent loan for a loan shark (Pileggi, 1985). At a middle level, Joseph Valachi, for example, after his apprenticeship period, ran a numbers bank, dabbled in loan-sharking, and eventually sold counterfeit ration stamps during World War II (Maas, 1968). Top entrepreneurs like Meyer Lansky had sufficient resources of money and entrepreneurial skills that they operated in regional and even international markets. Such persons might have interests in casinos, race tracks, and hotels in Miami, Havana, and Las Vegas (Haller, 1985a; Messick, 1967, 1971).

For many illegal entrepreneurs, the distinction between legal and illegal business activities is blurred. Their own careers move from one to the other, and their ventures often bridge the two worlds. Furthermore, illegal entrepreneurs often deal with "legitimate" businessmen. They know that many retailers will buy stolen goods, that some bankers will make loans with stolen securities as collateral (Teresa, 1973), that businesses ranging from the garment industry to antique dealers borrow regularly from loan sharks (Goldstock and Coenen, 1980: 157-159; Haller and Alviti, 1977; Seidl, 1968: Ch. 2, 3), and that various legitimate businessmen will make investments in shady deals or help launder the funds from illegal enterprises (President's Commission on Organized Crime, 1984; Karchmer, 1985).[19] Illegal entrepreneurs may also have ongoing political contacts, ranging from a prostitute's bribery of a policeman on the beat to the linkage of international drug traffickers with the Central Intelligence Agency and the foreign policy establishment (Cockburn, 1987; Kwitney, 1987; Sharkey, 1988). Criminal entrepreneurs act within a world of money-making, deals, and favors; all the "wise guys" have rackets, and they see little difference between their rackets and the rackets of those who look down on them (Haller, 1971-72).

Finally, as this final chapter has argued, the cooperation that sometimes emerges within illegal enterprise is seldom based on hierarchy or bureaucratic specialization. The urban underworld of small firms, hustling, and deal-making has a structure that reflects the necessity to avoid prosecution and to find a niche within the interstices of a larger and more bureaucratic society. Especially in the late nineteenth and early twentieth centuries, local ward leaders and local police often intervened to bring a certain amount of order to the illegal activities of a neighborhood or a ward. Seldom did that order extend even to an entire city. Furthermore, particularly since World War II, the ability of police and politicians to coordinate at the local level has weakened as a result of changes in both police and politics. Another source of coordination has derived from those entrepreneurs with the resources to participate in multiple and overlapping partnerships. In the nineteenth century, partnerships provided a structure for coordination primarily at the local level. But the experience of dealing bootleg liquor within an international market in the 1920s and the improvements in communication and transportation of the twentieth century have increasingly meant that some entrepreneurs used partnerships to exercise influence within regional and even international operations. Finally, economic factors within some illegal activities—whether the networks that transferred alcohol from foreign countries to the streets of American cities or the syndicates that assumed the risks in policy and numbers gambling—have resulted in a variety of cooperative relationships. The internal economic characteristics of such activities have led to cooperation at the same time that their illegality has worked against formal or bureaucratic solutions to the need for cooperation.

Notes

1. Smith (1971, 1975) has developed the concept of "illicit enterprise," which probably includes what I have called "illegal enterprise" but also includes a much wider range of activities. For discussions of the illegal enterprises of "organized crime" from a variety of perspectives, see Albini (1971: Ch. 7); Cressey (1969: Ch. 5); Ianni (1972: Ch. 5, 1974: Pt. III); Lasswell and McKenna (n.d.: Ch. 4); Rubin (1973); Schelling (1967); and especially Anderson (1979) and Reuter (1983).

2. Information on Chicago gambling is chiefly from the Herman F. Schuettler Scrapbooks of Newspaper Clippings, in Chicago Historical Society; also Citizens Association of Chicago, *Bulletin* No. 13 (June 10, 1904). Secondary sources are cited in the text.

3. For a description of the varied criminal activities within a redlight district, see investigative reports of the Bureau of Social Morals in New York City, found in the Judah L. Magnes Archives, Central Archives of the Jewish People, Jerusalem, Israel; see also, Block (1979).

4. Teasdale Commission Papers, Series No. 2/3/1/3-8, Box 19, Wisconsin State Historical Society, Madison.

5. Committee to Investigate Allegations of Corruption (1972). For an interesting discussion of the relation between police and gambling before and after the Knapp Commission, see Rubinstein and Reuter (1982: 60-93) and Reuter (1984). For a situation in Philadelphia similar to that found by Knapp in New York, see Pennsylvania Crime Commission (1974: 166-216). On the other

hand, the continuation of the traditional system of corrupt political control over the police is documented for the town of Chester in Pennsylvania Crime Commission (1989); see also Bellis (1985). Sherman (1978) provides a general discussion of police corruption and reform in recent years. The corruption from recent drug enforcement has generally not resulted in systematic licensing or regulation but has chiefly consisted of opportunistic shakedowns by police (McCormack, 1988).

6. The section on the Colonial Inn is based on a variety of sources. Investments are discussed in testimony before the Kefauver Committee; see U.S. Congress, Senate, Special Committee to Investigate Organized Crime in Interstate Commerce, *Investigation of Organized Crime in Interstate Commerce,* Hearings 81st Cong., 2nd Sess., 1950, and 82nd Cong., 1951, Part 1: 9-10, 115, 154-155, 480-481. Wertheimer's role is described in a memorandum from James E. Anderson to Special Agent in Charge, September 19, 1951, in the Guzik-Accardo income tax investigation file, File No. 42739-FR, Internal Revenue Service (IRS), Washington, D.C. The Colonial Inn is also mentioned in several secondary sources: Conrad (1982: 7-14); Eisenberg et al. (1979: 280, 292, 319); Fox (1989: 314); Messick (1971: 139-114). According to testimony before the Kefauver Committee (Part 1: 155), the Detroit group had a one-third interest in the Colonial Inn rather than the 50% interest claimed by Wertheimer.

7. Analysis of the Capone group businesses in Cicero is based on a number of sources: raw data in Capone income tax investigation, IRS File No. SI 7085-F; extensive newspaper clippings and investigative reports at Chicago Crime Commission, File Nos. 65, 65-50A, 3482-2, 8685, and 11654; also *Transcript of Record* in U.S. Circuit Court of Appeals for the Seventh Circuit, Oct. Term 1930, in Central Files of Department of Justice, No. 5-23-283, in National Archives; and Lipschultz income tax prosecution file, No. 5-23-11, in National Archives. See also two recent and careful journalistic biographies: Kobler (1971) and McPhaul (1970).

8. Capone's attorney estimated that each of the four senior partners received one-sixth of their joint profits, while one-third went to cover overhead expenses (rent on a headquarters, payment to bodyguards and entourage, etc.); see Lawrence P. Mattingly to C.W. Herrick, September 20, 1930, in IRS File No. SI 7085-F. In the IRS files there are different estimates of how profits from the Cicero operations were split but everyone—intelligence agents and crooks—agreed that the structure involved partnerships; see memorandum of Frank J. Wilson, December 21, 1933, in Env. No. I of the above file.

9. Pope quit the Smoke Shop in late 1926 because he believed that the senior partners had cheated him of his 18% share of the money ($84,000) in the safe at the time of a police raid in April of that year. Later, though, he engaged in various gambling activities with Guzik. Among documents on the Smoke Shop are "Testimony of Peter P. Penovich before Federal Grand Jury" in U.S.

vs. Ralph Capone et al., November 25, 1930, Env. 76, and memorandum of Frank J. Wilson, December 21, 1933, Env. 1, in IRS file on Capone.

10. In 1923 Louis LaCava and his brother Rocco represented Torrio when Torrio began setting up gambling in Cicero, much as Alterie represented the O'Banion group. (See "Record of Interview with Cornelius J. Sullivan, March 9, 1931," in IRS file on Capone, Env. No. 29.) LaCava was ostensibly in Chicago as a sales representative for a New York lithographer. In appearance before a federal grand jury, he claimed that, in his gambling activities, he had fronted for various deceased leaders of the Unione Siciliana. This story was presumably to protect Torrio. ("Testimony of Louis LaCava before the Federal Grand Jury, March 5, 1931," in IRS file on Capone, Env. No. 79.) On his activities with Torrio in New York in the 1930s, see McPhaul (1970: 274, 311, 320).

11. For descriptions of the Harlem Inn and other Stickney resorts, see Russell (1931: Ch. 2); also K.B. Alwood and J.L. Munday, "Stickney," student term paper (March 1930), in Ernest W. Burgess papers, University of Chicago Library. On involvement of the senior partners, see "Memorandum Relative to Houses of Prostitution under Control of the Capone Organization," June 29, 1931, and other materials in IRS file on Capone.

12. For a description of Burnham under Mayor Patton, see Mezzrow and Wolfe (1946: Ch. 5). The story of the Hawthorne Kennel Club is based on "Memorandum of Interview with Mae Baker, November 24, 1930," unnumbered envelope; memorandum of Frank J. Wilson, June 22, 1930; and correspondence in Env. No. 68 and two unnumbered envelopes, in IRS file on Capone; also typewritten report (1930) in Chicago Law and Order League papers, Chicago Historical Society. For a somewhat different version, see Kobler (1971: 23 238, 331-332). O'Hare was killed, gangland style, in November 1939.

13. Since Patton was a partner with O'Hare in the Florida track, it is probable that some of the senior partners were also involved.

14. The discussion of the economics of bootlegging is based on a number of sources: Coast Guard Intelligence files, National Archives, Washington, D.C.; clippings and investigative reports in files of Chicago Crime Commission, Chicago. See also Haller (1976a, 1985b); Mormino (1986); Nelli (1976: Ch. 6); and Vyhnanek (1979: Ch. 3).

15. For analyses of similar problems of risk among bookmakers, see Reuter (1983: Ch. 2) and Scott (1968: Ch. 7).

16. Of course, Italian-American crime families have served a number of functions, in addition to aiding the members' business interests. They are also like benevolent societies, such as the Elks or Masonic lodges, in having (more or less) secret memberships and rituals. And, since membership is by invitation only, members enjoy the prestige on the street from having been selected to join the elite of their profession. Thus, the place of the crime family in the lives of many members goes well beyond a consideration of rational business interest.

17. This distinction between independent businesses and the Cosa Nostra outfit is the same as the distinction that Anderson (1979: 2) makes between "the firm" and the "organized crime group." I believe it also parallels the distinction made by Ianni (1988: 89) between "two different systems of organization. One is an informal system in which people have prestige. The other is business."

18. Conversation of Bruno and DeCavalcante, February 11, 1962, in "Transcripts of Organized Crime Phone Taps," Papers of Citizens Crime Commission of Philadelphia, in Urban Archives, Temple University Library, Vol. 13: 14.

19. The same merging of illegal and legal activities can occur in fencing; see Klockars (1974) and Steffensmeier (1986). These two studies of fences provide models for the types of studies that should be done for illegal enterprises.

References

Abadinsky, Howard
    1983   The Criminal Elite: Professional and Organized Crime. Westport, Conn.: Greenwood Press.

Adler, Patricia A.
    1985   Wheeling and Dealing: An Ethnography of an Upper-Level Drug Dealing and Smuggling Community. New York: Columbia University Press.

Albini, Joseph L.
    1971   The American Mafia: Genesis of a Legend. New York: Appleton-Century Crofts.

Anderson, Annelise
    1979   The Business of Organized Crime: A Cosa Nostra Family. Stanford, Calif.: Hoover Institution Press.

Asbury, Herbert
    1938   Sucker's Progress: An Informal History of Gambling in America from the Colonies to Canfield. New York: Dodd, Mead.

Bellis, David J.
    1985   Political corruption in small, machine-run cities. In Herbert E. Alexander and Gerald E. Caiden (eds.), the Politics and Economics of Organized Crime. Lexington, Mass.: Lexington Books.

Best, Joel
- 1987 Business is business: Regulating brothel prostitution through arrests, St. Paul 1865-83. Research in Social Policy 1: 1-20.

Best, Joel and David S. Luckenbill
- 1982 Organizing Deviance. Englewood Cliffs, N.J.: Prentice-Hall.

Block, Alan A.
- 1979 The snowman cometh: Coke in progressive New York. Criminology 17: 75-99.
- 1983 East Side-West Side: Organising Crime in New York, 1930-1950. New Brunswick, N.J.: Transaction.

Blumberg, Leonard U., Thomas E. Shipley, and Stephen F. Barsky
- 1978 Liquor and Poverty: Skid Row as a Human Condition. New Brunswick, N.J.: Rutgers Center for Alcohol Studies.

Burnham, John
- 1971a Medical inspection of prostitutes in America in the nineteenth century: The St. Louis experiment and its sequel. Bulletin of the History of Medicine 45: 203-218.
- 1971b The social evil ordinance-A social experiment in nineteenth century St. Louis. The Bulletin of the Missouri Historical Society 27: 203-217.

Caldwell, Lewis A.H.
- 1940 The policy game-Chicago. Master's thesis, Northwestern University, Evanston, Ill.

Carlisle, Jack
- 1976 Gambling in Detroit: An informal history. In Commission on the Review of National Policy Toward Gambling, Gambling in America. Washington, D.C.: Government Printing Office. Appendix 1.

Carlson, Gustav G.
- 1940 Number gambling: A study of a culture complex. Ph.D. dissertation, University of Michigan, Ann Arbor.

Chambliss, William J.
- 1978 On the Take: From Paltry Crooks to Presidents. Bloomington: Indiana University Press.

Cockburn, Leslie
- 1987 Out of Control: the story of the Reagan Administration's secret war in Nicaragua, the illegal arms pipeline, and the Contra drug connection. New York: Atlantic Monthly Press.

Commission to Investigate Allegations of Police Corruption and the City's Anti-Corruption Procedures
   1972   Commission Report. New York: George Braziller.
Conrad, Harold
   1982   Dear Muffo: 35 Years in the Fast Lane. New York: Stein and Day.
Cressey, Donald R.
   1969   Theft of the Nation: The Structure and Operations of Organized Crime in America. New York: Harper & Row.
Eisenberg, Dennis, Uri Dan, and Eli Landau
   1979   Meyer Lansky, Mogul of the Mob. New York: Paddington Press.
Ekland-Olson, Sheldon, John Lieb and Louis Zurcher
   1984   The paradoxical impact of criminal sanctions: Some microstructural findings. Law & Society Review 18: 160-178.
Flexner, Abraham
   1969   Prostitution in Europe. Montclair, N.J.: Patterson Smith.
Fogelson, Robert M.
   1977   Big-City Police. Cambridge: Harvard University Press.
Fox, Stephen
   1989   Blood and Power: Organized Crime in Twentieth-Century America. New York: William Morrow.
Gardiner, John A.
   1970   The Politics of Corruption: Organized Crime in an American City. New York: Russell Sage Foundation.
Goldstock, Ronald and Dan T. Coenen
   1980   Controlling the contemporary Loanshark: The law of illicit lending and the problem of witness fear. Cornell Law Review 65: 127-185.
Haller, Mark H.
   1971-72 Organized crime in urban society: Chicago in the twentieth century. Journal of Social History 5: 210-234.
   1976a Bootleggers and American gambling, 1920-1950. In Commission on the Review of National Policy Toward Gambling, Gambling in America. Washington, D.C.: Government Printing Office. Appendix 1.
   1976b Historical roots of police behavior: Chicago, 1890-1925. Law & Society Review 10: 303-324.

1985a Bootleggers as businessmen: From city slums to city builders. In David E. Kyvig (ed.), Law, Alcohol, and Order: Perspectives on National Prohibition. Westport, Conn.: Greenwood Press.

1985b Philadelphia bootlegging and the report of the Special August Grand Jury. Pennsylvania Magazine of History and Biography 104: 215-233.

1988 Policy gambling, entertainment, and the emergence of black politics: Chicago, 1900 to 1940. Unpublished paper.

Haller, Mark H. and John V. Alviti
1977 Loansharking in American cities: Historical analysis of a marginal enterprise. American Journal of Legal History 21: 125-156.

Ianni, Francis A.J.
1972 A Family Business: Kinship and Social Control in Organized Crime. New York: Russell Sage Foundation.
1974 Black Mafia: Ethnic Succession in Organized Crime. New York: Simon & Schuster.
1988 Ethnic factors in drug networks. In Pennsylvania Crime Commission, Organized Crime Narcotics Enforcement Seminar. Conshohocken: Pennsylvania Crime Commission.

Johnson, David R
1981 American Law Enforcement: A History. St. Louis: Forum Press.

Karchmer, Clifford L.
1985 Money laundering and the organized underworld. In Herbert E. Alexander and Gerald E. Caiden (eds.), The Politics and Economics of Organized Crime. Lexington, Mass.: Lexington Books.

Kleiman, Mark
1985 Drug enforcement and organized crime. In Herbert E. Alexander and Gerald E. Caiden (eds.), The Politics and Economics of Organized Crime. Lexington, Mass.: Lexington Books.

Klockars, Carl B.
1974 The Professional Fence. New York: Free Press.

Kobler, John
1971 Capone: The Life and World of Al Capone. New York: G.P. Putnam's Sons.

Kwitney, Jonathan
  1987   The Crimes of Patriots: A True Tale of Dope, Dirty Money, and the CIA. New York: W.W. Norton.
Landesco, John
  1968   Organized Crime in Chicago. Chicago: University of Chicago Press.
Lasswell, Harold D. and Jeremiah B. McKenna
  n.d.   The Impact of Organized Crime on an Inner City Community. New York: Policy Sciences Center.
Light, Ivan
  1974   From vice district to tourist attraction: The moral career of American Chinatowns, 1880-1940. Pacific Historical Review 43: 367-394.
  1977   The ethnic vice industry, 1880-1944. American Sociological Review 42: 464-479.
Maas, Peter
  1968   The Valachi Papers. New York: G.P. Putnam's Sons.
Mackey, Thomas C.
  1987   Red Lights Out: A Legal History of Prostitution, Disorderly Houses, and Vice Districts, 1870-1917. New York: Garland.
McCormack, Robert
  1988   Perspectives on police corruption. In Pennsylvania Crime Commission, Organized Crime Narcotics Enforcement Seminar. Conshohocken: Pennsylvania Crime Commission.
McPhaul, Jack
  1970   Johnny Torrio: First of the Gang Lords. New Rochelle, N.Y.: Arlington House.
Merton, Robert K.
  1957   Social Theory and Social Structure. New York: Free Press.
Messick, Hank
  1967   The Silent Syndicate. New York: Macmillan.
  1971   Lansky. New York: G.P. Putnam's Sons.
Mezzrow, Mezz and Bernard Wolfe
  1946   Really the Blues. Garden City, N.Y.: Doubleday.
Mollenhoff, Clark R.
  1972   Strike Force: Organized Crime and the Government. Englewood Cliffs, N.J.: Prentice-Hall.

Moore, Mark
    1977   Buy and Bust. Lexington, Mass.: Lexington Books.
Mormino, Gary
    1986   A still on the hill: Prohibition and cottage industry. Gateway Heritage 7: 2-13.
Murray, George
    1965   The Madhouse on Madison Street. Chicago: Follett.
Nelli, Humbert J.
    1976   The Business of Crime: Italians and Syndicate Crime in the United States. New York: Oxford University Press.
Pennsylvania Crime Commission
    1974   Report on Police Corruption and the Quality of Law Enforcement in Philadelphia. St. Davids: Pennsylvania Crime Commission.
    1989   The Limits of the Criminal Sanction: The Case of John Nacrelli. Public Hearings Re: Chester, Pa. Conshohocken: Pennsylvania Crime Commission.
Pileggi, Nicholas
    1985   Wise Guy: A Life in a Mafia Family. New York: Simon & Schuster.
Pledge, Joe
    1956   Bombshell: From Boxer to Bookmaker. New York.
President's Commission on Organized Crime
    1984   The Cash Connection: Organized Crime, Financial Institutions, Money Laundering. Interim report to the President and Attorney General. Washington, D.C.: Government Printing Office.
Reppetto, Thomas A.
    1978   The Blue Parade. New York: Free Press.
Reuter, Peter
    1983   Disorganized Crime: The Economics of the Visible Hand. Cambridge, Mass.: MIT Press.
    1984   Police regulation of illegal gambling: Frustrations of symbolic enforcement. Annals of the American Academy of Political and Social Sciences 474: 36-47.
    1988   A profile of major drug traffickers. In Pennsylvania Crime Commission, Organized Crime Narcotics Enforcement Seminar. Conshohocken: Pennsylvania Crime Commission.

Reuter, Peter and John Haaga
- 1989 The Organization of High-Level Drug Markets: An Exploratory Study. Santa Monica, Calif.: Rand.

Reuter, Peter and Mark Kleiman
- 1986 Risks and prices: An economic analysis of drug enforcement. In Michael Tonry and Norval Morris (eds.), Crime and Justice: An Annual Review of Research. Vol. 7. Chicago: University of Chicago Press.

Richardson, James F.
- 1970 The New York Police: Colonial Times to 1901. New York: Oxford University Press.

Rosen, Ruth
- 1982 The Lost Sisterhood: Prostitution in America, 1900-1918. Baltimore: Johns Hopkins University Press.

Rubin, Paul H.
- 1973 The economic theory of the criminal firm. In Simon Rottenberg (ed.), The Economics of Crime and Punishment. Washington, D.C.: American Enterprise Institute.

Rubinstein, Jonathan and Peter Reuter
- 1982 Illegal Gambling in New York: A Case Study in the Operation, Structure, and Regulation of an Illegal Market. Washington, D.C.: Government Printing Office.

Russell, Daniel
- 1931 The road house: A study of commercialized amusements in the environs of Chicago. Master's thesis, University of Chicago.

Schelling, Thomas C.
- 1967 Economic analysis of organized crime. In President's Commission on Law Enforcement and Administration of Justice, Task Force Report: Organized Crime. Washington, D.C.: Government Printing Office.

Scott, Marvin B.
- 1968 The Racing Game. Chicago: Aldine.

Seidl, John Michael
- 1968 "Upon the hip"—A study of the criminal loan-shark industry. Ph.D. dissertation, Harvard University, Cambridge, Mass.

Sharkey, Jacqueline
    1988   The Contra-drug trade off. Common Cause Magazine 14: 23-33.

Sherman, Lawrence W.
    1978   Scandal and Reform: Controlling Police Corruption. Berkeley: University of California Press.

Shumsky, Neil Larry
    1980   Vice responds to reform: San Francisco, 1910-1914. Journal of Urban History 7: 31-47.

Smith, Dwight C., Jr.
    1971   Some things that may be more important to understand about organized crime than Cosa Nostra. University of Florida Law Review 24: 1-30.
    1975   The Mafia Mystique. New York: Basic Books.

Steffensmeier, Darrell J.
    1986   The Fence: In the Shadow of Two Worlds. Totowa, N.J.: Rowman & Littlefield.

Tarr, Joel A.
    1967   The urban politician as entrepreneur. Mid-America 49: 55-67.

Teresa, Vincent with Thomas C. Renner
    1973   My Life in the Mafia. Garden City, N.Y.: Doubleday.

Vice Commission of Chicago
    1911   The Social Evil in Chicago. Chicago: City of Chicago.

Vyhnanek, Louis A.
    1979   The seamier side of life: Criminal activity in New Orleans during the 1920s. Ph.D. dissertation, University of South Florida, Tampa.
    1981   "Muggles," "inchy," and "mud": Illegal drugs in New Orleans during the 1920s. Louisiana History 22: 253-279.

Walker, Samuel
    1980   Popular Justice: A History of American Criminal Justice. New York: Oxford University Press.

Wendt, Lloyd and Herman Kogan
    1943   Lords of the Levee: The Story of Bathhouse John and Hinky Dink. Indianapolis: Hobbs-Merrill.

Whyte, William Foote
    1955   Streetcorner Society. Chicago: University of Chicago Press.

Wooldridge, Clifton R.
   1901   Hands Up! In the World of Crime, Or 12 Years a Detective. Chicago: Charles C. Thompson.

Woolston, Howard B.
   1969   Prostitution in the United States. Montclair, N.J.: Patterson Smith.

Index

Throughout this index, *f* indicates a figure on the page.

A

Abbandondo, Frank, 182–183
Abrams, Hy, 157, 208, 210*f*, 212
Accardo, Tony
  DeStefano and, 187
  gambling and, 210*f*, 229*f*
  Guzik partnership, 207
  Las Vegas financial backing by, 211–212
  tactics of, 70, 146
Acculturation, 46–47
Administration of Justice, 78
Adonis, Joe, 66, 228, 229*f*
Advertising by salary lenders, 169–170
Aiello gang, 44, 48–49
Alcatraz Penitentiary, 64
Alcohol
  denatured, 86, 94, 95
  diversion of, 75, 85–90, 94–95, 201*f*
  diversity of, 200
  industrial, 75, 86–88, 94–96
  quality of, 89
  sources of, 89–90
Alcohol companies/industry
  business after repeal, 203–206
  cooperation within, 215, 236
  diversion by, 75, 85–90, 94–95, 201*f*
  investigations of, 94, 97
  Volstead Act and, 86
  See also Bootlegging; Breweries
Alky cookers, 48–49, 87
  See also Breweries
Alliance Distributors, Inc., 206
Alo, Vincent "Jimmy," 66, 228, 229*f*
Alterie, Louis, 230
Amberg, Louis, 182
Anastasia, Albert, 65, 144
Annalore, Angelo Bruno. *See* Bruno, Angelo "Ange"
Annenberg, Max, 150
Annenberg, Moses "Moe," 150–151, 158
Annenberg, Walter, 151
Anti-Racket Bureau, 182
Arcadia Gym, 74
Armstrong, Louis, 45
Army Air Force, 157, 211
Assassinations

Angelo Bruno, xiv, 122
Benjamin Siegel, 157, 212
Colosimo, Big Jim, 44, 62
Hugh McLoon, 84
Sam DeStefano, 187
William McSwiggin, 63
Associated Numbers Bankers, 146
Association of Commerce, 4, 8
Atlantic City, 87
Attell, Abe, 72–73
Authority, suspicions of, 46
Avery, Sewell L., 4, 9

B

Baer, Moishe, 188
Bail bondsmen, 16f, 45
Baker Bowl, 74
Bankers Trust Building, 86
Barbarians in Our Midst (Peterson, 1952), 71
Batista, Fulgencio, 66, 67, 156, 209
Bawler-out, 173
Beckman, Captain, 93
Beiderbecke, Bix, 45
Bell Telephone, 230
Bellevue-Stratford Hotel, 84
Benson, Louis "Tiny," 184
Betting, 147, 184, 185, 209
 See also Gambling
Beverly Club (New Orleans, LA), 66, 207
Beverly Hills Club, 207
Black Americans
 boxing and, 37
 entertainment industry and, 37, 45–46
 numbers gambling introduction by, 143
 as organized crime leaders, 36, 47, 146
 politics and, 143, 145, 146, 224
 prostitution and, 45
 suspicions of government authority, 46
 vice districts and, 46
Black ghettos
 numbers gambling in, 138, 143, 158
 policy gambling in, 43, 48, 145
 rise of gambling syndicates in, 43, 146, 158–159
 See also Ghettos
"Black Sox" scandal, 72–73
Blackburn, Jack, 74
Boats, smuggling, 87–88
Bongiovanni, Joseph, 128
Bookmakers
 career as, 240
 early, 137
 Hawthorne Smoke Shop and, 231
 interrelationships of, 141
 off-track, 77
 overview of, 147–152
 political corruption and, 223–224
 technology and, 158
 See also Off-track bookmaking
Bootleggers
 bookmaking and, 151
 Capone gang and, 44, 62–63, 69
 cooperation and partnerships between, 39, 200, 214–215, 235–236
 ethnicity of, 16, 44, 79

gambling and, 141–142, 152–160, 203
hijacking, 140, 200
importance of in founding of Las Vegas, 206–214
"King" of, 87, 91, 94
loan sharks and, 181–182
looking for respectability, 215–216
society, 89
Special August Grand Jury on, 96
typical ages of, 158, 200, 207
typical backgrounds of, 199–200, 214–215
upward mobility and, 35–42, 139
See also Entrepreneurs
"Bootleggers as Businessmen: From City Slums to City Builders" (Haller), xiii
Bootlegging
business challenges faced by, 202–203
complex structure of, 88, 89–90, 201*f*
conflicts between gangs of, 41
creation of idea of "mafia," xi, 78–79
developing into legal companies, 203–206
development of organized crime around, 77
economic impact and, 48–49
growth of syndicates, 188
rise of, 85
Special August Grand Jury on, 95–98
structure of, 138–142
wars, 44, 69, 77, 85, 95–98
See also Alcohol companies/industry
Boss, in the crime family, xi, 104
Boston, 210*f*
Bowen, Louise de Koven, 9
Boxing, 37, 74–75
See also Prizefighting
Breweries, 90, 140, 200, 203–205
See also Alcohol companies/industry; Alky cookers
Bribery
Philadelphia Grand Jury investigation and, 91–93, 99–101
police and politicians, 49, 75, 100–101
railroad employees, 94–95
Bronfman, Samuel, 204
Brown, Rachel, 72–73
Browne Vintners, 206
Brownsville Brewery, 182
Bruce, Andrew A., 4, 10
Brunder, William, 143–144
Bruno, Angelo "Ange"
assassination of, xiv
background of, 103
on business, 239
Gambino family and, 115
Bruno, Sue, 115
Bruno family
characteristics of, 115–117
drugs and, 109
Frank Sindone and, 129–131
functions of, 110–115
gambling and, 107
Harry Riccobene, 125–128
illegal businesses of, 105–109
legal businesses of, 109–110

loan sharking and, 106, 122–123
markets involved in, 109
network of, 115
as a regulatory agency, 103, 105, 110, 117, 122, 132
rise of, 103–104
structure of, 104–105
See also Crime families/groups; Regulatory systems
"The Bruno Family of Philadelphia" (Haller), xiii
Bullet-proof vests, 98
Burgess, Ernest W., ix, 11, 32
Businesses
  alcohol production and distribution, 200, 201*f*, 202, 203–206, 236
  blurred lines in, 241
  illegal enterprise as, 105–109, 220–221
  in illegal goods, 235–236
  legal/illegal partnerships, 241
  loan sharking as, 124–125
  loan sharking to legal, 106, 122, 129, 185–186
  relationships/partnerships within, 85, 116, 140, 202
  after repeal, 204–205
  running legal and illegal, 109–110
  structure of, 104
Butler, Rush C., 4, 9, 11
Butler, Smedley D., 83–84

C

Cabarets, 45–46
Campbell, Johnny "King of the Bootleggers," 87–88
Capone, Al "Snorky"
  background of, 61–65
  bootlegging and, 44
  in Cicero, 230, 232*f*
  media and, 77
Capone, Gabriel, 62
Capone, Ralph, 62, 230–231, 232*f*
Capone, Salvatore (Frank), 62
Capone gang
  alky cookers, 48–49
  bootlegging and, 44, 62–63, 69
  dog racing and, 39, 64
  entertainment industry and, 63–64
  formation of, 62
  gambling and, 152–153
  as a set of partnerships, 230–231, 233
  systematization of organized crime by, 29–30
  violence and, 63, 65
  See also Gangs
Capone: The Life and World of Al Capone (Kobler, 1971), 71
Capos (capis), 104, 112
Captive City (Demaris, 1968), 71
Carbo, Frankie, 76
Career patterns
  bootlegging, 85
  ethnicity, 36, 42
  in illegal enterprises, 47–50, 240
  loan sharking, 181
Carnegie Foundation, ix
Carroll, James J., 155
Caruso, Enrico, 40
Casino industry, 66–67, 68, 212–214, 228–229, 229*f*

See also Las Vegas, NV
Castro, Fidel, 67, 209
Cayton, Horace R., 52
Central States Pension Fund, 213
Cermak, Anton, 145
Cerone, Jackie, 187
Chain debt, 172
Chamberlin, Henry B., 5, 7-8
Chattell lender, 168
Chicago
  famous bootleggers from, 83
  gambling in, 146-147, 152-153, 158-159, 210*f*
  loan sharking in, 177
  organized crime compared to other cities, 38
  racketeer loan sharking in, 185-189, 191
  salary lending in, 177-178
  success of black gamblers in, 146
  types of gambling in, 143
Chicago Association for Criminal Justice, 6-9
Chicago Bar Association, 4
Chicago Church Federation, 4
Chicago Council of Social Agencies, 5
Chicago Crime Commission
  contracts with Illinois Association for Criminal Justice, 10
  Illinois Crime Survey recommendations and, 18
  impact of McSwiggin Murders on, 8
  opposition to state organization, 7-8
  Ryerson Committee views on, 5
Chicago School of Urban Sociology, ix, xiv, 11, 17, 24
Chicago *Tribune*, 12
Chicago White Sox, 72-73
Ciancaglini, Joseph "Chickie," 129
Cicero, IL
  Capone gang activities in, 69, 152, 208, 230-233, 232*f*
  controlled election in, 62-63, 69
  gambling in, 38, 43
Cincinnati Reds, 72-73
Citron, Anne (Lansky), 67
Civil liberties, 30-31
Civil War gambling, 77, 137
C.J. Rich and Company, 155
Clark, Wilbur, 212
Claybaugh, Hinton T., 11
Clearfield, Morris, 91-92
Cleveland, OH, 210*f*
Cleveland Browns, 151
Coast Guard, 88, 155, 209
Cocaine, 235
Coccozza, Vincent, 84
Code, as information source, 151
Cohen, Charles, 92
Cohen, Mickey, 211
Collateral, 166
Collections. *See* Debt collection
Colonial Inn (Hallandale, FL), 66, 228-230, 229*f*
Colosimo, James "Big Jim," 29, 40, 44, 62
Commission agents, 105
Commission on Law Enforcement, 78
Committee of Fifteen, 5
Competition
  alcohol companies, 95-96

bootlegging and, 90, 140
families/groups rules on, 112–114, 117, 123
in the national race wire, 151–152
using corruption to limit, 221, 223
using partnerships as protection against, 80–81, 123, 147
using police and courts against, 41
Consentino, Louis, 232*f*
Consigliere, 104
Consolidated Ethyl Solvents Corporation, 97
Constitutional issues, 30
Contacts, 36, 104
Continental Press, 151, 157, 208
Cook County Real Estate Board, 4
Cornero, Tony, 212
Corruption
 changes causing reduction in, 227
 police and political corruption, 221–222
 politics and gambling, 223–224
 reasons for, 221–222
 red-light districts, 224–225
Cosa Nostra groups, xi, 239–240
 See also Crime families/groups; Regulatory systems
Costello, Frank
 backing of Alliance Distributors, 206
 casino investments of, 66, 157, 212, 228
 casino partnerships of, 210*f*, 229*f*
 gambling regions of, 210*f*
 Las Vegas and, 207
 Rothstein and, 73, 148
 slot machines and, 153
Cotton Club, 232*f*
Coughlin, John "Bathhouse," 68–69, 224
Coughlin, Mary "Mae" (Capone), 62
"Cover-up" houses, 95
Covington, Kentucky, 155, 210*f*
Crap games, 108–109
Credit
 betting on, 148, 149
 loan sharks and, 188
 loans and, 185
 numbers gambling and, 108
 salary lending and, 167, 189
Cressey, Donald R., x–xi
Crimaldi, Charles, 187
Crime
 history of from only certain cities, 154–155
 Landesco's report on, 24, 26–30
 Shaw's report on, 25–26
 social roots of, 24–30
 traditions of, 23–24
Crime families/groups
 Donald Cressey's corporate model, xi
 network of, 114–115
 partnerships outside the family, 115–116
 as a regulatory agency, 103, 105, 110, 117, 122, 132, 239–240
 structure of, xiv, 104
 See also Bruno family; Cosa

Nostra groups; Regulatory systems
Crime in America (Kefauver, 1951), 71
Criminal behavior, 29
Criminal defense lawyers, 16
Criminal justice
  of the 20's and 30's, 31
  as another racket, 41
  Illinois Crime Survey views on, 32
  interrelationships with crime groups, 41
  traditional views of, 23
Criminal laws and processes, 15, 31–32
Criminals
  community ambiguity about, 51–52
  lending operations and, 179
  loan sharking to, 185
  Mark Haller on, xii
  participating in organized crime, 76
  prohibition creating entrepreneurial, 215
  social world of, 40–41
  turning to the racket, 96
  wealth of, 47
Criminology (Sutherland, 1924), ix
Crowe, Robert, 12
Crowell, Henry P., 4, 5
Cugat, Xavier, 212
Culture
  diversity in, 17
  impact on criminal activities, 46–47
  juvenile delinquency and, 25
  loan sharking and, 132
  male, 125
  See also Ethnicity; Immigrant/ethnic groups
Cusick, Elsie, 68
Customers for illegal goods and services, 50, 62, 215–216

D

Daily Racing Form, 150
Dalitz, Morris "Moe," 155–156, 207, 210f, 212, 215–216
D'Andrea, Anthony, 29
Daniels, Josephus, 39
Davis, Dixie, 144
Davis, Harry A., 93
Dawes, William R., 4, 146
Deaths, family assistance and, 114
Debt collection
  loan sharking and, 124–125
  profit increase tactics, 189
  salary lenders tactics, 172–174
  use of violence in, 107, 165–166, 180–181
DeCavalcante, Sam, 239
Decentralization, partnerships and, 106, 234
Defense attorneys, 45
Del E. Webb, 214
Dempsey, Jack, 75
Denatured alcohol, 86, 94, 95
DePriest, Oscar, 145
Desert Inn (Las Vegas, NV), 212, 213–214
DeStefano, Sam, 186–188
Detroit, MI, 143, 146–147
Dewey, Thomas E., 166

Diamond, Jack "Legs," 73
Distribution of alcohol, 200, 201f, 202, 203–206, 236
Divorce in Nevada, 211
Dog racing
  Abrams investment in, 208
  Capone gang and, 39, 64, 69
  in Cicero, 231, 232f, 233
  Jack Guzik and, 70
Drake, St. Clair, 52
Drug cartels, 80
Drug selling
  Bruno family, 109, 111
  Frank Sindone, 129
  Harry Riccobene, 125
  partnerships and, 235
  See also Smuggling
Druggan, Terry, 44
Duffy, Mickey, 87, 90, 145
Durante, Jimmy, 76, 212
Dwyer, Bill, 73, 209
Dwyer, William, 153

E

Eastern State Penitentiary, 64
Eastman, Monk, 179
Economics
  bootlegging networks and, 85–86, 90
  horse racing and, 147
  in illegal enterprises, 221
  impact of organized crime, 47–50
  Las Vegas gambling and, 156–157, 160, 213
  in partnerships, 235–238
  policy racket and, 47–48
  red light districts and, 225
  subaltern, xii
  Volstead Act and, 138–139
Education campaign on organized crime, 33
Ehrenreich, Joseph L., 99–100
Entertainment industry
  Black achievements in, 45–46
  Bruno family and, 109–110
  Capone gang and, 63–64
  immigrant groups and, 37, 38
  interrelationships within, 39
  Las Vegas and, 213
  post Civil War period and, 138
Entrepreneurs
  advantages of business partnerships, 227–228, 234–235
  backgrounds of, 159
  cultivating business contacts, 239
  factors contributing to cooperation between, 219, 221
  as heroes, 50
  levels of, 240–241
  prohibition and, 85, 215
  youth of, xiii, 85
  See also Bootleggers; Gambling entrepreneurs
Erickson, Frank
  casino investments of, 148, 228
  casino partnerships of, 229f
  gambling regions of, 210f
  racing investments of, 209
  slot machines and, 154
Ethnicity, 14–15, 16, 36, 42–47
  See also Culture; Immigrant/ethnic groups
Eugenics: Hereditarian Attitudes in American Thought (Haller, 1963), viii

F

Fallucio, Frank, 61
Favors, 104, 114–116, 122
Federal Bureau of Investigation (FBI), 67, 126, 130
Felony charges, 12
Felony waiver, 31
Fences (stolen goods), 45, 73
Fischer, Gustave F., 11
Fitzgerald, F. Scott, 71, 73
Fitzgerald, Lincoln, 228, 229*f*
The Flamingo (Las Vegas, NV), 66, 157, 199, 212, 214
Flegenheimer, Arthur (Dutch Schultz), 83, 144
Florida, 155, 209, 210*f*
Flynn, Helen (Hoff), 74
Fogel, Benjamin, 97
Forty-Two Gang, 186–187
Franklin Mortgage and Investment Company, 75, 86
Frank's Cabana, 128–129
Friendship. *See* Loyalties/friendship

G

Gambino, Carlo, 115
Gambling
  in the Civil War, xii, 77, 137
  development of organized crime around, 76–77
  See also Betting; Numbers gambling; Policy gambling/racket
Gambling entrepreneurs
  ages of, 207, 214
  Arnold Rothstein, 71–73
  background of, 159
  ethnic specialization of, 42–43
  Jack Guzik, 69, 70
  Meyer Lansky, 66–67, 68
  Moe Dalitz, 207
  upward mobility and, 35–42
  See also Entrepreneurs
Gambling syndicates
  in the black ghetto, 43, 146, 158–159
  bootleggers and, 142, 203
  Bruno family and, 107
  conflicts between, 41
  coordination of, 152–157
  creation of idea of "mafia" and, 79
  loan sharking and, 185
  Philadelphia Grand Jury investigation and, 91, 100–101
  political corruption and, 223–224
  post Civil War period and, 138
  relationships/partnerships within, 141, 159, 188, 210*f*, 236–238
  structure of, 142, 158
The Gang (Thrasher, 1929), ix
Gang warfare
  in Cicero, 230
  to protect bootleg operations, 44, 69, 77, 85, 95–98
Gangs
  Aiello, 44, 48–49
  conflicts between, 41
  Forty-Two Gang, 186–187
  Gennas, 44
  Northside, 69
  producing bootleggers, 139
  rivalries between, 200
  Shaw's analysis and, 25

See also Capone gang
Gangsters
    Al Capone, 61–65
    conflicts between, 41
    John Landesco's views on, x
    politics and, 28–29
    as a product of surroundings, 28
    Special August Grand Jury on, 96
Gelhke, C. E., 10
General News Bureau, 150, 151
Gennas gang, 44
German Americans, 37, 42, 46
The Ghetto (Wirth, 1928), ix
Ghettos, 36
    See also Black ghettos
Giancana, Sam, 146
Glenwood Industrial Alcohol Company, 75, 95–96
Glimco, Joey, 187
The Godfather (1972), 78
Gold, Rose, 183–184
The Gold Coast and the Slum (Zorbaugh, 1929), ix
Golder, Benjamin M., 75, 86
Goldstein, Phil "Bugsy," 182–183
Gooderham and Worts, 204
Goods and services
    customers for, 50, 62, 215–216
    illegal, 50
    partnerships and, 235–236
Gordon, Waxey, 73
Gore, Edward, 7–8, 9
Graft, 90–93, 99–100
Grand Jury investigation, Philadelphia. *See* Philadelphia Grand Jury investigation

The Great Gatsby (Fitzgerald, 1953), 71
Greek Americans, 37, 45
Greene, Carolyn (Rothstein), 73
Guns, 98
Gusenberg brothers, 44
Guzik, Harry, 68
Guzik, Jack "Jake"
    background of, 68–71, 159
    Capone gang and, 44, 63, 69, 146, 230–231
    Colonial Inn investment, 228, 229
    gambling and, 153, 207, 210*f*
    James Ragen rivalry, 151
    partnerships of, 229*f*, 232*f*
Guzik, Max, 68
Guzik, Rose, 70
Guzik, Sam, 69, 231, 232*f*

H

H.A. Courtright, 177
Haim, Charles, 88, 97
Haim, Irving, 88, 97, 206
Hall, James Parker, 4
Haller, Mark H.
    background of, viii
    on crime family structure, xiii–xiv
    on criminal partnerships, xiii
    introduction into world of organized crime, ix
    on the origins of organized crime, xii–xiii
    reprinting Landesco's publication, vii
    study of urban crime, x
    view on Donald Cressey's model, xi

views on how crime was studied, xii
Harlem Inn, 232f
Harno, Albert J., 4, 10, 11
Harno, Bruce, 11
Harrison, Carter H. II, 223
Hartzell, Alexander, 130–131
Hassel, Max, 90
Hassel, Max "Millionaire Newsboy," 87
Hatch, Harry C., 204
Havana, Cuba, 156, 209, 210f
Hawthorne Kennel Club, 64, 69, 231, 232f
Hawthorne Smoke Shop, 231
Healy, John J., 11
Hearst organization, 150
Hendrie, Al, 88–89
Heroin, 235
Heroism within organized crime, 50–52
Hijacking, 140, 200
  See also Violence
Hines, Jimmy, 72, 144
Hinton, E.W., 10, 11
Hiram Walker and Sons, 204–205
The Hobo (Anderson, 1923), ix
Hoff, Harry, 74
Hoff, Helen Flynn, 74
Hoff, Margaret (Kaher), 76
Hoff, Max "Boo-Boo"
  alcohol diversion by, 86
  background of, 74–76
  bodyguards, 98
  gambling and, 100–101
  interests in Delaware Valley area, 86
  Philadelphia Grand Jury investigation and, 91, 94, 97

Hoff, Sara, 74
Holden, Charles R., 4
Hoover, Herbert, 64
Horse racing, 39, 77, 147, 158
Hot Springs, AR, 207, 210f
Hotel Nacional (Havana, Cuba), 67, 156, 209
Hughes, Howard, 213–214
Hunt, Nicholas, 223–224
Hyatt Corporation, 214

I

Illegal enterprise
  business partnerships in, 227–228
  careers in, 240
  compared to organized crime, 220
  coordination within, 241–242
  defined, 219–220
  extent of police and politician coordination, 226–227
  impact of corruption on, 222
  internal economic factors, 235–238, 242
  Mark Haller's study on, xi–xii
  police and political corruption, 221–222
  politics and gambling, 223–224
  red-light districts, 224–225
  structure of, 241–242
  typical informality of, 240
"Illegal Enterprise" (Haller), xiii
Illegal search and seizure, 30
Illinois Association for Criminal Justice
  academic contacts within, 15–16
  contracts with Chicago Crime

Commission, 10
crime survey experts recruited, 10–11, 17
crime survey results publication, 12
December meeting, 11–12
dissolution of, 12–13
domination of Chicago metro persons, 13–14
elite reformers within, 14–15
financial backing of, 9–10
formation of, ix, 3, 6–7
Illinois Crime Survey recommendations to, 33
impact of McSwiggin Murder on, 8–9
lack of support for the *Illinois Crime Survey*, 17
opening of, 10
opposition to, 7–8
politics and, 31
recognizing limitations of, 17
unrepresentative of Chicago, 13–15
views on Constitutional issues, 30
Illinois Crime Survey (1929)
emphasis of, 31
felony waiver issue, 31
influence of, 17–18
Landesco's contribution, vii, ix–x, 27
media coverage of, 12
missing topics from, 30–31
Prohibition in, 31
recommendations of, 24–25, 32
scope and size of, 23
Shaw's contributions in, 26
support behind, 17–18
traditions exhibited in, 23–24, 32
Illinois State Bar Association, 3
Illinois State Commerce Commission, 145
Illinois Vigilance Association, 5
Immigrant/ethnic groups
ambiguity about criminals, 51–52
criminal heroes within, 50–51
with deep suspicions of authority, 46
economic impact of organized crime, 47–50
impact of ethnic life style on criminal activities, 46–47
juvenile delinquency and, 25–26
movement of, 35
See also Culture; Ethnicity
Immigration Services, 67
Importing
business challenges of, 202
cooperation and, 85
partnerships and, 236
ports for, 155
after repeal, 204–205
specializing in, 200
syndicates, 153
Incarceration
Al Capone, 64
Annenberg and Ragen, 151
crime family assistance during, 114
D.H. Tolman, 170
Frank Sindone, 129
for gambling, 148
Harry Riccobene, 125
Jack Guzik, 69
Joel Kerper, 89

Jones brothers, 146
Sam DeStefano, 187
Income in a partnership, 106
Industrial alcohol, 75, 86–88, 94–96
Industrial Club, 9–10
Institute for Juvenile Research, 11, 24
Institute of Criminal Law and Criminology (Northwestern University), 11
Insurance, casino, 229f, 230
Interest rates, 167, 171, 176, 177–178
Internal Revenue Service (IRS), 64, 67, 144
International markets. *See* Markets, national and international
Interrelationships. *See* Relationships
Investigators/investigations, 96–98, 166–167, 180–181, 182
Investment fraud, 80
Investments
  casino partnerships and, 229f
  Colonial Inn (Hallandale, FL), 228, 229–230
  gambling centers, 155–156, 207, 208, 209
  Las Vegas, NV, 66, 157, 211–213
Ippolito, Carl "Pappy," 115
Irish Americans
  bootleggers, 44, 85, 139, 199
  boxing and, 37
  entertainment industry and, 37
  gambling and, 42–43, 159
  impact of ethnicity on criminal activities, 46
  labor unions and, 36
  organized crime leaders, 36
  in police and politics, 223
  post Civil War period and, 138
  suspicions of government authority, 46
Ison, "Big Joe," 144
Italian Americans
  bootleggers, 44, 85, 139, 199
  gambling and, 43, 159
  impact of ethnicity on criminal activities, 46–47
  loan sharks, 181
  "mafia," 78–80
  organized crime leaders, 36
  prostitution and, 43, 45
  suspicions of government authority, 46

J

The Jack-Roller (Shaw, 1931), 26
Jackson, Dan, 145
Jackson, William "Action," 187
James, William, 130–131
Jazz music, 45
Jeffries, Jim, 211
Jerome, William Travers, 176
Jewish Americans
  bootleggers, 44–45, 85, 139, 199, 214
  boxing and, 37
  entertainment industry and, 37
  gambling and, 43, 146, 159
  loan sharks, 181
  "mafia," 79
  organized crime leaders, 36
  prostitution and, 45
  suspicions of government

authority, 46
Johnny Torrio: First of the Gang Lords (McPhaul, 1970), 71
Johns Hopkins University, viii
Johnson, Jack, 211
Johnson, John "Mushmouth," 224
Johnson, William, 153
Jones, Edward, 146
Jones brothers, 145–146
Joseph E. Seagram and Sons, Ltd, 204
Juice racket. *See* Racketeer loan shark
Juvenile delinquency, 24–26
Juvenile Delinquency and Urban Areas (Shaw, McKay, 1942), 26
Juvenile Protective Association, 5, 9

K
Kaelker, Charles, 101
Kaelker, Richard, 101
Kaher, Margaret (aka Kaier), 76
Kahn, Esther (Rothstein), 72
Kastel, Phil "Dandy," 154, 207, 210f
Kefauver, Estes, 66–67
Kefauver Committee, 78, 213
Kendrick, W. Freeland, 83
Kenna, Michael (Hinky Dink), 40, 68–69, 70, 224, 232f
Kerper, Joel, 89
Kidnapping, 111, 146
  See also Violence
King, Patrick J. "Patsy," 223
Klenha, Joe, 232f, 233
Knapp Commission, 227
Knickerbocker Hotel, 73
Knight, William D., 11

L
Labor unions
  conflicts between, 41
  criminal heroes within, 50
  employment in, 36–37
  immigrant groups and, 38
  racketeer controlled, 49
  Rothstein and, 73
LaCava, Louis, 231, 232f, 233
LaGuardia, Fiorello, 154, 207
Lake, Frankie, 44
Landesco, John
  background of, ix, 11, 26–27
  organized crime report, vii, 24
  research methods of, 27
  on slum neighborhoods, 28
  using "organized crime" term, 77
  views on causes of crime, x, 24, 27–28
Lansky, Jake, 66, 228, 229f
Lansky, Meyer
  background of, 65–68, 159
  casino partnerships, 229f
  Colonial Inn (Hallandale, FL), 228–230
  financial backing in Las Vegas, 157
  gambling and, 156, 210f
  investments of, 208, 209, 212
  as a top level entrepreneur, 241
Lanzetti brothers, 87, 144
Las Vegas, NV
  economic growth of, 213
  importance of ex-bootleggers in success of, 156–157, 160,

212–213
  legislature on casino licenses, 214
  major investors in, 211–213
  rise of, 199, 207–209
  special environment of, 211
  See also Casino industry
Lashly, Arthur, 10, 18, 31–32
Law and Order League, 5
Law enforcement, 226–227, 240
  See also Police officers; Regulatory systems
Laws
  complex attitudes towards, 41
  salary lenders and, 167–168, 170
  on small loans, 176
  views on cooperation with, 41
Lay-off bookmakers, 148–149
Lazar, Samuel, 75, 94, 97
Legal Aid Society, 174–175
Legislation, 176–177, 178–179
Levin, Hymie, 70, 153
Lewis, Joe E., 38
Life-styles, 106, 109
Lindy's restaurant, 73
Lippman, Walter, vii
Lipschultz, Louis, 69, 231, 232*f*, 233
Liquor. *See* Alcohol
Little Caesar (1932), 77
Lively Levee, 224
Loan markets, 176, 186, 188, 190, 191
Loan sharking
  Bruno family and, 106, 122–123
  as a business, 124–125
  debt collections and, 106–107

examples of, 105–106
history of, 166
major syndicate figures investing in, 191–192
rise of, 121
structure of, 107
two types of, 165
use of violence in, 124–125, 191
Loan sharks
  backgrounds of, 181–182
  Frank Sindone, 129–131
  gambling and, 185
  Harry Riccobene, 125–128
Loesch, Frank J., 18, 41–42
Long, George, 88
Long, Huey, 154, 207
Lookout House, 207
Loop district, 43, 224, 232*f*
Los Angeles, CA, 155, 210*f*
Loyalties/friendship
  crime families and, 104, 111
  customer, 50, 141
  value of, 27, 28, 37, 41
Luciano, Lucky, 65, 67, 79

M

Machine guns, 98
Mackey, Harry A., 93
Madden, Owney, 210*f*
Mafia, ideal of, xi, xiv, 78–80, 167, 214
Maione, Harry, 182
Management, casino, 229*f*
Manpower, 37
Marchettie, Louis "Babe," 113
Markets, national and international
  alcohol and, 200, 201*f*, 204–

205
  bootlegging and, 78, 140, 202, 242
  high-risk loans, 185
  for loan sharks, 183–184
  Philadelphia, 87–88
Maryland Athletic Club, 208
Master Barbers Association, 49–50
Mathis, Reuben, 228, 229f
McBride, Arthur B. "Mickey," 151
McClellan Hearings (1963), xi
McDonough brothers, 154–155
McGinnis, Tom, 224
McKay, Henry, 11, 26
McLoon, Hughie, 84
McManus case, 96–98
McSwiggin, William H., 8, 63
Media
  emphasizing gang rivalries, 200
  focusing on Philadelphia bootlegging, 83
  portrayal of Las Vegas, 213
  portrayal of organized crime, 77, 78
  publishing crime survey results, 12
Merlino, Salvatore, 112
Metro-Goldwyn Mayer, 214
Miami *Tribune*, 150
Middle classes, ambiguity about gangsters, 52
Midwest Distributing Company, 206
Military Sales Company, 75
Mill Creek Distillery, 88
Miller, Amos C., 3–4, 6, 9, 10, 12

Miller, Davy, 51
Miller brothers, 51
"Millionaire Newsboy," 87
Mills Novelty Company, 153
Milwaukee *Journal*, 150
Miro, Jose Enrique "Henry," 143–144
Missouri Association for Criminal Justice, 7
Moley, Raymond, 10, 18
Monaghan, John, 92, 99
Money, political, 37
Money laundering, 80
Montgomery, John R., 3, 4, 9
Mooney, John, 155
Moran, George "Bugs," 44, 61
Moretti, Willie, 154
Morning Telegraph, 150
Morning World, 169
Morris, Norval, ix
Morris Plan Banks, 176
Muni, Paul, 77
Murder
  families/groups code on, 112
  loan sharking and, 182–183
  See also Violence
Murder Incorporated, 65
Murphy, Charles, 72

N
National Commission, xiv
National race wire. *See* Race wire
Nationwide News Service, 151
Nelli, Humbert S., 52, 206
Nevada, 211
New Jersey, 210f
New Orleans, LA, 207, 210f
New York City, NY
  famous bootleggers from, 83

gambling in, 146–147, 153, 158–159
loan sharking in, 177
main ex-bootlegger gambling operator in, 210f
racketeer loan sharking in, 166, 180–185
types of gambling in, 143
usury laws and, 176–177
Newport, KY, 155, 210f
Nitti, Frank, 63, 69, 207, 230–231, 232f
Northside gang, 69
Northwestern University, 4, 11
Nugent, Rolf, 181
Number banks, 107–108
Numbers gambling, 105, 107–108, 142–147, 236–237
See also Gambling

O

O'Banion, Dion, 44, 63, 230
O'Donnell brothers, 44
O'Dwyer, William, 183
Off-track bookmaking, 77, 137, 147–148
See also Bookmakers
O'Hare, Edward J., 64, 69, 231, 232f
O'Leary, James, 223–224
Oliver, King, 45
Olson, Harry, 4
Organized crime
  bootlegging and, 77
  Capone gang and, 29–30
  compared to illegal enterprise, 220
  decentralized system of, 69
  development of, 137
  development of term, 76–80
  Donald Cressey's corporate model, xi
  economic impact of, 47–50
  ethnic specialization in, 16, 42–47
  focus on model of, 238
  heroism within, 50–52
  influence and reflection of urban life, 52
  interrelationships within, 39, 41
  Landesco's views on, 27–28
  Mark Haller's study and, xi–xii
  origins of, 139–140
  public opinion and, 32–33
  as a regulatory agency, xii, 103, 105, 110, 117, 122, 132, 239–240
  structure of, 234
  upward mobility from, 35–42, 139
Organized Crime in Chicago (Landesco, 1929), vii, x, 77
"Organized Crime in Urban Society: Chicago in the Twentieth Century" (Haller), xii
Organized Crime Task Forces, 79
Overhead expenses of illegal enterprise, 106

P

Panetta, Vincent "Tippy," 130–131
Partnerships
  among bootleggers, 39, 200, 202, 214–215, 235–236, 242
  Capone gang, 69, 71, 230–231, 233

in the casino industry, 160, 228–229, 229f
Cicero, 230–233, 232f
Colonial Inn (Hallandale, FL), 228–230
compared to organized crime structure, 234
within families, 105, 106
forced, 144
gamblers and bootleggers, 142, 147, 148–149, 154
gamblers and loan sharks, 185
in illegal enterprises, 221, 227–228
internal economic factors and, 235–238
outside the families, 115–116
overview of, 227–228
violence and, 235
See also Relationships
Patterson, Matthew, 99–100
Patton, Johnny, 208, 209, 232f, 233
Pawnshops, 168
Payne, John, 150
Payne News Agency, 150
Payoffs (payments), 222
Penovich, Pete, 231, 232f, 233
Peters, William G., 100
Philadelphia, PA
  background of bootlegging operations in, 84–85
  Butler's raids in, 83–84
  complex bootlegging structure within, 88, 89–90
  dominance of bootlegging in, 144–145
  famous bootleggers from, 83
  gambling in, 146–147
  importance of for diversion of industrial alcohol, 85–87
  international markets and, 87–88
  as major alcohol diversion center, 75, 85–86
  police/politician relationships to bootleggers in, 89
  society bootleggers, 89
  types of gambling in, 143
Philadelphia Grand Jury investigation
  on the alcohol industry, 94–99
  convening of, 84
  facts reported by, 90–91
  gambling overlords, 100–101
  guns and, 98
  on police wealth, 91–93
  on politics and graft, 99
  saloons and speakeasies investigated, 99
Philadelphia *Inquirer*, 150
Philadelphia Warriors, 76
Philanthropist, criminal entrepreneurs viewed as, 50
Piccadilly Nightclub, 76
Pineapple Primary, 12, 17, 63
Piping Rock nightclub, 66
Plantation casino (Hallandale, FL), 66
Police officers
  associated with Max Hoff, 75–76, 86
  buying protection against, 100–101
  corruption, 221–222, 227
  ethnicity of, 16, 43
  harassment by, 30
  interrelationships, 141

moonlighting, 49
Philadelphia Grand Jury investigation and, 90–93
political ties and, 84
post Civil War period and, 137–138
regulating red-light districts, 224–226
Sam DeStefano and, 187
See also Law enforcement
Policy gambling/racket, 47–48, 77, 137, 142–147, 236–238
See also Gambling
Polish Americans, 37, 44, 85, 139, 199
Politics/politicians
  banquets and, 40
  black organizations and, 143, 145, 146
  bootlegging networks and, 85–86, 90
  Capone gang and, 62–63
  corruption, 221–222, 223–224, 227, 230
  Cuban, 156
  ethnicity of, 43
  gambling and, 154
  gangsters and, 28–29
  Hoff's payments to, 86
  illegal entrepreneurs and, 241
  Illinois Crime Survey and, 17–18, 31, 33
  interrelationships, 141
  linked with vice and graft, 91–93, 99–100
  organized crime and, 37
  police officers and, 84
  post Civil War period and, 137–138
  providing protection, 144
  regulating red-light districts, 224–225
  urban machine, 36
Pope, Frankie, 231, 232*f*, 233
Ports and smuggling, 155, 156
Poverty, 25
Prendergast and Davies, 206
President's Commission on Law Enforcement and Administration of Justice (1967), xi
Prestige
  from being a criminal, 25, 45
  from belonging to a crime family, 104, 122–123, 132
Primerano, Frank, 127
Prizefighting, 86, 211
  See also Boxing
Prizzi's Honor (1985), 78
Profits
  bootlegging, 140
  gambling, xiii, 43, 63, 141
  loan sharking and, 185, 189
  salary lenders, 178
  sharing, 105
  skimming, 67, 213
Prohibition
  alky cookers, 48–49
  Capone gang and, 63–64
  creating a group of criminal entrepreneurs, 215
  creation of idea of "mafia," 78
  impact of, 84–85
  lack of coverage of in the *Illinois Crime Survey*, 31
  Landesco's views on organized crime and, 27–28
  liquor business after repeal of, 203–206

loan sharking and, 181
opening of business opportunities by, 43–44
public attitude and, 32
Prostitution
Bruno family taboo on, 111
development of organized crime around, 77
economic impact and, 48
ethnic specialization of, 43, 45
interrelationships within, 39
Jack Guzik and, 68–69
regulation of, 224–226
Social Evil Ordinance, 225–226
See also Red light districts
Protection
of bootlegging, 95
casino partnerships and, 228, 229f
crime family, 113–114, 123
against hijacking, 140
loan sharks and, 124, 182
numbers syndicate, 144
policy racket and, 137, 145
political, 28, 39, 43, 144
for retailers, 89–90, 91
through gunmen, 200
See also Violence
Public opinion, 32–33, 172–173
Puppo, Ralph, 115

Q

Quaker Industrial Alcohol Company, 75, 86, 94, 95–96

R

Race wire
Ben Siegel and, 157
changing ownership of, 138, 149–150
competition in, 151–152
interrelationships in, 141
Jake Guzik and, 151–152, 208
Moe Annenberg and, 151, 158
Racing, 70, 77, 209
Racketeer loan shark
advantages of over salary lenders, 191
changes leading to rise of, 190–191
in Chicago, 185–189, 191
customers of, 183–184
increasing coordination of, 188, 191
minimum population for, 189
in New York City, 180–185, 191
origins of, 179–180
overview of, 165–166
profit increase tactics, 189
types of, 185
typical backgrounds of, 186, 191
work environment of, 184–185
Racket/racketeers
Capone gang and, 39
economic impact and, 49–50
life-style of, 106
Rothstein and, 73
Special August Grand Jury on, 96
view of whole world as, 41–42
Raft, George, 212
Ragen, James, 70, 151, 152
Ragtime music, 45
Railroads, 86, 94–95

Raiola, Teresa, 62
Reading Railroad, 86, 95
Real estate, 73, 75
Red light districts, 77, 138, 224–226
  See also Prostitution
Reforms, 17
Regulatory systems
  Cosa Nostra groups and, 239–240
  gambling and politics, 223–224
  organized crime as, xii, 103, 239–240
  in red light districts, 225
  See also Bruno family; Cosa Nostra groups; Crime families/groups; Law enforcement
Reinfeld Syndicate, 205–206, 208
Relationships
  in the bootlegging industry, 90, 140–142
  criminal justice institutions and criminal groups, 41
  government and salary lending, 176
  in the loan sharking business, 125, 184–185
  organized crime, 37, 39–40
  salary lenders and employers, 190
  See also Partnerships
Reles, Abe, 182–183
Repeal, liquor business after, 203–206
Research Bureau of the University of Chicago, 11
Respect. *See* Values/beliefs
Retailers

  for alcohol purchases, 90
  as front for gambling, 238
  in the policy racket, 237
  providing extra services, 49
  system for acquiring alcohol, 88–89
Reuter, Peter, 220, 238
Ricco, Inc., 126
Riccobene, Harry, 113, 114, 116, 121, 125–128
Riccobene, Mario "Sonny," 125
Riccobene, Robert, 125, 126
Risk assumption, 237
The Riviera (Las Vegas, NV), 67, 70
Robinson, Edward G., 77
Rockefeller Foundation, ix
Rosen, Harry "Nig," 145, 208, 210f
Rosensteil, Lewis, 205
Rosenwald, Julius, 5
Rotary Club, 4
Rothstein, Abraham, 72
Rothstein, Arnold, 66, 71–74, 148, 179
Rothstein, Carolyn (Greene), 73
Roxborough, John, 146
Rules/expectations
  Cosa Nostra groups providing, 239–240
  families/groups and, 104–105, 111–112, 117, 122, 132
  loan sharking, 132
Runyon, Damon, 72
Russell Sage Foundation, 166, 175, 177, 181
Ryerson, Joseph T., 4, 9
Ryerson Committee, 4–7, 13

S

S&G Syndicate, 70
Salary lenders
  advantages of loan sharks over, 191
  changes in, 189–190
  customers of, 168, 171–172
  debt collection tactics, 172–174
  demise of, 178–179
  entanglement and, 172–173
  history of, 166, 168
  law and, 167–168, 173–174
  movement against, 174–176
  offices of, 169
  overview of, 165
  process of, 170–171
  profit increase tactics, 189
  public attitudes towards, 172–173
  purpose of, 167
  as roots to racketeer loan sharking, 179–180
  size of, 170
Saletko, Morris, 188
Saloons and restaurants, 40, 46, 49, 99, 109–110
Saltis, Joe "Pollack," 44
The Sands (Las Vegas, NV), 212
Saratoga Springs (New York), 66
Satinover, Eddie, 88
Satinover, Ella, 88
Scalleat, Albert, 111
Scalleat, Joseph, 111, 116
Scandinavian Americans, 42
Scarface. *See* Capone, Al "Snorky"
Scarface (1932), 77
Scarfo, Nicky, xiv
Schenley Products Company, 205
Schoenleber, Charles, 99–100
Schultz, "Dutch" (Arther Flegenheimer), 83, 144, 182, 238
Schwartz, Charlie, 75, 86, 94, 97, 100
Schwartz, Thelma "Teddy" (Lansky), 67
Seabury investigation, 143–144
Seagram, 204
Shadow Inn, 232*f*
Shaw, Clifford R., 11, 24, 25–26
Siegel, Benjamin "Bugsy," 65–66, 157, 208, 210*f*, 211–212
Siegel, Sam "Dapper," 183–184
Simone, Robert, 131
Sinatra, Frank, 212
Sindone, Frank, 112, 116, 121, 129–131
69th Street Mob, 145
Skidmore, William (Billy or Skid), 39–40, 153, 223
Skinner, Edward M., 4, 5
Slot machines, 153–154, 207, 231, 232*f*
Slums, 28
Small businesses. *See* Businesses
Smith, Bruce, 10–11
Smuggling, 73, 80, 155, 156, 209
  See also Drug selling
Snorky. *See* Capone, Al "Snorky"
Social disorganization, 25
Social Evil Ordinance, 225–226
Social factors, criminal behavior and, 28–29
Social mobility, 35–42, 139
South Side (Chicago), 45–46
Speakeasies, 45–46, 84, 88–89,

99
Special Committee on Enforcement of Criminal Law, 3–4, 6–7, 13
Special Committee on the Crime Situation appointment, 4
Special Committee to Investigate Organized Crime. *See* Kefauver Committee
Sports
  Guzik and Levin and, 70
  horse racing, 77
  Max Hoff and, 74–75, 86
  organized crime and, 37
  social mobility and, 38–39
  World Series fixing, 72–73
St. Louis, MO, 143, 155
St. Valentine's Day Massacre, 61, 63, 69, 77
The Stardust (Las Vegas, NV), 212
Stills, alcohol, 87, 89–90
Stock market, 73
Stoneham, Charles, 72
Storyville district (New Orleans), 45
Strauss, Phil "Pittsburgh," 182–183
Suchowljansky, Max, 65
Suchowljansky, Meyer. *See* Lansky, Meyer
Suchowljansky, Yetta, 65
Sullivan, Danny, 228, 229f
Sullivan, Joseph "Sport," 72–73
Sullivan, Tim, 72
Superior Wines and Liquor Company, 206
Swope, Bayard, 72
Sylvania Hotel, 86

Syndicates. *See* Crime families/groups; Gambling syndicates

T
Takeovers, gambling, 144
Talent agency, 126
Tammany Hall, 72, 153
Task Force Report: Organized Crime, xi
Tax evasion charges
  Annenberg and Ragen, 151
  Bill Skidmore, 223
  Capone gang, 64
  Jones brothers, 146
  Miro and Brunder, 144
  Skidmore and Johnson, 153
Teamster Union, 157, 213
Telephones, 138, 148, 149, 158
Temple University, xi
Tennes, Mont, 150
Testa, Phil, 115, 129
Theft of a Nation: The Structure and Operation of Organized Crime in America (Cressey, 1969), x–xi
Third degree, 30
Thompson, William Hale "Big Bill," 63, 145
Thrasher, Frederic, x
Thrasher, Samuel, 5
Three Star Hennessy Chemical Company, 88
The Thunderbird (Las Vegas, NV), 212
Tolman, Daniel H., 170, 173
Torrio, John
  bootlegging interests, 44, 206
  Capone working for, 62
  Jack Guzik and, 69

rise of Cicero, 230
shooting of, 63
Torture, 187
Trans-America Publishing and News Service, 70, 152, 157, 208
The Tropicana (Las Vegas, NV), 212
Tru-Mint Company, 154, 207
Tucker, Sophie, 76
Tunney, Gene, 75
Tyrone DeNittis Talent Agency, 126

U

Underboss, in the crime family structure, 104
University of Chicago, vii, ix, 4
University of Chicago Department of Sociology, 24
University of Maryland, viii
University of Wisconsin, Madison, viii
"The Untouchables," 83
Upward mobility, 35–42, 139

Urban life
　corrupt political organizations and, 222
　crime and mobility, 35–42
　economic impact of organized crime, 47–50
　ethnicity and, 42–47
　heroism within, 50–52
　Landesco's views on, 27–28
　tradition viewing social structure of as major cause of crime, 24
Urban machine politics, 36

U.S. Army, viii, 129
U.S. Supreme Court, 64
Usury laws, 167–168, 171, 175, 176–177, 190

V

Valachi, Joseph, xi, 78, 241
The Valachi Papers (1968), xi
Values/beliefs
　causing ambiguity towards criminals, 52
　criminal behavior and, 29
　families/groups and, 104–105, 111–112
　influence on opportunities for criminal activities, 46
　linking the criminal social world, 40–41
　loans and, 128, 132
　loyalties/friendship in, 27, 28, 37, 41
　shared from backgrounds, 124–125
　stool pigeons, 41
Venereal diseases, 225–226
Vice districts, 43, 44–45, 68–69, 99–100
Vice in Chicago (Reckless, 1933), ix
Villa DiRoma, 126
Village Barn, 76
Vineyards/wineries, 203
Violence
　bootleggers and, 140, 158, 200
　Capone gang and, 63, 65
　debt collection and, 107, 165–166, 180–181
　"Dutch" Schultz and, 144
　loan sharking and, 124–125,

191
machine guns, 98
national wire competition and, 152
organized crime contributing to, 52
Sam DeStefano, 187
shaping partnership behavior, 235
Special August Grand Jury on, 96
threats of, 129–131
See also Hijacking; Kidnapping; Murder; Protection
Vogel, Eddie, 232*f*
Vollmer, August, 11
Volstead Act, 84, 138

W

Walker, Hiram, 204
War on Drugs, 80
Ward committeemen, 16
Ward leaders, 223–224
Warrington, Charles "Chickie," 112–113
Washington D.C., 210*f*
Watson, Everett, 146
Weinbeck, Moses, 101
Weinberg, George, 144
Wertheimer, Mert, 228–230, 229*f*
Wesleyan University, viii
West Indians, 142
Western Electric Company, 230
Western Union, 149
Whiskey supply, 93–94
Whisky Trust, 202
White Americans, 36, 159
Wholesale arrest, 30
Wholesalers in the alcohol industry, 236
Wickersham Commission, 26
Wiess, Earl "Hymie," 44
Wigmore, John H., 4, 23–24
Wilson, Woodrow, 223
Wire services. *See* National race wire
Women in the loan sharking culture, 125, 169
World Series fixing, 72–73
World War II, 67, 78–79, 157
Writers
  high employment of, 37, 43, 48, 146
  location selling from, 106, 108
  numbers, 105, 108
  policy, 137

Y

Yellow Cab Company (Cleveland), 151
Yesteryear Lounge, 126

Z

Zanghi, Joseph, 84
Zignetti games, 108–109
Zuta, Jack, 44
Zwillman, Abner "Longie," 205–206, 208, 210*f*, 212

About the Author

Born in Washington, D.C., Mark Haller spent his formative years in the Nation's capitol and in neighboring Bethesda, Maryland. He took a bachelor's degree in English from Wesleyan University in Connecticut in 1951; and followed it with a master's in history from University of Maryland in 1954. After finishing military service overseas, he matriculated to the University of Wisconsin, Madison, for his history doctorate and finished in 1959.

He would spend the next decade at the University of Chicago, where his dissertation was published as *Eugenics: Hereditarian Attitudes in American Thought* (Rutgers University Press, 1963). In 1966, he obtained a grant to study crime and policing in early twentieth century Chicago. This led to a study of organized crime in Chicago, and the publication of John Landesco's *Organized Crime in Chicago* (University of Chicago Press, 1968), in which Haller contributed an introduction and was the moving force behind the re-issue of this 1929 classic.

In 1968, Professor Haller moved to Temple University in Philadelphia, where he joined both the history and criminal justice departments. For almost five decades, he has been researching and publishing articles on illegal enterprise—commonly referred to as organized crime. Professor Haller passed away at the age of 83 in September 2012. This book represents a compendium of his major work on illegal enterprise.

About the Editor

Matthew G. Yeager obtained his bachelor's degree in criminology from the University of California at Berkeley in 1972. There, while a teaching assistant in the School of Criminology's course on organized crime, he was introduced to Mark Haller and the reprint of John Landesco's classic research on *Organized Crime in Chicago*. Mr. Yeager completed a master's degree from the State University of New York at Albany (1975), and a doctorate in sociology from Carleton University, Ottawa, Canada, in 2006. Dr. Yeager is currently an associate professor in the Department of Sociology, King's University College, which is part of Western University Canada. He lives with his family in London, Ontario.